Bloom's Modern Critical Interpretations

Herman Melville's
MOBY-DICK
Updated Edition

Edited and with an introduction by
Harold Bloom
Sterling Professor of the Humanities
Yale University

BLOOM'S LITERARY CRITICISM
An imprint of Infobase Publishing

Bloom's Modern Critical Interpretations: Moby-Dick, Updated Edition

Copyright © 2007 Infobase Publishing
Introduction © 2007 by Harold Bloom

ISBN-10: 0-7910-9363-8
ISBN-13: 978-0-7910-9363-4

Bloom's Literary Criticism
An imprint of Infobase Publishing
132 West 31st Street
New York NY 10001

Library of Congress Cataloging-in-Publication Data
Herman Melville's Moby-Dick / Harold Bloom, editor. — Updated ed.
   p. cm — (Bloom's modern critical interpretations)
  Includes bibliographical references and index.
  ISBN 0-7910-9363-8 (hardcover)
 1. Melville, Herman, 1819–1891. Moby Dick. 2. Sea stories, American-History criticism.
I. Bloom, Harold. II. Title: Moby-Dick. III. Series
PS2384.M62H385 2007   ·
813'.3—dc22   2006031155

Contributing Editor: Amy Sickels

Cover Illustration: Ben Peterson

Printed in the United States of America

Bang EJB 10 9 8 7 6 5 4 3 2 1

Contents

Editor's Note

My Introduction argues for Captain Ahab as the American Promethean hero, and as a Gnostic visionary, rather like Herman Melville himself.

Alfred Kazin rather curiously sees Melville as taking nature's side against the human, while Patrick McGrath accurately discerns a powerful homoeroticism pulsating throughout the great American prose epic.

The allegory of a hypocritical America—enslaving and self-aggrandizing—is persuasively interpreted by Homer B. Pettey, after which Fred V. Bernard suggests that Ahab and Ishmael both may be mulattos.

Carolyn L. Karcher invokes the renegade prophet Jonah, as the model for Ishmael's voyage, while David S. Reynolds foregrounds *Moby-Dick* in the popular culture of its day.

Ahab's monomania is read by Henry Nash Smith as a mode of transcendence, and as a path to wisdom, after which Carolyn Porter juxtaposes the two polarities of the book, Ahab's self-generated authority and Ishmael's miraculous salvation.

The poet Charles Olson uncovers Melville's Shakespearean heritage, while Christopher Sten proclaims the epic triumph of Melville's masterwork.

In this volume's final essay, John Bryant studies the origins of *Moby-Dick* in the American Revolution, so that the mingling of Ahab's and Ishmael's voices causes a revolving in the reader that becomes consonant with the purposeful theme of revolution itself.

HAROLD BLOOM

Introduction

"Canst thou draw out leviathan with a hook?," God's taunting question to Job. Can be said to be answered by Captain Ahab with a "Yes!" in thunder. Job's God wins, Ahab loses, and the great white leviathan swims away, harpooned yet towing Ahab with him. But Ahab's extraordinary last speech denies that Moby-Dick is the conquerer:

> I turn my body from the sun. What ho, Tashtego! Let me hear thy hammer. Oh! Ye three unsurrendered spires of mine; thou uncracked keel; and only god-bullied hull; thou firm deck. And haughty helm, and Pole-pointed prow,—death-glorious ship! Must ye then perish, and without me? Am I cut off from the last fond pride of meanest shipwrecked captains? Oh, lonely death on lonely life! Oh, now I feel my topmost greatness lies in my topmost grief. Ho, ho! from all your furthest bounds, pour ye now in, ye bold billows of my whole foregone life, and top this one piled comber of my death! Towards thee I roll, thou all-destroying but unconquering whale; to the last I grapple with thee; from hell's heart I stab at thee; for hate's sake I spit my last breath at thee. Sink all coffins and all hearses to one common pool! and since neither can be mine, let me then tow to pieces, while still

1

chasing thee, though tied to thee, thou damned whale! *Thus*, I give up the spear!

Beyond the allusions—Shakespearean, Miltonic, Byronic—what rings out here is Melville's own grand self-echoing, which is of Father Mapple's sermon as it concludes:

> He drooped and fell away from himself for a moment; then lifting his face to them again, showed a deep joy in his eyes, as he cried out with a heavenly enthusiasm,—"But oh! shipmates! on the starboard hand of every woe, there is a sure delight; and higher the top of that delight, than the bottom of the woe is deep. Is not the main-truck higher than the kelson is low? Delight is to him—a far, far upward, and inward delight—who against the proud gods and commodores of this earth, ever stands forth his own inexorable self. Delight is to him whose strong arms yet support him, when the ship of this base treacherous world has gone down beneath him. Delight is to him, who gives no quarter in the truth, and kills, burns, and destroys all sin though he pluck it out from under the robes of Senators and Judges. Delight,—top-gallant delight is to him, who acknowledges no law or lord, but the Lord his God, and is only a patriot to heaven. Delight is to him, whom all the waves of the billows of the seas of the boisterous mob can never shake from this sure Keel of the Ages. And eternal delight and deliciousness will be his, who coming to lay him down, can say with his final breath—O Father!—chiefly known to me by Thy rod—mortal or immortal, here I die. I have striven to be Thine, more than to be this world's, or mine own. Yet this is nothing; I leave eternity to Thee; for what is man that he should live out the lifetime of his God?"

Father Mapple's intensity moves from "a sure delight, and higher the top of that delight" through "a far, far upward. And inward delight" on to "Delight,—top-gallant delight is to him," heaven's patriot. Ahab's equal but antithetical intensity proceeds from "unsurrendered spires of mine" through "my topmost greatness lies in my topmost grief" to end in "top this one piled comber of my death." After which the *Pequod* goes down with Tashtego hammering a hawk to the mainmast, an emblem not of being "only a patriot to heaven" but rather of a Satanic dragging of "a living part of heaven along with her." Admirable as Father Mapple is, Ahab is certainly the hero, more Promethean than Satanic, and we need not conclude (as so many critics do) that Melville chooses Mapple's stance over Ahab's. William Faulkner, in 1927, asserted that the book he most wished he had written was *Moby-Dick*, and called Ahab's fate "a sort of Golgotha of the heart become immutable as bronze in the sonority of its plunging ruin," characteristically adding: "There's a death for a man, now."

As Faulkner implied, there is a dark sense in which Ahab intends his Golgotha, like Christ's, to be a vicarious atonement for all of staggering Adam's woes. When Melville famously wrote to Hawthorne: "I have written a wicked book," he was probably quite serious. The common reader does not come to love Ahab, and yet there is a serious disproportion between the reader's awe of, and admiration for, Ahab, and the moral dismissal of the monomaniacal hero by many scholarly critics. Ahab seems to provoke academic critics rather more even than Milton's Satan does. Ishmael, presumably speaking for Melville, consistently emphasizes Ahab's greatness. And so does Ahab himself, as when he confronts the corposants or St. Elmo's fire, in the superb Chapter 119, "The Candles":

> Oh! thou clear spirit of clear fire, whom on these seas I as Persian once did worship, till in the sacramental act so burned by thee, that to this hour I bear the scar; I now know thee, thou clear spirit, and I now know that thy right worship is defiance. To neither love nor reverence wilt thou be kind; and e'en for hate thou canst but kill; and all are killed. No fearless fool now fronts thee. I own thy speechless, placeless power; but to the last gasp of my earthquake life will dispute its unconditional, unintegral mastery in me. In the midst of the personified impersonal, a personality stands here. Though but a point at best; whencesoe'er I came; wheresoe'er I go; yet while I earthly live, the queenly personality lives in me, and feels her royal rights. But war is pain, and hate is woe. Come in thy lowest form of love, and I will kneel and kiss thee; but at thy highest, come as mere supernal power; and though thou launchest navies of full-freighted worlds, there's that in here that still remains indifferent. Oh, thou clear spirit, of thy fire thou madest me, and like a true child of fire, I breathe it back to thee.

If Ahab has a religion, it is Persian or rather Parsee, and so Zoroastrian, but Melville has not written a Zoroastrian hymn to the benign light for Ahab to chant. Ahab's invocation is clearly Gnostic in spirit and in substance, since the light is hailed as being both ambiguous and ambivalent. Ahab himself knows that the clear spirit of clear fire is not from the Alien God but from the

Demiurge, and he seems to divide the Demiurge into both the "lowest form
of love" and the "highest. . . mere supernal power." Against this dialectical
or even self-contradictory spirit, Ahab sets himself as personality rather than
as moral character: "In the midst of the personified impersonal, a personality
stands here." As a personality, Ahab confronts "the personified impersonal,"
which he astonishingly names as his father, and defies, as knowing less than
he, Ahab, knows:

> I own thy speechless, placeless power; said I not so? Nor was
> it wrung from me; nor do I now drop these links. Thou canst
> blind; but I can then grope. Thou canst consume; but I can
> then be ashes. Take the homage of these poor eyes, and shut-
> ter-hands. I would not take it. The lightning flashes through
> my skull; mine eye-balls ache and ache; my whole beaten brain
> seems as beheaded, and rolling on some stunning ground. Oh,
> oh! Yet blindfold, yet will I talk to thee. Light though thou be,
> thou leapest out of darkness; but I am darkness leaping out of
> light, leaping out of thee! The javelins cease; open eyes; see, or
> not? There burn the flames! Oh, thou magnanimous! now I do
> glory in my genealogy. But thou art but my fiery father; my sweet
> mother, I know not. Oh, cruel! what hast thou done with her?
> There lies my puzzle; but thine is greater. Thou knowest not
> how came ye, hence callest thyself unbegotten; certainly know-
> est not thy beginning, hence callest thyself unbegun. I know that
> of me, which thou knowest not of thyself, oh, thou omnipotent.
> There is some unsuffusing thing beyond thee, thou clear spirit, to
> whom all thy eternity is but time, all thy creativeness mechanical.
> Through thee, thy flaming self, my scorched eyes do dimly see it.
> Oh, thou foundling fire, thou hermit immemorial, thou too hast
> thy incommunicable riddle, thy unparticipated grief. Here again
> with haughty agony, I read my sire. Leap! leap up, and lick the
> sky! I leap with thee; I burn with thee; would fain be welded with
> thee; defyingly I worship thee!

The visionary center of *Moby-Dick*, and so of all Melville, as critics
always have recognized, is chapter 42, "The Whiteness of the Whale." It
is Ishmael's meditation, and not Ahab's, and yet how far is it from Ahab?
Ishmael is himself half a Gnostic:

> Though in many of its aspects this visible world seems formed in
> love, the invisible spheres were formed in fright.

Closer to Carlyle than to Emerson, this extraordinary sentence is the prelude to the final paragraph of Ishmael's reverie:

> But not yet have we solved the incantation of this whiteness, and learned why it appeals with such power to the soul; and more strange and far more portentous—why, as we have seen, it is at once the most meaning symbol of spiritual things, nay, the very veil of the Christian's Deity; and yet should be as it is, the intensifying agent in things the most appalling to mankind.
>
> Is it that by its indefiniteness it shadows forth the heartless voids and immensities of the universe, and thus stabs us from behind with the thought of annihilation, when beholding the white depths of the milky way? Or is it, that as in essence whiteness is not so much a color as the visible absence of color, and at the same time the concrete of all colors; is it for these reasons that there is such a dumb blankness, full of meaning, in a wide landscape of snows—a colorless, all-color of atheism from which we shrink? And when we consider that other theory of the natural philosophers, that all other earthly hues—every stately or lovely emblazoning—the sweet tinges of sunset skies and woods; yea, and the gilded velvets of butterflies, and the butterfly cheeks of young girls; all these are but subtile deceits, not actually inherent in substances, but only laid on from without; so that all deified Nature absolutely paints like the harlot, whose allurements cover nothing but the charnel-house within; and when we proceed further, and consider that the mystical cosmetic which produces every one of her hues, the great principle of light, for ever remains white or colorless in itself, and if operating without medium upon matter, would touch all objects, even tulips and roses, with its own blank tinge—pondering all this, the palsied universe lies before us a leper; and like wilful travellers in Lapland, who refuse to wear colored and coloring glasses upon their eyes, so the wretched infidel gazes himself blind at the monumental white shroud that wraps all the prospect around him. And of all these things the Albino whale was the symbol. Wonder ye then at the fiery hunt?

Ishmael's "visible absence of color" becomes the trope of whiteness, "a dumb blankness," similar to its descendant in the beach-scene of Wallace Stevens's "The Auroras of Autumn":

Here, being visible is being white,
Is being of the solid of white, the accomplishment
Of an extremist in an exercise. . .

The season changes. A cold wind chills the beach.
The long lines of it grow longer, emptier,
A darkness gathers though it does not fall.

And the whiteness grows less vivid on the wall.
The man who is walking turns blankly on the sand.

Melville and Stevens alike shrink from "a colorless, all-color of atheism," not because they are theists, but precisely because they both believe in and fear the Demiurge. When Ishmael cries out: "Wonder ye then at the fiery hunt?" he refutes all those critics, moral and psychoanalytic, who condemn Ahab as being immoral or insane. It was Melville, after all, who wrote two memorable quatrains, in the mode of Blake, which he entitled "Fragments of a lost Gnostic Poem of the 12th Century":

Found a family, build a state,
The pledged event is still the same:
Matter in end will never abate
His ancient brutal claim.

Indolence is heaven's ally here,
And energy the child of hell:
The Good Man pouring from his pitcher clear,
But brims the poisoned well.

There the Gnosticism is overt, and we are left a little cold, since even a heretical doctrine strikes us as tendentious, as having too clear a design upon us. Perhaps "The Bell-Tower" is a touch tendentious also. *Moby-Dick*, despite its uneven rhetoric, despite its excessive debt to Shakespeare, Milton, and Byron, is anything but tendentious. It remains the darker half of our national epic, complementing *Leaves of Grass* and *Huckleberry Finn*, works of more balance certainly, but they do not surpass or eclipse Melville's version of darkness visible.

ALFRED KAZIN

Introduction to Moby-Dick

Moby-Dick is not only a very big book, it is also a peculiarly full and rich one, and from the very opening it conveys a sense of abundance, of high creative power, that exhilarates and enlarges the imagination. This quality is felt immediately in the style, which is remarkably easy, natural and "American," yet always literary and which swells in power until it takes on some of the roaring and uncontainable rhythms with which Melville audibly describes the sea. The best description of this style is Melville's own, when he speaks of the "bold and nervous lofty language" that Nantucket whaling captains learn straight from nature. We feel this abundance in heroic types like the Nantucketers themselves, many of whom are significantly named after Old Testament prophets and kings, for these, too, are mighty men, and the mightiest of them all, Captain Ahab, will challenge the very order of the creation itself. This is the very heart of the book—so much so that we come to feel that there is some shattering magnitude of theme before Melville as he writes, that as a writer he had been called to an heroic new destiny.

It is this constant sense of power that constitutes the book's appeal to us, that explains its hold on our attention. *Moby-Dick* is one of those books that try to bring in as much of life as a writer can get both hands on. Melville even tries to create an image of life itself as a ceaseless creation. The book is written with a personal force of style, a passionate learning, a steady insight

From *Moby-Dick: Or, The Whale* by Herman Melville, Alfred Kazin, ed., pp. v–xiv. © 1956, renewed 1984 by Alfred Kazin.

7

into our forgotten connexions with the primitive. It sweeps everything before it; it gives us the happiness that only great vigour inspires.

If we start by opening ourselves to this abundance and force, by welcoming not merely the story itself, but the manner in which it speaks to us, we shall recognize in this restlessness, this richness, this persistent atmosphere of magnitude, the essential image on which the book is founded. For *Moby-Dick* is not so much a book *about* Captain Ahab's quest for the whale as it is an experience *of* that quest. This is only to say, what we say of any true poem, that we cannot reduce its essential substance to a subject, that we should not intellectualize and summarize it, but that we should recognize that its very force and beauty lie in the way it is conceived and written, in the qualities that flow from its being a unique entity.

In these terms, *Moby-Dick* seems to be far more of a poem than it is a novel, and since it is a narrative, to be an epic, a long poem on an heroic theme, rather than the kind of realistic fiction that we know today. Of course Melville did not deliberately set out to write a formal epic; but half-consciously, he drew upon many of the traditional characteristics of epic in order to realize the utterly original kind of novel he needed to write in his time—the spaciousness of theme and subject, the martial atmosphere, the association of these homely and savage materials with universal myths, the symbolic wanderings of the hero, the indispensable strength of such a hero in Captain Ahab. Yet beyond all this, what distinguishes *Moby-Dick* from modern prose fiction, what ties it up with the older, more formal kind of narrative that was once written in verse, is the fact that Melville is not interested in the meanness, the literal truthfulness, the representative slice of life, that we think of as the essence of modern realism. His book has the true poetic emphasis in that the whole story is constantly being meditated and unravelled through a single mind.

"Call me Ishmael," the book begins. This Ishmael is not only a character in the book; he is also the single voice, or rather the single mind, from whose endlessly turning spool of thought the whole story is unwound. It is Ishmael's contemplativeness, his *dreaming*, that articulates the wonder of the seas and the fabulousness of the whale and the terrors of the deep. All that can be meditated and summed up and hinted at, as the reflective essence of the story itself, is given us by Ishmael, who possesses nothing but man's specifically human gift, which is language. It is Ishmael who tries to sum up the whole creation in a single book and yet keeps at the centre of it one American whaling voyage. It is Ishmael's gift for speculation that explains the terror we come to feel before the whiteness of the whale, Ishmael's mind that ranges with mad exuberance through a description of all the seas; Ishmael who piles up image after image of "the mightiest animated mass that has survived the flood." It is Ishmael who, in the wonderful chapter on the masthead, embodies for us man as a thinker, whose reveries transcend space and time as he stands watch high above the seas. And of course it is Ishmael, both actually and as the symbol of man, who is the one survivor of the voyage. Yet utterly alone as he is at the end of the book, floating on the Pacific Ocean, he manages, buoyed up on a coffin that magically serves as his life-buoy, to give us the impression that life itself can be honestly confronted only in the loneliness of each human heart. Always it is this emphasis on Ishmael's personal vision, on the richness and ambiguity of all events as the sceptical, fervent, experience-scarred mind of Ishmael feels and thinks them, that gives us, from the beginning, the new kind of book that *Moby-Dick* is. It is a book which is neither a saga, though it deals in large natural forces nor a *classical* epic, for we feel too strongly the individual who wrote it. It is a book that is at once primitive, fatalistic, and merciless, like the very oldest books, and yet peculiarly personal, like so many twentieth-century novels, in its significant emphasis on the subjective individual consciousness. The book grows out of a single word, "I," and expands until the soul's voyage of this "I" comes to include a great many things that are unseen and unsuspected by most of us. And this material is always tied to Ishmael, who is not merely a witness to the story—someone who happens to be on board the *Pequod*—but the living and germinating mind who grasps the world in the tentacles of his thought.

The power behind this "I" is poetical in the sense that everything comes to us through a constant intervention of language instead of being presented flatly. Melville does not wish, as so many contemporary writers do, to reproduce ordinary life and conventional speech. He seeks the marvellous and the fabulous aspects that life wears in secret. He exuberantly sees the world through language—things exist as his words for them—and much of the exceptional beauty of the book lies in the unusual incidence of passages that, in the most surprising contexts, are so piercing in their poetic intensity. But the most remarkable feat of language in the book is Melville's ability to make us see that man is not a blank slate passively open to events, but a mind that constantly seeks meaning in everything it encounters. In Melville the Protestant habit of moralizing and the transcendental passion for symbolizing all things as examples of "higher laws" combined to make a mind that instinctively brought an inner significance to each episode. Everything in *Moby-Dick* is saturated in a mental atmosphere. Nothing happens for its own sake in this book, and in the midst of the chase, Ishmael can be seen meditating it, pulling things apart, drawing out its significant point.

But Ishmael is not just an intellectual observer; he is also very much in the story. He suffers, he is there. As his name indicates, he is an estranged and solitary man; his only friend is Queequeg, a despised heathen from the South Seas. Queequeg, a fellow "isolato" in the smug world of white middle-class Christians, is the only man who offers Ishmael friendship; thanks to Queequeg, "no longer my splintered heart and maddened hand were turned against the wolfish world. This soothing savage had redeemed it." Why does Ishmael feel so alone? There are background reasons, Melville's own: his father went bankrupt and then died in debt when Melville was still a boy. Melville-Ishmael went to sea—"And at first," he tells us, "this sort of thing is unpleasant enough. It touches one's sense of honour, particularly if you come of an old established family in the land." But there is a deeper, a more universal reason for Ishmael's apartness, and it is one that will strangely make him kin to his daemonic captain, Ahab. For the burden of his thought, the essential cause of his estrangement, is that he cannot come to any conclusion about anything. He feels at home with ships and sailors because for him, too, one journey ends only to begin another; "and a second ended, only begins a third and so on, for ever and for aye. Such is the endlessness, yea, the intolerableness of all earthly effort."

Ishmael is not merely an orphan; he is an exile, searching alone in the wilderness, with a black man for his only friend. He suffers from doubt and uncertainty far more than he does from homelessness. Indeed, this agony of disbelief *is* his homelessness. For him nothing is ever finally settled and decided; he is man, or as we like to think, modern man, cut off from the certainty that was once his inner world. Ishmael no longer has any sure formal belief. All is in doubt, all is in eternal flux, like the sea. And so condemned, like "all his race from Adam down," to wander the seas of thought, far from Paradise, he now searches endlessly to put the whole broken story together, to find a meaning, to ascertain—where but in the ceaselessness of human thought?—"the hidden cause we seek." Ishmael does not perform any great actions, as Ahab does; he is the most insignificant member of the fo'c'sle and will get the smallest share of the take. But his inner world of thought is almost unbearably symbolic, for he must think, and think, and think, in order to prove to himself that there is a necessary connexion between man and the world. He pictures his dilemma in everything he does on board the ship, but never so clearly as when he is shown looking at the sea, searching a meaning to existence from the inscrutable waters.

What Melville did through Ishmael, then, was to put man's distinctly modern feeling of "exile," of abandonment, directly at the centre of his stage. For Ishmael there are no satisfactory conclusions to anything; no final philosophy is ever possible. All that man owns in this world, Ishmael would say, is his insatiable mind. This is why the book opens on a picture of the dreaming contemplativeness of mind itself: men tearing themselves loose from their jobs to stand "like silent sentinels all around the town ... thousands of mortal men fixed in ocean reveries." Narcissus was bemused by that image which "we ourselves see in all rivers and oceans," and this, says Ishmael when he is most desperate, is all that man ever finds when he searches the waters—a reflection of himself. All is inconclusive, restless, an endless flow. And Melville's own style rises to its highest level not in the neo-Shakespearean speeches of Ahab, which are sometimes bombastic, but in those amazing prose flights on the whiteness of the whale and on the Pacific where Ishmael reproduces, in the rhythms of the prose itself, man's brooding interrogation of nature.

II

But Ishmael is a witness not only to his own thoughts, but also a witness to the actions of Captain Ahab. The book is not only a great skin of language stretched to fit the world of man's philosophic wandering, it is also a world of moral tyranny and violent action, in which the principal actor is Ahab. With the entry of Ahab a harsh new rhythm enters the book, and from now on two rhythms—one reflective, the other forceful—alternate to show us the world in which man's thinking and man's doing each follows its own law. Ishmael's thought consciously extends itself to get behind the world of appearances; he wants to see and to understand everything. Ahab's drive is to *prove*, not to discover; the world that tortures Ishmael by its horrid vacancy has tempted Ahab into thinking that he can make it over. He seeks to dominate nature, to impose and to inflict his will on the outside world—whether it be the crew that must jump to his orders or the great white whale that is essentially indifferent to him. As Ishmael is all rumination, so Ahab is all will. Both are thinkers, the difference being that Ishmael thinks as a bystander, has identified his own state with man's utter unimportance in nature. Ahab, by contrast, actively seeks the whale in order to assert man's supremacy over what swims before him as "the monomaniac incarnation" of a superior power:

> "If man will strike, strike through the mask! How can the prisoner reach outside except by thrusting through the wall? To me, the white whale is that wall, shoved near to me. Sometimes I think there's naught beyond. But 'tis enough. He tasks me, he heaps me; I see in him outrageous strength, with an inscrutable malice sinewing it. That inscrutable thing is chiefly what I hate, and be the white whale agent, or be the white whale principal, I will wreak that hate upon him. Talk not to me of blasphemy, man;

I'd strike the sun if it insulted me. For could the sun do that, then could I do the other, since there is ever a sort of fair play herein, jealousy presiding over all creations. But not my master, man, is even that fair play. Who's over me? Truth hath no confines."

This is Ahab's quest—and Ahab's magnificence. For in this speech Ahab expresses more forcibly than Ishmael ever could, something of the impenitent anger against the universe that all of us can feel. Ahab may be a mad sea captain, a tyrant of the quarter deck who disturbs the crew's sleep as he stomps along on his ivory leg. But this Ahab does indeed speak for all men who, as Ishmael confesses in the frightening meditation on the whiteness of the whale, suspect that "though in many of its aspects this visible world seems formed in love, the invisible spheres were formed in fright." So man, watching the sea heaving around him, sees it as a mad steed that has lost its rider, and looking at his own image in the water, is tortured by the thought that man himself may be an accident, of no more importance in this vast oceanic emptiness than one of Ahab's rare tears dropped into the Pacific.

To the degree that we feel this futility in the face of a blind impersonal nature that "heeds us not," and storm madly, like Ahab, against the dread that there's "naught beyond"—to this extent all men may recognize Ahab's bitterness, his unrelentingness, his inability to rest in that uncertainty which, Freud has told us, modern man must learn to endure. Ahab figures in a symbolic fable, he is acting out thoughts which we all share. But Ahab, even more, is a hero; we cannot insist enough on that. Melville believed in the heroic and he specifically wanted to cast his hero on American lines— someone noble by nature, not by birth, who would have "not the dignity of kings and robes, but that abounding dignity which has no robed investiture." Ahab sinned against man and God, and like his namesake in the Old Testament, becomes a "wicked king." But Ahab is not just a fanatic who leads the whole crew to their destruction, he is a hero of thought who is trying, by terrible force, to reassert man's place in nature. And it is the struggle that Ahab incarnates that makes him so magnificent a *voice*, thundering in Shakespearian rhetoric, storming at the gates of the inhuman, silent world. Ahab is trying to give man, in one awful, final assertion that his will *does* mean something, a feeling of relatedness with his world.

Ahab's effort, then, is to reclaim something that man knows he has lost. Significantly, Ahab proves by the bitter struggle he has to wage that man is fighting in an unequal contest; by the end of the book Ahab abandons all his human ties and becomes a complete fanatic. But Melville has no doubt—nor should we!—that Ahab's quest is *humanly* understandable. And the quest itself supplies the book with its technical *raison d'être*. For it leads us through all the seas and around the whole world; it brings us past ships of every nation. Always it is Ahab's drive that makes up the *passion* of *Moby-Dick*, a passion that is revealed in the descriptive chapters on the whale, whale-fighting, whale-burning, on the whole gory and fascinating industrial process aboard ship that reduces the once proud whale to oil-brimming barrels in the hold. And this passion may be defined as a passion of longing, of hope, of striving: a passion that starts from the deepest loneliness that man can know. It is the great cry of man who feels himself exiled from his "birthright, the merry May-day gods of old," who looks for a new god "to enthrone ... again in the now egotistical sky, in the now unhaunted hill." The cry is Ahab's—"Who's to doom, when the judge himself is dragged to the bar?"

Behind Ahab's cry is the fear that man's covenant with God has been broken, that there is no purpose to our existence. The *Pequod* is condemned by Ahab to sail up and down the world in search of—a symbol. But this search, mad as it seems to Starbuck the first mate, who is a Christian, nevertheless represents Ahab's real humanity. For the ancient covenant is never quite broken so long as man still thirsts for it. And because Ahab, as Melville intended him to, represents the aristocracy of intellect in our democracy, because he seeks to transcend the limitations that good conventional men like Starbuck, philistine materialists like Stubb, and unthinking fools like Flask want to impose on everybody else, Ahab speaks for the humanity that belongs to man's imaginative vision of himself.

Yet with all this, we must not forget that Ahab's quest takes place, unceasingly, in a very practical world of whaling, as part of the barbaric and yet highly necessary struggle by man to support himself physically in nature. It is this that gives the book its primitive vitality, its burning authenticity. For *Moby-Dick*, it must be emphasized, is not simply a symbolic fable; nor, as we have already seen, can it possibly be construed as simply a "sea story." It is the story of agonizing thought in the midst of brutal action, of thought that questions every action, that annuls it from within, as it were—but that cannot, in this harsh world, relieve man of the fighting, skinning, burning, the back-breaking row to the whale, the flying harpoons, the rope that can take you off "voicelessly as Turkish mutes bowstring their victims." *Moby-Dick* is a representation of the passionate mind speaking, for its metaphysical concerns, out of the very midst of life. So, after the first lowering, Queequeg is shown sitting all night in a submerged boat, holding up a lantern like an "imbecile candle in the heart of that almighty forlornness ... the sign and symbol of a man without hope, hopelessly holding up hope in the midst of despair." Melville insists that our thinking is not swallowed up by practical concerns, that man constantly searches for a reality equal to his inner life of thought—and it is his ability to show this in the midst of a brutal, dirty whaling voyage that makes *Moby-Dick* such an astonishing book. Just as Ahab is a hero, so *Moby-Dick* itself is a heroic book. What concerns Melville is not merely the heroism that gets expressed in physical action, but the heroism of thought itself as it rises above its seeming insignificance and proclaims, in the very teeth of a seemingly hostile and malevolent creation, that man's voice *is* heard for something against the watery waste and the deep, that man's thought has an echo in the universe.

III

This is the quest. But what makes *Moby-Dick* so fascinating, and in a sense even uncanny, is that the issue is always in doubt, and remains so to the end. Melville was right when he wrote to Hawthorne: "I have written a wicked book, and feel as spotless as the lamb." And people who want to construe *Moby-Dick* into a condemnation of mad, bad Ahab will always miss what Melville meant when he wrote of his book: "It is not a piece of fine feminine Spitalfields silk—but it is of the horrible texture of a fabric that should be woven of ships' cables & hawsers. A Polar wind blows through it, & birds of prey hover over it." For in the struggle between man's effort to find meaning in nature, and the indifference of nature itself, which simply eludes him (nature here signifies the whole external show and force of animate life in a world suddenly emptied of God, one where an "intangible malignity" has reigned from the beginning), Melville often portrays the struggle from the side of nature itself. He sees the whale's view of things far more than he does Ahab's: and Moby-Dick's milk-white head, the tail feathers of the sea birds streaming from his back like pennons, are described with a rapture that is like the adoration of a god. Even in the most terrible scenes of the shark massacre, where the sharks bend around like bows to bite at their own entrails, or in the ceaseless motion of "my dear Pacific," the "Potters' fields of all four continents," one feels that Melville is transported by the naked reality of things, the great unending flow of the creation itself, where the great shroud of the sea rolls over the doomed ship "as it rolled five thousand years ago." Indeed, one feels in the end that it is only the necessity to keep one person alive as a witness to the story that saves Ishmael from the general ruin and wreck. In Melville's final vision of the whole, it is not fair but it is entirely *just* that the whale should destroy the ship, that man should be caught up on the beast. It is just in a cosmic sense, not in the sense that the prophet (Father Mapple) predicts the punishment of man's disobedience in the telling of Jonah's story from the beginning, where the point made is the classic reprimand of God to man when He speaks out of the whirlwind.

What Melville does is to speak for the whirlwind, for the watery waste, for the sharks.

It is this that gives *Moby-Dick* its awful and crushing power. It is a unique gift. Goethe said that he wanted, as a writer, to know what it is like to be a woman. But Melville sometimes makes you feel that he knows, as a writer, what it is like to be the eyes of the rock, the magnitude of the whale, the scalding sea, the dreams that lie buried in the Pacific. It is all, of course, seen through human eyes—yet there is in Melville a cold, final, ferocious hopelessness, a kind of ecstatic masochism, that delights in punishing man, in heaping coals on his head, in drowning him. You see it in the scene of the whale running through the herd with a cutting spade in his body, cutting down his own; in the sharks eating at their own entrails and voiding from them in the same convulsion; in the terrible picture of Pip the cabin boy jumping out of the boat in fright and left on the Pacific to go crazy; in Tashtego falling into the "honey head" of the whale; in the ropes that suddenly whir up from the spindles and carry you off; in the final awesome picture of the whale butting its head against the *Pequod*. In all these scenes there is an ecstasy in horror, the horror of nature in itself, nature "pure," without God or man: the void. It is symbolized by the whiteness of the whale, the whiteness that is not so much a colour as the absence of colour. "Is it that by its indefiniteness it shadows forth the heartless voids and immensities of the universe, and thus stabs us from behind with the thought of annihilation, when beholding the white depths of the milky way?" And it is this picture of existence as one where man has only a peep-hole on the mystery itself, that constitutes the most remarkable achievement of Melville's genius. For as in the meditation on the whiteness of the whale, it becomes an uncanny attempt to come to grips with nature as it might be conceived with man entirely left out; or, what amounts to the same thing, with man losing his humanity and being exclusively responsive to primitive and racial memories, to the trackless fathomless nothing that has been from the beginning, to the very essence of a beginning that, in contradiction to all man's scriptures, had no divine history, no definite locus, but just *was*—with man slipped into the picture much later.

This view of reality, this ability to side with nature rather than with man, means an ability to love what has no animation, what is inhumanly still, what is not in search, as man himself is—a hero running against time and fighting against "reality." Here Melville puts, as it were, his ear to reality itself: to the rock rather than to the hero trying to get his sword out of the rock. He does it by constantly, and bitterly, and savagely in fact, comparing man with the great thing he is trying to understand. Ahab may be a hero by trying to force himself on what is too much for him, but Melville has no doubt that man is puny and presumptuous and easily overwhelmed—in short, drowned—in the great storm of reality he tries to encompass.

This sense of scale lies behind the chapters on the natural history of the whale, and behind the constant impressing on our minds of the contrast between man and the whale—man getting into a small boat, man being overwhelmed by his own weapons. The greatest single metaphor in the book is that of bigness, and even when Melville laughs at himself for trying to hook this Leviathan with a pen—"Bring me a condor's quill! Bring me Vesuvius' crater for an inkstand!"—we know that he not merely feels exhilaration at attempting this mighty subject, but that he is also abashed, he feels grave; mighty waters are rolling around him. This compelling sense of magnitude, however, gets him to organize the book brilliantly, in a great flood of chapters—some of them very small, one or two only a paragraph long, in the descriptive method which is the great homage that he pays to his subject, and which so provides him with an inexhaustible delight in devoting himself to every conceivable detail about the whale. And, to go back to a theme mentioned earlier, it is this sense of a limitless subject that gives the style its peculiarly loping quality, as if it were constantly looking for connectives, since on the subject of the whale no single word or statement is enough. But these details tend, too, to heap up in such a staggering array as to combine into the awesomeness of a power against which Ahab's challenge is utterly vain, and against which his struggle to show his superiority over the ordinary processes of nature becomes blasphemous. The only thing left to man, Melville seems to tell us, is to take the span of this magnitude—to feel and to record the power of this mighty torrent, this burning fire.

And it is this, this poetic power, rather than any specifically human one, this power of transcription rather than of any alteration of life that will admit human beings into its tremendous scale, that makes up the greatness of the book—by giving us the measure of Melville's own relation to the nature that his hero so futilely attempts to master or defy. For though Melville often takes a grim and almost cruel pleasure in showing man tumbling over before the magnitude of the universe and though much of the book is concerned, as in the sections on fighting and "cooking" the whale, with man's effort to get a grip on external nature, first through physical assault and then by scientific and industrial cunning, man finds his final relatedness to nature neither as a hero (Ahab) nor by heeding Father Mapple's old prophetic warning of man's proper subservience to God. Though all his attempted gains from nature fail him and all goes down with the *Pequod*—all man's hopes of profit, of adjustment to orthodoxy (Starbuck), even of the wisdom that is in madness (Pip)—man, though forever alien to the world, an Ishmael, is somehow in tune with it, with its torrential rhythms, by dint of his art by the directness with which his words grasp the world by the splendour of his perceptions, by the lantern which he holds up "like a candle in the midst of the almighty forlornness". Man is not merely a waif in the world, he is an ear listening to the sea that almost drowns him; an imagination, a mind, that hears the sea in the shell, and darts behind all appearance to the beginning of things, and runs riot with the frightful force of the sea itself. There, in man's incredible and unresting mind, is the fantastic gift with which we enter into what is not our own, what is even against us—and for this, so amazingly, we can speak.

PATRICK McGRATH

Introduction to Moby Dick

There is nothing more sardonic than a good Melvillean joke, and *Moby Dick*, for all its tragic grandeur, is full of them. In the first paragraph our narrator, Ishmael, speaking of the 'damp, drizzly November in my soul', reports that one of the symptoms of this mild depression of his is an involuntary tendency to hang about in front of coffin warehouses. There's a lovely morbid humour to the picture this evokes, particularly when coupled with his inclination to bring up the rear of every funeral procession he meets. Ishmael then tells us how he intends to deal with his depression: he will go to sea, he will have a look at 'the watery part of the world'. So he does; but he is still not free of coffins, they continue to haunt him, although ultimately to benign effect. For a coffin will save Ishmael's life. It will allow him, alone of all the crew of the *Pequod*, to survive an encounter with the White Whale and come home to tell the story.

There is a moment, late in *Moby Dick*, when the *Pequod* is caught in a typhoon somewhere off Japan. After one of her boats is stove in by a great rolling sea, the second mate turns to the first mate and says: 'You see, Mr. Starbuck, a wave has such a great long start before it leaps, all round the world it runs, and then comes the spring!' The same might be said of Herman Melville. He was only 30 when he began writing *Moby Dick*, but he had crammed a great deal of living into those years. Born in 1819, he

---

From *Moby Dick* by Herman Melville, pp. v–xi. © 1999 by Patrick McGrath.

19

came of good New York stock: his mother was a Gansevoort, and both his grandfathers were heroes of the American Revolution. But as Herman was growing up the family business began to founder, and at 19 he went to sea. Over the next six years he saw much of the world, and then sat down at his desk to write up his experiences. In short order he produced five novels and found himself a famous author.

And then comes the spring! He sets to work on *Moby Dick*, and in under two years completes what is now considered by many to be the best novel ever written in the English language.

Contemporary readers did not altogether see it that way, however. Much that we now recognize to be magnificent about the book—its complex unities, its digressive coherence, its deep metaphysical soundings—these qualities put off many nineteenth-century readers, and Melville never recovered the popularity he had known with his first books. In later years he produced masterpieces of the order of *Benito Cereno* and *Billy Budd, Sailor*, but was plagued by ill-health, financial uncertainty, and bouts of depression. In 1863 he left his farm in Pittsfield, Massachusetts, unable to keep it going, and returned with his family to New York. He died there in 1891, a forgotten man, and it would be another thirty years before the Melville revival got under way and *Moby Dick* entered the canon as the towering masterpiece it is now acknowledged to be.

It is with melancholy Ishmael, then, and his intention to go to sea that the novel opens. Arriving in New Bedford, Ishmael befriends that extraordinary giant of a man from the South Seas, that comprehensively tattooed harpooneer of whales, Queequeg. The two share a bed in the Spouter-Inn, Ishmael setting aside his misgivings with the words, 'Better sleep with a sober cannibal than a drunken Christian'. They take the ferry to Nantucket, where Ishmael finds a vessel whose bulwarks are decorated with sperm whale teeth, and whose tiller is carved from a sperm whale's jaw. This of course is the *Pequod*, fitted out, like her master, with the bones of her enemy.

Ishmael wants to meet the master of the *Pequod*. That man, he learns, is Captain Ahab. He is 'a grand, ungodly, god-like man' who has apparently had a recent brush with insanity, brought on by the pain in the stump of his leg where a whale took it off. And what whale was that? A whale Ishmael has already glimpsed, so he tells us, in his inmost soul: 'one grand hooded phantom, like a snow hill in the air.'

It will be hundreds of pages before we meet that grand hooded phantom, and not a few before we meet the ungodly, godlike man who has sworn to kill it. What happens in the mean time is very curious. For we seem to lose Ishmael, after he and Queequeg have secured their berths aboard the

Pequod he seems to dissolve in a sea of knowledge about whales and whaling. He turns into one of those romantic young men he himself sneers at, who ship out on whalers and sink into such reverie up at the mast-head that they lose their identity—until, that is, they come to, and discover that they are hovering 'over Descartian vortices'.

To read the novel today is oddly like making a sea voyage; often we find ourselves adrift in passages of learned discourse about the whale: the historical aspect of the whale, the mythological aspect, the zoological, biological, and culinary aspects, and so on—the *bibliographical* aspect, even, as we see the whale family divided into folio, octavo, and duodecimo editions, Melville thus turning on its head his grand formal metaphor, that the book is a whale of a thing, with the idea that each whale is a sort of a book. 'Give me a condor's quill! Give me Vesuvius' crater for an inkstand! Friends, hold my arms! ... To produce a mighty book, you must choose a mighty theme.'

The effect of these multiple perspectives is to overwhelm the reader with the intractable question of how we are to think of the whale, if the creature looks different with every distinct point of view from which it is observed. Whatever the truth of the whale, clearly language cannot contain it, the reality of any phenomenon for Melville lying deeper than language, deeper even than the appearance of the thing.

Small wonder then that we lose Ishmael in this ocean of metaphysical instability, for in all the vastness of the world, and the systems of knowledge man has devised to apprehend it, the individual is but a speck, invisible; and it is Melville's genius to expand on this mighty theme with such vigour and erudition and humour that we allow ourselves to be carried far into the alien seas of the novel, until, from out of the great, obliterating, oceanic sweep of it all emerges—old Ahab: 'In the midst of the personified impersonal, a personality stands here.'

And what a personality. Ahab is one of the giants of literature. Rigid in his obsession, he has been called an ego without a self, a will without a character—a partial man because a man identified entirely with that part of himself that is injured and will not heal: his 'torn body and gashed soul bled into one another; and so interfusing, made him mad.' But for all that he is still a man, a stern Quaker sea-captain from Nantucket with forty years experience hunting whales, and recently married to a young wife who has given him a son. He is capable of arousing fierce loyalty in his crew, if not affection; and he is not immune to pathos, he can shed a tear of grief at his own desperate predicament: 'nor did all the Pacific contain such wealth as that one wee drop.'

With the appearance of Ahab, and his ritualistic declaration of war upon the White Whale, the novel moves forward with new purpose, but by no means in a straight line; the course remains digressive, the narrative cumulative, as encounters with other vessels, and the brute realities of ocean and weather, as well as incidents aboard the *Pequod* herself, all pile meaning upon meaning until the impending struggle of man and whale is so heavily loaded with significance that nothing but this epic structure could possibly bear it without buckling under the strain. For with his insistence that 'some certain significance lurks in all things', Melville opens the way for not only spiritual essences to inhere in the physical world, but for myriad metaphorical connections to be brought into play. Sharks are seen as 'the strong, troubled, murderous thinkings of the masculine sea'. 'All men,' reflects Ishmael, 'live enveloped in whale-lines.' There is in man's soul 'one insular Tahiti'; and this, on the subject of whiteness: 'all deified Nature absolutely paints like the harlot, whose allurements cover nothing but the charnel-house within.' This relentless stream of figuration contributes heftily to Melville's sceptical interrogation of the world of appearances, which endures as the central philosophical thrust of the novel.

The *Pequod* enters the Pacific Ocean with whales ahead of her and pirates behind, and the final encounter with Moby Dick is imminent. It is still not too late for Ahab to turn back from his mad project, as Starbuck attempts to persuade him to do; and as though to underline the allure of home, Melville has the *Pequod* encounter another American ship, Nantucket-bound, her holds full to bursting with spermaceti. The contrast between them is striking, 'one all jubilations for things passed, the other all forebodings as to things to come', and the captains are equally starkly differentiated: the one benignly overseeing his men as they dance on deck with olive-hued native girls, while the other, Ahab, is 'shaggy and black, with a stubborn gloom'. In short, the one ship, the *Pequod*, is full of death, and the other is full of sperm oil. And what is it called, this vital, spermy ship? The *Bachelor*.

Another good joke from Melville. In this world of men, here is the *Bachelor* with sperm not only filling her holds, but barrels of the stuff hanging from the rigging, stowed on every deck, crowding the state-rooms, even filling the steward's spare coffee-pot and the sockets of the harpoons. It is everywhere, in short, except in the captain's trouser pockets—'and those he reserved to thrust his hands into, in self-complacent testimony of his entire satisfaction'. It is a bitter, misogynistic joke, one guaranteed to provoke a bark of laughter in the gloom of a seamen's tavern. It is also the culmination of a punning association Melville has sustained all through the novel, of sperm whale oil with sperm; in fact sex is all over this vast book that has no women in it.

But how to speak of the sex in *Moby Dick*? The only observed act of coitus is performed by whales and merely hinted at, with a great discretion of circumlocution, in terms of 'Leviathan amours' and 'inscrutable creatures' who 'serenely revelled in dalliance and delight'—a sight that has Ishmael reflecting that 'amid the tornadoed Atlantic of my being, do I myself still for ever centrally disport in mute-calm'—thus turning whale sex into a metaphor for a certain 'mildness of joy' in the depths of his own narcissistic being.

Even so, a powerful homoerotic current surges through the book. It is there in Ishmael's embraces with Queequeg in the Spouter-Inn; it is sustained through their linkage at either end of a monkey-rope; and it continues to the final image of Ishmael, sole survivor of the wreck of the *Pequod*, clutching Queequeg's coffin which, carved as it is with all the complex symbols of its owner's tattoos, is thus identified with the harpooneer's body. Ishmael saves himself, then, by figuratively embracing the body of his heathen friend.

But here, too, the meanings pile up inexorably, and if the relationship of Ishmael and Queequeg seems an implicitly sexual bond, so also does it suggest a wider fraternity, a brotherhood among the races, an idea of America as the place where such disparate men as Ishmael and Queequeg—and Daggoo, and Tashtego, and Fedallah the Parsee—brown, black, red, and yellow skins, as well as white—might live in democratic harmony, 'federated along one keel'. In this view the *Pequod* stands as a symbol of America herself; but an America bent on self-destruction, and why? Because under the sway of an obsession with whiteness. At which point we remember that in the early 1850s, when Melville was writing *Moby Dick*, it was already clear to many that the argument between the states over the question of slavery must end in a bloody civil war, and that America would tear herself apart precisely because of her obsession with whiteness.

There is no neat summary possible for a book so sprawlingly alive with ideas and imagery, and so fiercely aflame with the passion of its author. A book that began with a joke about coffins ends with a man clinging to a coffin in the middle of the ocean. The ultimate symbol of death is transformed into a life-raft, and a life-raft, moreover, covered with 'grotesque figures and drawings', all copied by Queequeg from the tattoos on his own body. And what of those tattoos? They 'had been the work of a departed prophet and seer of his island, who, by those hieroglyphic marks, had written out on [Queequeg's] body a complete theory of the heavens and the earth, and a mystical treatise on the art of attaining truth.'

This may be the bleakest of all the bleak jokes in the book; certainly it is an idea that most pungently expresses the spirit of robust and mocking scepticism with which Melville assaults all received ideas concerning the nature of reality. It is the idea that the answers to the large questions that most sorely perplex us are under our very noses—are inscribed on our skin—but we lack the wit to decode them.

HOMER B. PETTEY

Cannibalism, Slavery, and
Self-Consumption in Moby-Dick

They were "slaves without masters," the little fish who were food for all
the larger.

George Fitzhugh, Cannibals All! or, Slaves Without Masters

In this vein, Maori cannibalism—well-documented from contemporary
nineteenth-century accounts—was set in a context of ritual warfare; the
consumption of human flesh paralleled that of birds and fish in hunting
rituals. Men consumed at cannibalistic feasts were referred to as "fishes,"
and "first fish" being eaten by a chief who thus acquired control over the
land of the vanquished.

I. M. Lewis, Religion in Context: Cults and Charisma

"Kill-e," cried Queequeg, twisting his tattooed face into an unearthly
expression of disdain,—"ah! him bery small-e fish-e; Queequeg no kill-e
so small-e fish-e; Queequeg kill-e big whale!"

Melville, "The Wheelbarrow," Moby-Dick

That Melville chose an unrepentant South Sea cannibal, Queequeg, to
be his narrator's spiritual guide and savior in *Moby-Dick* (1851) certainly
must have disturbed his nineteenth-century readers. Equally disconcerting,
the novel's narrator assumes the allegorical guise of Ishmael, slave son of

From *Arizona Quarterly* 59, no. 1 (Spring 2003): 31–58. © 2003 by Arizona Board of Regents.

Abraham: symbol of alienated, social outcasts from the bosom of Abraham; progenitor of enemies to Israel, whose tribe conspires with the nations of Edom, Moab, Ammon, and Assyria for Israel's destruction (Ps. 83); and in literature, wild man father (Gen. 16:12) of the enemies of Christianity, the "Africk" in Spenser's *Faerie Queene*, as well as father of Native Americans in Longfellow's *Evangeline* (1847).[1] By pairing Queequeg with Ishmael in *Moby-Dick*, Melville unites barbarous cannibal with outcast slave. Barbarity and slavery would also be recognizable in the ship's name, *Pequod*: these Amerindians, viewed by Puritan sages as "Bloody *Salvages*" (Mather, *Magnalia* 166), were nearly decimated in a genocidal military campaign by New England settlers in 1637.[2] Pequot survivors were forced into the peculiar institution of Puritan slavery, sold to plantations in the Caribbean, given a status comparable to African slaves, and inhumanely branded for running away.[3] Historically, Pequots were faced with vicious New England slavers to the north and east and had nowhere to go westward, because beyond the Connecticut Valley lived hostile Mohawks, whose name also meant cannibals.[4] Puritans collected war trophies—severed heads and hands—of the Pequots as evidence to Bay Colony officials that their capital had been well invested in military protection; Thomas Hooker adopted a cannibalistic metaphor when preaching on these body parts, stating that "the Indians would be 'bread for us,'" a recognition of, if not praise for, New England's Christian brand of bloodthirsty aggression (Shuffelton 237–38). In the nineteenth century, numerous examples of Christians resorting to cannibalism at sea pre-dated *Moby-Dick*, among them, the *Medusa* in 1816, subject of Gericault's *Raft of the Medusa* (1819), and the *Essex* in 1820, subject of Chase's *Narrative* cited in his "Extracts."[5] Melville distrusted hypocritical condemnations of savages or cannibals by Christian culture, whose pieties he viewed as more gruesome than the rituals of so-called primitives.

In *Moby-Dick*, Melville uses cannibalism in order to attack the cruel institutions of slavery and capitalism which were eating away at American culture. Aware of the political rhetoric of slavery, particularly the denigration of African-Americans as savages by pro-slavery Southerners, Melville recognized the equally savage conditions imposed by Northern industrialism and American expansionism, not just upon indigenous and slave populations, but also upon Northern workers.[6] Cannibalism, then, served Melville as a sociopolitical metaphor by which he could attack America's hypocritical system of values. It also afforded Melville an allegorical and symbolic mode for representing acts of appropriation, subjugation, and consumption. For Melville, the whaling industry itself was a perfect symbol of American capitalism and expansion of his day; the enterprise of whaling also shared similarities with cannibalism—hunting, killing, possessing, dismembering,

and consuming. Fish, sharks, and whales often function as metaphorical
substitutes for mankind in *Moby-Dick*; as most readers recognize, the
anatomy, dissection, and consumption of the whale thinly veil analogies to
human beings.

Most certainly, Melville was fascinated with ethnography of primitive
peoples, especially how these cultures were both set apart from American
culture and paradoxically reflected it. Standard typology of cannibalism
includes exocannibalism, the killing and eating of outsiders, usually in
warfare; endocannibalism, kinship killing or kinship feeding that reinforces
life process and regeneration; and autocannibalism, ingestion of one's own
body.[7] Melville is keenly aware of just these sorts of cultural distinctions,
as evidenced by Ishmael drawing literal and figurative distinctions between
Queequeg and the other crew members of the *Pequod*. Melville populates
the *Pequod* with cannibals, making the very vessel a symbol of cannibalistic
urges. The voyage of the *Pequod* results in increasing stages of grotesque
consumption, particularly evident from the cetological and cannibalistic
centers of the novel. Structurally, the novel moves from ritualized
exocannibalism to narcissistic autocannibalism. Rhetorically, cannibalism
results in self-consuming fictions, by which political and economic structures
based upon oppression lead inevitably to their own self-destruction.

Melville's approach to cannibalism in *Moby-Dick* and his characterization
of Queequeg rely upon his reading of Montaigne's "Of Cannibals."[8]
Montaigne provides a template for the novel's thematic dichotomy between
savagery and civilization, as well as for Ishmael's *olla podrida* of allusions—
biblical, classical, modern European and New World examples of barbarity.
Like Montaigne, Melville recognized that civilized men had "changed
artificially" and were "led astray from the common order" of Nature by
their belief that others were inhuman, savage, and wild based on the paltry
evidence that they practiced different customs (152). This sanctimonious
bias by Christianity develops from its fervent belief that it will always have
"the perfect religion, the perfect government, the perfect and accomplished
manners in all things" (152). Montaigne uses as his counterexample the New
World cannibal community whose way of life surpasses poetic visions of the
classical golden age. Melville similarly uses Queequeg to underscore the
hypocrisy of Christian morality. Michel de Certeau explains the structure of
Montaigne's essay in terms that can be seen to parallel Ishmael's adventure
in *Moby-Dick*. The essay lays out a narrative topography in the form of "a
travel account" with three movements: the outbound journey that distances
the narrator from his culture, intellectually and socially; the excursion among
the savages in which "the discourse that sets off in search of the other with
the impossible task of saying the truth returns from afar with the authority

to speak in the name of the other"; and the return of the native, the now savage-minded narrator (69–70). Initially, Ishmael's tale maps out boundaries between cultures of land and sea; he adopts the pose of authority and often speaks for Queequeg, his cannibalistic alter ego; and the novel, as the reader discovers, is his retrospective account that is somewhat in sympathy with his cannibal's worldview. Distinctions occur in *Moby-Dick* among types of cannibalism; often Ishmael contrasts Queequeg's cannibalistic humanism to Ahab's Christian monomania. In *Moby-Dick*, however, sociopolitical topography demarcating civilized and savage worlds soon becomes less distinct as unchecked barbarism aboard the *Pequod* increases.

"Of Cannibals" sympathetically treats the practices of this New World savage community—symbolic warfare, enslavement, headhunting, communal killing, communal feasts on human flesh—that seem inimical to Western culture. Melville agreed with Montaigne's assertion that "treachery, disloyalty, tyranny, and cruelty" are "our ordinary vices" (156). By juxtaposing this civilized savagery with incidents of Christian barbarism such as the Inquisition, Montaigne renders these savage acts less barbarous than Western customs: "Truly here are real savages by our standards; for either they must be thoroughly so, or we must be; there is an amazing distance between their character and ours" (158). To add accuracy to his account, he informs his reader that he spoke with a New World warrior cannibal, "our sailors called him a king" (159), comparable to Queequeg's seafaring, royal heritage. Montaigne concludes his essay on a comical note concerning this distinguished spokesman of the cannibals, reminding his reader of culturally based prejudices: "All this is not too bad—but what's the use? They don't wear breeches" (159). Of course, Queequeg "staving about with little else but his hat and boots on" comes immediately to mind (35). For both Melville and Montaigne, those who denigrate the practice of cannibal cultures do so from the standpoint of blindness to their own culture's savage heritage. Montaigne demonstrates that contradictory images—utopian ideals and cannibalism, Christian pieties and savagery—are "interdependendent mechanisms" (Klarer 395). In *Moby-Dick*, this interdependence first occurs in the marriage between Ishmael and Queequeg; Ishmael awakens in the Spouter-Inn in Queequeg's "bridegroom clasp," as though "I had been his wife" (33, 32). In Melville's comic marriage, Ishmael is wedded to paganism and divorces himself from the hypocrisies and barbarity of Western culture.

Queequeg's sign of exocannibalism, like that of Montaigne's New World primitives, is the New Zealand head he peddles about New Bedford, a town whose economy already has a surplus of shrunken heads, and where "actual cannibals stand at street corners; savages outright; many of whom yet carry on their bones unholy flesh" (37). Trophies of exocannibalism also present themselves in the patrician society of New Bedford, which "is a queer place" with a "bony" appearance placed upon a "scraggy scoria" of land; the skeletal and excremental puns are worth noting here in comparison with the cannibals in the streets (38). New Bedford, as Ishmael tells us, is no promised land, no land of milk and honey, "not like Canaan," but "a land of oil" (38), a symbol of nineteenth-century American capitalism. Natives of New Bedford, not unlike their pagan counterparts, engage in symbolic rituals, giving "whales for dowers to their daughters" (38). Like Queequeg's shrunken head, whales are trafficked in a kind of exocannibalism, serving as trophies of enemies to New Bedford warriors. Melville pointedly connects whale rituals with capitalism. Surplus profit and accumulation mark the conspicuous consumption of the New Bedford population, who "have reserves of oil in every house" and "recklessly bum" spermaceti candles (38). American consumption far outweighs that of the primitives. It is in New Bedford where Ishmael stands before gable-ended Spouter-Inn and recalls the New Testament parable of class division-Lazarus and Dives. Ishmael transforms Dives into a modern-day New England capitalist, who "lives like a Czar in an ice palace made of frozen sighs, and being a president of a temperance society, he only drinks the tepid tears of orphans" (19). By "temperance society" Melville probably means the Washingtonians, a charitable association devoted solely to moral suasion to rid society of the evils of drink, but not its more pressing needs; such as dismal poverty.[9] Melville's taste for liquor and his distaste for sanctimonious Christians explains his characterization for this Dives. The cannibalistic metaphor of living off the tears of orphans inverts the meaning of Luke's parable. In Luke 16, Dives ignores the suffering of the poor man Lazarus and his indifference results in his burning in Hades, while Lazarus ascends into the arms of father Abraham after death. Moreover, like Tantalus, Dives suffers from an unquenchable thirst in Hades, which Melville inverts by having him cannibalistically drink the sorrows of the poor. In New England's cruel system of amassing wealth and class division, Melville cynically sees no salvation for the poor and no punishment for callous, autocratic capitalists.

Queequeg's encounters with Christian culture are rarely harmonious as well. According to his biographical tale, he set out from Kokovoko in order "to learn among the Christians, the arts whereby to make his people still happier," but soon discovers "that even Christians could be both miserable and wicked; infinitely more so, than all his father's heathens" (57). Ishmael concurs. Without proselytizing, Queequeg converts Ishmael. In "A Bosom Friend," Ishmael works out a moral logic for transforming himself into Queequeg's pagan reflection:

> But what is worship?—to do the will of God—that is worship. And what is the will of God?—to do to my fellow man what I would have my fellow man to do to me—that is the will of God. Now, Queequeg is my fellow man. And what do I wish that this Queequeg would do to me? Why, unite with me in my particular Presbyterian form of worship. Consequently, I must then unite with him in his; ergo, I must turn idolator. (54)

Ishmael embraces Queequeg's customs, but he does so as an act of rebellion against American Christian prejudices, summed up in Ishmael's logic of inversion: "Better sleep with a sober cannibal than a drunken Christian" (31). Here, Ishmael's rejection of his culture echoes Satan's rebellion against God in Milton's *Paradise Lost*: "Better to reign in Hell, than serve in Heav'n" (1.263). Idolatry, however, does not mean becoming a religious fanatic. By explaining to Queequeg the history of religion from "the primitive religions, and coming down to the various religions of the present time," Ishmael hopes to dissuade his friend from fasting, since "all these Lents, Ramadans, and prolonged ham-squattings in cold, cheerless rooms were stark nonsense; bad for the health; useless for the soul; opposed, in short, to the obvious laws of Hygiene and common sense" (81). What eats at Ishmael is the emptiness of rituals. Religious self-punishment, as Ishmael sarcastically puts it, is based upon indigestion: "hell is an idea first born on an undigested apple-dumpling; and since then perpetuated through the hereditary dyspepsias nurtured by Ramadans" (82). This "apple-dumpling," the forbidden fruit of Eden, recalls the action of the "two orchard thieves" (15) whose consumption brings sin and death into the world. Moreover, their desire to possess and to consume brings about their self-destruction. Religion, then, reminds us of our self-consuming impulses. In "Loomings," Ishmael has wryly warned his readers from the outset that myth of Narcissus "is the key to it all" (14).

Ishmael shows signs of transforming into a cannibal long before he sets sail aboard the *Pequod*. In "Chowder," Ishmael experiences a comic foreshadowing of the whale dissections and meals from the cannibalistic center of *Moby-Dick*: "Chowders for breakfast, and chowder for dinner, and chowder for supper, till you began to look for fish-bones coming through clothes" (65). From the first moment that Ishmael feasts his eyes upon the "ivory" *Pequod* (199), the narrative portends the cannibalism to come: "A cannibal of a craft, tricking herself forth in the chased bones of her enemies" (6–7). Captain Peleg warns Ishmael that Ahab has tasted the civilized and savage worlds: "Mark ye, be forewarned; Ahab's above the common; Ahab's been in colleges, as well as 'mong the cannibals" (76). Like the *Pequod* with its "jaw-bone tiller" (420), Ahab bears the symbols of his own cannibalistic urges, his "ivory leg had at sea been fashioned from the polished bone of a sperm whale's jaw" (110).

Dining experiences aboard the *Pequod* always include cannibalism. Even Ahab's "ivory-inlaid" cabin dining table is formed from the body of the whale (131). As opposed to the mealtime segregation of kingly Ahab and his knights, the "three savages"—Queequeg, Tashtego, and Daggoo—create an "almost frantic democracy," though they "dined like lords" (133). Melville's comic paradox of hierarchical stations reverses the presumed aristocracy of the "their masters, the mates," who are afraid of the "ungentlemanly" manners and hideous sounds of rapacious feeding coming from Queequeg, the Polynesian, and Tashtego, the Native American, and are perhaps surprised, as Ishmael's depictions suggest, by the "baronial," "dainty" manners of the "noble savage," the African Daggoo (133). Melville also provides comic scenes of the harpooners' "portentous appetites" that produce panic in the Dough-Boy, "the progeny of a bankrupt banker and a hospital nurse" (152), who represents American culture and its ridiculous ethnocentric dread of other cultures. Of course, this heir to a failed economic system and diseased morality cannot understand the ways of cannibal, slave, and savage. Tashtego, like Queequeg and Daggoo, is "unmixed," a pure specimen and "inheritor of the unvitiated blood" of his race of "proud warrior hunters" (107); and yet, his "snaky limbs" are reminders of the "superstitions of some of the earlier Puritans" who considered redmen to be sons of the "Prince of the Powers of the Air" (107). That satanic imagery will appear again when the *Pequod* sinks and Tashtego acts in a manner similar to the Devil himself. Daggoo, "a gigantic, coal-black negro-savage," is no slave, but freely volunteered to join a whaler's crew. Like Queequeg and Tashtego, he has "retained all his barbaric virtues," so much so that his very presence frightens American white men, who "standing before him seemed a white flag come to beg truce of a fortress" (107, 108).

From the outset of the *Pequod*'s voyage, Melville draws our attention to associations between types of cannibalism and slave labor in order to show the corrupt economic foundation of nineteenth-century American capitalism. Into his discussion of the lineage of the harpooners, Ishmael interjects an ironic anatomy of labor:

> Herein it is the same with the American whale fishery as with the American army and military and merchant navies, and as with the engineering forces employed in the construction of the American Canals and Railroads. The same, I say, because in all these cases the native American liberally provides the brains, the rest of the world as generously the muscles. (108)

America's Manifest Destiny and its military and commercial expansionist policies exploit the bodies of other cultures. As a scion of American superstition and racial prejudice, Dough-boy experiences the great American phobia—that the victims of rapacious American capitalism will turn the tables on him. He is consumed with fear of these savages: Queequeg's "barbaric smack" causes Dough-Boy "to see whether any marks of teeth lurked in his own lean arm"; Tashtego sings out for the frightened Steward "that his bones might be picked" (134). Reversing the roles of master and slave, capitalist and laborer, Ishmael wryly points out the dilemma awaiting America: "hard fares the white waiter who waits upon cannibals" (134).

Ishmael's theory of race in America is evident in "The Wheelbarrow." Here, he dismisses artificial racial distinctions "as though a white man were anything more dignified than a whitewashed negro" (60). By analogy, a Christian is hardly more virtuous than a cannibal. In this chapter, Ishmael speculates on the high moral character of Queequeg, a humane cannibal isolated among Christian heathens. Melville contextualizes racial issues with the description of the little *Moss* among the waves "as a slave before a Sultan" (60), metaphorically preparing the reader for the racial issues to come and prefiguring the crew before tyrannical Ahab. A greenhorn bumpkin aboard the little *Moss* mocks Queequeg on the sea journey from New Bedford to Nantucket; Queequeg responds with his own biting cannibalistic mockery, "Queequeg no kill-e so small-e fish-e" (60), but the Christians do not understand his joke. When the insolent man falls overboard and while good Christians gaze but do not stir to help him, the cannibal risks his life to save the very man who had offended him. Ishmael narrates Queequeg's thoughts after the rescue: "Was there ever such unconsciousness? He did not seem to think that he at all deserved a medal from the Humane and Magnanimous Societies.... and mildly eyeing those around him, seemed to be saying to himself—'It's a mutual, joint-stock world, in all meridians. We cannibals must help these Christians'" (61). Queequeg's cannibalism, then, is not a savage taking of life, but a reverence for life. His religion has nothing to do with Christian cannibalism, that oppressive obsession with death which Ishmael equates with faith: "But Faith, like a jackal, feeds among the tombs, and even from these dead doubts she gathers her most vital hope" (41). In contrast to the white, Christian world of suspicious xenophobes, Queequeg's indifference to race and his reverence for life attracts Ishmael. Critics often argue that Ishmael clings to Queequeg as an affirmation of a natural brand of humanism, Lockean ideals, and democratic gestures of racial and cultural inclusion.[10] We need to be wary of Ishmael's motives, since from the outset he simply seems fed up with his own culture.

Melville contrasts this scene of pagan altruism with Bulkington's death at sea in "The Lee Shore." One white Christian bigot is saved from the engulfing sea, while another white man is swallowed by it. In a howling gale, Bulkington stands at the *Pequod*'s helm, piloting its "vindictive bows in cold malicious waves" (97). Here, the *Pequod* attempts to master the sea, in sharp contrast to the little *Moss* which seems a slave before the Sultan sea in "The Wheelbarrow." But who is this Bulkington and why is he killed off so early in the novel? Scholars have made claims that Bulkington is an actual figure from Melville's own time, from the Missouri Senator Thomas Hart Benton to the British artist J. M. W. Turner.[11] William V. Spanos has politicized Bulkington as a symbol of Melville's "differential" and "disinherited" American (155). Most likely, though, this short epitaph of a chapter can be read as Melville's contempt for slave-abiding America. After all, Ishmael tells us in "The Spouter-Inn" that Bulkington's voice "at once announced that he was a Southerner" (23). Bulkington, even though he stands aloof from his mates, is among those "arrantest topers" in whose heads "liquor soon mounted" (23). Two enigmatic characters command Ishmael's attention and fascination at the Spouter-Inn—Bulkington and Queequeg. In that chapter, Ishmael's off-hand comic remark about preferring to sleep with a sober cannibal rather than a drunken Christian also can be read as his drawing distinctions between these two men—the humane cannibal and the white man from the enslaving South. Bulkington's demise is a misanthropic ritual sacrifice, the first of Melville's many death—wishes for America and its institutions.

Too often "The Lee Shore" is read as somehow lacking Ishmael's usual irony. Bulkington's apotheosis is no affirmation at all, but a bitterly sarcastic denunciation of what the man represents. Ishmael's topography betrays Melville's political context for this Southerner: even though it seems he will die in the infinite sea like a demigod, the waves and winds, the conspiring forces of heaven and earth against which the *Pequod* sails, will toss his body toward "the treacherous, slavish shore" (97). Bulkington's death sets a pattern of cosmic political retributions in *Moby-Dick*, followed by the sea deaths of Radney in "The Town-Ho's Story" and of Ahab himself. In the final chapters of the novel, whenever Moby-Dick emerges from the sea and brings about death to whalers, it is worth recalling that he does so on the "leeward" side (433, 451, 465), an allegorical reprisal against those from that "slavish" shore. And, like *Moby-Dick*'s warnings, the Bulkington chapter prophetically signals the inevitable self-destruction awaiting the unyielding "slavish" shores of America, in the South as well as in New England.

Melville concentrates his most explicit attacks upon Western slavery and cannibalism in those chapters often considered the cetological center of the novel. Ishmael's prolonged discussions of depictions of whales, whale anatomy, and whaling practices allegorize social and political problems in Melville's America. Western culture's penchant for order—social, political, economic, and artistic structures—Ishmael playfully undercuts. Edgar A. Dryden's overview of *Moby-Dick* as self-consciously generating fictions is worth mentioning in this context: "The hierarchical social structure aboard a well-ordered ship, the constructs of science and pseudo-science, pagan and Christian religious systems, even the concepts of space and time—all of the forms which man uses to assure himself that everything which happens follow certain laws—are revealed, in *Moby-Dick*, as 'passing fables'" (83). It is not merely the constructs, but their interpretation and justification that Ishmael calls into question. For Ishmael, misinterpretation reveals the underlying presuppositions of America's attitudes toward race. In his observation of the obscured oil painting he tries to decipher at the Spouter-Inn, Ishmael initially misperceives its subject matter as figures of blackness: a portentous "black mass," "the Black Sea in a midnight gale" (20). His inability to see blackness occurs when he first enters New Bedford; Ishmael stops before a "Negro church and at first perceives it to be "the great Black Parliament sitting in Tophet" (18). Ironically, Ishmael has difficulty at first recognizing the reality of blackness, but few problems distinguishing many variations of whiteness, as demonstrated in "The Whiteness of the Whale." Eventually, he arrives at an interpretation of the painting: "an exasperated whale, purposing to spring clean over the craft, is in the enormous act of impaling himself upon the three mastheads" (21). This final interpretation grandly portends self-destructive death, recalling Ishmael's suicidal impulses from "Loomings." After this episode of misconceptions, Ishmael sees "a heathenish array of monstrous clubs and spears," which make him shudder at the thought of "what monstrous cannibal and savage could ever have gone a death-harvesting with such a hacking, horrifying implement" (21). Ishmael's misinterpretation of the "monstrous cannibal and savage" Queequeg corresponds to his readers' and America's cultural misconceptions. In fact, the comedy of the bedroom scene at the Spouter-Inn would not work without the reader empathizing to some degree with Ishmael's fears.

In chapter 57, Ishmael addresses true portraits created by the barbaric whale hunters: "As with the Hawaiian savage, so with the white sailor-savage" (232). Ishmael concludes that the further one is removed from Christian, civilized depiction of whales, the closer one comes to their true representation. By the same token, the further one travels away from Christian culture, the closer one comes to exhibiting the inherent condition of man-savagery:

> Long exile from Christendom and civilization inevitably restores
> a man to that condition in which God placed him, i.e. what is
> called savagery. Your true whale-hunter is as much a savage as an
> Iroquois. I myself am a savage, owning no allegiance but to the
> King of the Cannibals; and ready at any moment to rebel against
> him. (232)

Here, two readings are suggested for the King of Cannibals: Ahab and the
Christian God. Ishmael vows both to serve and to rebel against the King of
Cannibals, or the king of Kings, since tyranny, especially the master and slave
relationship, is the primary form of political cannibalism for Ishmael. Aboard
the *Pequod*, Ahab commands supreme authority over his crew. Ishmael
regards Ahab's tyranny as "sultanism that became incarnate in an irresistible
dictatorship" (129) and he likens him to "Belshazzar, King of Babylon," ruler
of the Old Testament's most profligate enslaving state (131). His allegorical
name recalls the most tyrannical king of ancient Israel. As king over Israel,
ruling from his "ivory" house (1 Kings 22:39), Ahab conducted unspeakable
acts of violence and apostasy. Through treachery, usurpation, and murder,
Ahab stole Naboth's vineyard, an act which American politicians viewed as
analogous to the cupidity of the country's expansionist policies during the
1840s.[12] Ahab's hypnotic, antidemocratic command over the crew of the
Pequod in "The Quarter-Deck" includes Starbuck, who viewed the Deity
as "centre and circumference of all democracy! His omnipresence, our
divine equality!" (104). Ahab's winning over of Starbuck has replaced the
democratic Lord of equality with a sultan, czar, or king.

Even more evident, the relationship between Ahab and Fedallah is
characterized as master and slave: "And yet, somehow, did Ahab—in his
own proper self, as daily, hourly, and every instant, commandingly revealed
to his subordinates,—Ahab seemed an independent lord; the Parsee but his
slave" (439). Fittingly, Fedallah's prophecy in "The Whale Watch" functions
as the slave's retribution by means of irony, for he condemns Ahab to see
two hearses before he dies, "the first not made by mortal hands; and the
visible wood of the last one must be grown in America" (410). Ahab's final
vision must be the product of that "slavish shore," America. The madness of
enslaving others, Ishmael views as a cannibalistic impulse of the darkest kind,
which will invariably degenerate into self-destruction. Ishmael suggests this
connection when he observes that Ahab's soul, like "the last of the Grisly
Bears ... fed upon the sullen paws of its gloom!" (134). Ahab's unrelenting
authority and tyrannical mastery of the *Pequod*, thus, signals the tragic
movement from exocannibalism to self-consumption in the novel.

Chapters 58–66 constitute the cannibalistic center of *Moby-Dick*. Melville introduces his reader to more grotesque and disturbing scenes of cannibalism which eventually become graphic depictions of autocannibalism. Like his earlier treatments of the subject in *Typee*, Melville tries "to demystify the practice of cannibalism and to defuse Western obsessions with cannibalism as the crucial sign of savagery" (Otter 47). Melville's method of demystification, though, is to infuse his cetology chapters with tropes of acquisition, feeding, and power. In short, he universalizes cannibalism. Ishmael concludes that the sea, like human world and God's universe, is governed by one principle—cannibalism: "Consider, once more, the universal cannibalism of the sea; all whose creatures prey upon each other, carrying on eternal war since the world began" (236). The sea conceals its monstrous violence in its loveliest hues, not unlike the way "all deified Nature absolutely paints like the harlot, whose allurements cover nothing but the charnel-house within" (170). That oceanic treachery corresponds to that "treacherous, slavish shore," which is Melville's not-too-subtle condemnation of tyrannical governments and enslaving leaders. Like the cannibalistic cruelty of the creatures of the sea, so too does mankind live by the dictates of cannibalism.

Rituals of exocannibalism are observed aboard the *Pequod*. After all, it is a whaling ship, aboard which the crew often dines cannibalistically on the brains of whale calves. Brain-feeding, as Herbert N. Schneidau aptly observes, is a prominent ritual among cannibals and provides "the dead and the living an interpenetrating identity" (83). Melville accentuates this point with a political metaphor of betrayal: "And that is the reason why a young buck with an intelligent looking calf's head before him, is somehow one of the saddest sights you can see. The head looks a sort of reproachfully at him with an 'Et to Brute!' expression" (255). Typical of Ishmael's treatment of flesh-eating, exocannibalism merges with endocannibalism; the enemy ingested by the whalers reflects their very natures. Ishmael concludes "The Whale As A Dish" by asserting that man has evolved into a cannibal, one who consumes that creature which once was considered to be his equal: "Go to the meat-market of a Saturday night and see the crowds of live bipeds staring at the long rows of dead quadrupeds. Does not that sight take a tooth out of the cannibal's jaw? Cannibals? who is not a cannibal?" (255). The marketplace and the economics of civilized consumption are more ghastly than headhunting and cannibal feasts. For Ishmael, insatiable desires to consume transform man into a cannibal.

The extent of Ishmael's misanthropy and condemnations of his own culture are evident in his depictions of sharks feeding. In Old Fleece's sermon, Stubb distinguishes Christianity at its essence. Oddly, Old Fleece's comic sermon is to sharks not men, but Ishmael has already alluded to the shark's vicious behavior as being analogous to men's aggressive consumption. Old Fleece admonishes the sharks gathering over the side of the *Pequod* to act with moral restraint and to correct their greedy natures: "'Your woraciousness, fellow-critters, I don't blame ye so much for; dat is natur, and can't be helped; but to gobern dat wicked nature, dat is the pint. You is sharks, sartin; but if you gobern de shark in you, why den you be angel; for all angel is not'ing more dan de shark well goberned'" (251). The sharks tear blubber out of their "neighbor's mout," which Old Fleece condemns, asking for a communal sharing of the whale: "'but to bite off de blubber for de small fry ob sharks, dat can't get into de scrouge to help demselves'" (251). But his admonitions are of no matter, as Old Fleece tells Stubb: "'no use a-preachin' to such dam g'uttons'" (251). The *Pequod*'s crew members are little better than these savage sharks.

This universal law of blind consumption bears out most fascinatingly in "The Shark Massacre." In order to save the whale's body from the sharks surrounding the *Pequod*, Queequeg strikes the sharks in their skulls with the whale-spade, although missing at times and causing more frenzied feeding. Universal cannibalism of the sea ultimately results in horrible self-consumption. Here, we should recall again Ishmael's prophetic statement in "Loomings" that the story of Narcissus "is the key to it all" (14). Narcissism is the basis for the kinds of consumption that Ishmael views with disgust and horror aboard the *Pequod*, in the sea, and in the universe.[13] Cannibalism is an unnatural extension of Ahab's monomania, as is that of all tyrants blindly consuming the labor, liberty, and life of others. This is brought home when a dead shark hauled aboard the ship of sharks nearly takes off Queequeg's hand, an action ironically reversing the harpooners' comic cannibalistic attacks upon the Dough-Boy. Queequeg simply cannot conceive of a god who would create such a beast as the shark: "'wedder Fejee god or Nantucket god; but de god war made shark must be one damn Ingin'" (257). Queequeg's comic irreverence and uncertainty about what power controls this aggressive universe is not shared by Ishmael, who already attributes this law of consumption to Western culture and its institutions.[14]

In "Loomings," Ishmael binds himself and his readers together as slaves: "Who aint a slave?" (15). Melville adopts a pose in this first chapter of the novel that is similar to the universal brotherhood of bondage that begins many slave narratives of the nineteenth century.[15] Quite cynically, he also forges a bond among all of mankind as cannibals. At this point, Ishmael's outrageous rhetorical questions—"Who aint a slave?" and "who is not a cannibal?"—have several affirmative responses, especially when the two concepts are conjoined—Who is not both a slave and a cannibal? Ishmael's association of slavery and cannibalism draws together two devastating social systems in nineteenth-century America: the institution of plantation slavery and its counterpart in industrial capitalism.

Idiosyncratic economic arguments against slavery were prevalent among Northern theorists in the nineteenth century. For example, Daniel Raymond's *The Elements of Political Economy* (1822) includes anticapitalist rhetoric but also upholds industrialization within limits, primarily to restrict its demoralizing power over laborers reduced to propertyless conditions (Kaufman 67–81). Southern endorsements of slavery saw the institution as more compatible with market capitalism than wage labor, as evidenced by the quirky works of Southerner Thomas Roderick Dew in the 1830s which viewed slavery, by means of racist logic, as epitomizing the evolution from barbarism to civilization.[16] As Laurence Shore points out in *Southern Capitalists*, William Gregg's *Essays on Domestic Industry* (1844) tried to shame Southern capitalists into developing their own manufacturing economy so that Southern states could maintain slavery at a profit, while Ellwood Fisher's famous lecture in 1849 claimed that statistically the Southern slave economy had attained a per capita wealth that "eclipsed the North" (32–33, 38). Shore also notes that Thomas Dew's very odd use of Adam Smith's capitalist theory revealed that "somehow, through market forces, slave labor and the black population would wither away" (27). In essence, for Dew, the marketplace will consume its own laborers.

George Fitzhugh's Virginia pamphlets of 1850 and 1851 propagandize the economic necessity of adopting Southern slavery and promulgated its social and moral advantages. His extended socialist rant against industrial capitalism favors the Southern slave system. As C. Vann Woodward explains, Fitzhugh's early Richmond pamphlets attack the failed concepts of liberty and equality, which he called "self-destructive and impracticable," and extolled the plantation system of slavery in the South against Northern capitalism: "To call free labor 'wage slavery' as the socialists did was 'a gross libel on slavery,' for the condition of free labor was 'worse than slavery.' The wage system was a contradiction of human needs" (xv). Fitzhugh maintains in *Cannibals All!, or Slaves Without Masters* (1856) that capitalistic exploitation results in "the White Slave Trade" which is far more cruel than its black counterpart, because "the master allows the slave to retain a larger share of the results of his own labor than do the employers of free labor" (15). Fitzhugh even compares his Northern capitalist reader to a cannibal: "You are a Cannibal! and if a successful one, pride yourself on the number of your victims quite as much as any Fiji chieftain, who breakfasts, dines, and sups on human flesh—and your conscience smites, you, if you have failed to succeed, quite as much as his, when he returns from an unsuccessful foray" (17). Such virulent racist rhetoric surfaced in the economic and political debates of Melville's day. In order to attack the hypocrisy of American sentiment for government by the consent of the governed, Fitzhugh proffers a number of examples in which the master and slave relationship must prevail, from fathers of families to military leaders and governmental officials who are little more than "self-elected despots," and, of interest for *Moby-Dick*, the dogmatic rule of sea captains (243). Fitzhugh's polemic somewhat fits Ahab's tyranny but not his cannibalistic urges, which contradict the illogical propaganda of *Cannibals All!* Of course, Melville uses cannibalism to attack exploitation; he does not limit it to capitalistic exploitation, but includes philosophical, legal, and religious exploitation. For Melville, the cannibal and the slave are aspects of the human condition, indeed shared by all alike.

To see Melville's enfolding of these two concepts, one needs to read carefully chapter 89, "Fast-Fish and Loose-Fish." Here, Melville uses the dislodging of a whale held fast to the ship, set adrift or made loose, then recovered by another ship as his metaphor for fugitive slave laws. Much mischief, Ishmael explains to the reader, has been played into this "masterly code" (331), an obvious reference to system of slavery. The specific loose-fish case that Ishmael cites reminds one of Fugitive Slave cases, for the whale was chased "in the northern seas" (332), but was lost when the chasers met peril and was captured by another vessel. In due course, the chasers, like Southern slavers, sue for recovery of their property. Melville's father-in-law, Chief Justice of the Supreme Judicial Court of Massachusetts Lemuel Shaw, had decided several points of law in the famous 1842 Latimer case in favor of the fugitive slave's captors; moreover, as Levy notes, "Shaw's opinion on the right of the states to provide machinery for the arrest of fugitives from justice became the law in every state in the country" (79, n.19). In 1851, the year of *Moby-Dick*'s publication, Chief Justice Shaw decided another fugitive slave case involving a runaway slave, Thomas Sims; again, he decided against freedom, upholding the Fugitive Slave Law of 1850. His decision caused a furor in Boston, as can be evidenced by the outcries from William Lloyd Garrison, Ralph Waldo Emerson, Theodore Parker, and Frederick Douglass.

The Latimer case had incited rioters to attack the arresting officials and moved several African Americans to execute an escape for Latimer.[17] Massachusetts citizens, some 50,000 in number, protested Shaw's decision in the case and signed "a petition which former President John Quincy Adams had tried—unsuccessfully—to present to Congress" (Simpson 26). Ultimately, Latimer's freedom was not contingent upon any Constitutional application. As Louis Filler explains in *The Crusade Against Slavery: 1830–1860*, Latimer's owner, James B. Grey of Virginia (the same state that

Ishmael assumes Bulkington hails from), faced with mounting court costs of more than Latimer's worth on the market, ironically sold his deed of emancipation to obliging abolitionists (171). In November of 1842 Frederick Douglass sent an alarming letter to Garrison concerning the Latimer case and the appearance of slavery in Massachusetts:

> Slavery, our enemy, has landed in our very midst, and commenced its bloody work. Just look at it; here is George Latimer a man—a brother—a husband, a father, stamped with the likeness of the eternal God, and redeemed by the blood of Jesus Christ, outlawed, hunted down like a wild beast, and ferociously dragged through the streets of Boston, and incarcerated within the walls of Leverett-st. jail.... Boston has become the hunting-ground of merciless men-hunters, and man-stealers. (*Liberator* 159)[18]

Douglass' depiction of "men-hunters, and man-stealers" certainly accords with Melville's cannibalistic depictions of the whaling industry, property rights of fast and loose fish, and the obsessive drive to possess. The "brutal overbearing" Radney of "The Town-Ho's Story" hypocritically slights Steelkilt without "common decency of human recognition which is the meanest slave's right" (210). Radney originates from Nantucket, which suggests Melville's allegorical condemnation of New England false piety. Radney's demise also recalls Bulkington's death at sea. This time, however, Moby-Dick consumes Radney in an act of cosmic justice and retribution. The scene foreshadows the political death of the tyrannical Ahab, the Massachusetts captain. Indeed, Starbuck, Stubb, and Flask all hail from Massachusetts: "every one of them Americans; a Nantucketer, a Vineyarder, and a Cape man" (109). Nineteenth-century Massachusetts never offered much in the way of tolerance: hence, Melville's revenge upon the Bay Colony crew of the *Pequod*.

Unlike the case before his father-in-law and the Massachusetts Supreme Court, in which a fugitive slave was ordered returned to Southern master, the loose whale of Ishmael's allegory was allowed to be kept by the northern vessel. A darker fugitive slave tale occurs in "The Castaway," when Pip, the Alabama cabin-boy, leaps out of Stubb's boat to become a loose-fish and only accidentally is recovered by the *Pequod*. Stubb ignores Pip in favor of hunting down whales, which are of greater economic value than the *Pequod*'s servant. Melville sternly allegorizes antebellum Massachusetts shipping and industrial interests outweighing African American and fugitive slaves' rights. Not content to end his analogy here, Melville expands upon the various conditions that exist for Fast-Fish and Loose-Fish throughout the world. Physically, Russian serfs and Republican slaves are caught fast to their masters; economically, the widow's last bit and the bankrupt man's interest on his loan are held by landlord and lender; religiously, the earnings of "broken-backed laborers" are seized in order to supplement the Church's already bloated income; and politically, hamlets, Ireland, and Texas are held in bondage by their oppressors and enslavers (333). Serf, slave, and pauper define for Melville the vicissitudes of misery imposed by economic oppression. Dives as a "Czar" again comes to mind. "Republican slaves" can mean both chattel slavery in the South and wage slavery in the North. Melville is also relying upon conventional treatment of the other cultures as animals, a trope found in numerous seventeenth-century British discussions of neighboring countries and colonial inhabitants, as Margaret Hodgen reminds us: "Whether Irishmen or Pequots, Scots or Iroquois, they were enemies, they were ignorant, and they were animal-like. The only way to regard them was through the lenses of a quasi-philosophical, quasi-religious, and quasi-political 'anti-primitivism,' unembarrassed either by any recognition of brotherliness or by a more austere theological assumption of common humanity" (364–65). Melville has taken a similar approach in *Moby-Dick*, but for the purpose of uplifting the primitive and denouncing the civilized along lines that recall Montaigne's arguments in "Of Cannibals."

Yet, for Melville, history will always prove that what was once a Loose-Fish will in fact be made fast, as America was to Columbus, India to England, Poland to Russia, Greece to the Ottomans, and most recently for Melville, Mexico to the United States. Melville would have been aware of the historical oppression suffered by these cultures. During his day, the political rhetoric of anti-slavery in Massachusetts, as attested to by David Walker's *Appeal to the Coloured Citizens of the World*, often included references to these enslaved cultures.[19] Of interest, several of the countries Ishmael lists have also been treated as realms of cannibals. The Americas of Columbus were inhabited by the Caribs, from whose name the word cannibal derives. Ireland, according the geographer Strabo, was inhabited by a people, as Arens reminds us, "more savage than the Britons, since they are man-eaters" (14). Claude Rawson explains that this treatment of the Irish as savage or cannibalistic is all too evident among English writers, such as Spenser and Camden: "there are significant parallels between English descriptions of the Irish and European descriptions of Africans and Amerindians, a standard colonial discourse" (345). Nineteenth-century Massachusetts citizens would have been inclined to the same sentiments: after all, Nativism against Irish immigrants in the mid-1830s caused a Charlestown, Massachusetts mob to set an Ursuline convent ablaze and Nativists joined forces with Whigs to place their candidate in the office of mayor of Boston in 1845 (Anbinder 9,

12). Mexico, ancestral home of the Aztecs, was viewed by the Spanish, from accounts by Diaz and from Prescott's *History of the Conquest of Mexico* (1843), as populated by cannibals: "The most famous of the Amerindians cannibals, were, of course, the Mexica, whose spectacular bouts of human sacrifice were assumed to have been followed by orgiastic feasts on the flesh of the victims" (Pagden 83). Melville, of course, is relying upon the mixing of metaphors in the rhetoric of Western political domination and con–quest. Associating cannibalism with enslaved peoples belongs to an overriding master–slave dialectic that, as Hayden White observes, "permeates the psychosocial pathology of all oppressive systems" (188).[20]

Since the 1830s the abolitionist cause had met with some resistance from capitalists in Massachusetts, as Reinhard O. Johnson explains: "Textile manufacturers and shipping interests had formed a close relationship with southern planters, and these industrialists and merchants were reluctant to countenance any activity which was critical of a basic southern institution" (238). Melville would also have been aware of the connection between slavery and ghoulish consumption from the antislavery rhetoric in Massachusetts in the 1840s, as evidenced by Joshua Leavitt's "Financial Power of Slavery" (1841): "Slavery takes value out of the pockets of the free, as well as out of the sinews of the enslaved, without rendering an equivalent. It is a vampyre which is drinking up the life blood of free industry" (245). Once again, Dives drinking the tears of orphans comes to mind.

Ishmael's rhetoric cynically applies momentary freedom to inevitable enslavement on a universal scale:

> What are the Right of Man and the Liberties of the World but Loose-Fish? What all men's minds and opinions but Loose-Fish? What is the principle of religious belief in them but a Loose-Fish? What to the ostentatious smuggling verbalists are the thoughts of thinkers but Loose-Fish? What is the great globe itself but a Loose-Fish?" (334)

Fitzhugh describes exploited labor in terms readily familiar to Melville: "To be exploitated ought to be more creditable than to exploitate. They were 'slaves without masters,' little fish who were food for all the larger" (38). While his major work postdates *Moby-Dick*, Fitzhugh took a number of expressions from Thomas Carlyle, among them the "slaves without masters" motif for alienated working class men reduced to a form of cannibalism; he also borrowed extensively from Carlyle's virulent attack in 1849 on British colonial policies supporting manumission in the West Indies.[21] Characteristically, Ishmael universally includes all humankind in this master and slave, cannibal and slave schema: "And what are you, reader, but a Loose-Fish and a Fast-Fish, too?" (334). Melville's answer to a Raymond, Dew, or Fitzhugh is not a choice between cannibal or slave, but the inevitability of suffering both fates at once.

In "Heads or Tails," Melville interjects a tale of English sailors losing the product of their labor—a whale and its market value—to the Duke of Wellington as a commentary on loose-fish capitalism. Antiquated laws of monarchical property extend privileges to those who "had nothing to do with taking this fish" (335). Ishmael condemns not just the exploitation of labor but the very appropriation of the product of that labor. Melville well understood the frenetic economy—bankruptcies, market downturns, depressions—facing Massachusetts workers during the 1840s and 1850s (Keyssar 31). Comparisons between the injustices of Southern slavery and the inhumane conditions of New England workers often resounded in the political battles of the period in attacks upon Lords of Lash and Loom (Laurie 4–7). In "The Tartarus of Maids" (1855), Melville denounced the factory system of New England capitalism: "Machinery—that vaunted slave of humanity—here stood menially served by humans, who served mutely and cringingly as the slave serves the Sultan" (328). Melville employed the same metaphor—the slave before the Sultan—for the little *Moss* before the sea and for the *Pequod*'s crew before Ahab. For Melville, slavery, like cannibalism, is an inevitable consequence of capitalism and expansionism, nowhere more evident than in the whaling industry.[22] Just as the Duke of Wellington took possession of the labor of his whalers, so too does Stubb, although comically, exploit the labors of the whalers aboard the *Rose-Bud* by appropriating a fast whale. Melville's point is that human nature lends itself readily to be exploiter and exploited, cannibal and slave.

The complex dialectic of cannibalism and slavery also can be observed in the novel's polarizing of angels and devils, as seen in Old Fleece's sermon to the shark. "The Fossil Whale" provides an intriguing account of a pre-adamite whale discovered in Alabama in 1842 (coincidentally, the year of the Latimer case) on the slave plantation of one Judge Creagh. This fossilized fast-fish had two interpretations: by the slaves, it was seen as "a fallen angel"; by the Alabama doctors, "a huge reptile" (380). Given the name Basilosaurus, derived from the Greek for King, this monster was rechristened by Owen Zeuglodon, from the Greek for the slave yoke. Master–slave metaphors are conjoined in this "antemosaic" whale, so ancient that Ishmael claims "to shake hands with Shem" upon seeing it (380). Ishmael obviously refers to Genesis 9–10 and its curse upon the descendants of Ham and Canaan to be slaves in perpetuity to the descendants of Shem. Melville interjects angelic imagery to cast it in his familiar opposition, as Ishmael describes the tail of the whale:

So in dreams, have I seen majestic Satan thrusting forth his tormented colossal claw from the flame Baltic of Hell. But in gazing at such scenes, it is all in all what mood you are in; if in the Dantean, the devils will occur to you; if in that of Isaiah, the archangels. (317)

The same opposition occurs at the conclusion of the final chase, when the sky-hawk enfolded in the flag, "with archangelic shrieks" disappears with the *Pequod* as Ahab "went down with his ship, which, like Satan, would not sink to hell till she had dragged a living part of heaven along with her" (469). Aboard the ship, the three harpooners remain aloft in the three masts, ready to be crucified. Although they were once princes in their domains, their contact with American commercial interests has reduced them to slaves. The Golgotha analogy has more cynical implications for Melville. Significantly, Queequeg is not on the main mast, the place of Christ, but along with Daggoo takes the position of one of the two malefactors.

Why does Melville not allow his noble cannibal the supreme sacrificial position in this final scene? No salvation of Queequeg's pagan variety is available to mankind. No humane cannibalism replaces the savagery of American economic, political, and social oppression. A lone survivor, Ishmael, the orphaned slave, returns quite the misanthrope. Reading the novel retrospectively, we discern the extent of Ishmael's cynicism. Ishmael sardonically recounts in allegorical terms his era of terrible slavery, bitter poverty, hypocritical Christian morality, cruel, monomaniacal expansionism, and of a Union on the verge of its own self-destruction. Melville, like Ishmael, simply could no longer stomach the corruption and hypocrisy of American culture. And who could blame him?

NOTES

1. Westenbroek provides an extensive list of the use of this name Ishmael in English letters.

2. In addition to his characterization of the Pequots in the *Magnalia*, in 1718 Cotton Mather upbraided colonists for allowing native peoples to continue practicing "pagan impieties": "that in the very heart of a colony renowned for the profession of Christianity, there should for fourscore years together be a body of the aboriginals persisting in the darkest and most horrid paganism" (*Selected Letters* 265).

3. Fickes provides an extensive record of Pequot enslavement in early New England, especially the accounts of branding—(75) and Captain Morris requesting from John Winthrop "compensation in 1647 so that he might replace his escaped Pequot captive with an African" (79). John Winthrop's diary entry of July 13, 1637 notes that Mr. Pierce sent fifteen Pequot boys and two women to Providence Isle (227). Thomas Hutchinson in his history admits that many Pequot "captives were sent to Bermuda and sold for slaves" (80).

4. For the Mohawk threat to Pequots, see Leach (21–22) and Johnson who relates that "Pequot sachems fled to the Mohawks seeking safety, but instead were executed" (34). For the etymological reference, see Sollers (27).

5. Crain provides detailed listings of incidents of cannibalism during nineteenth-century naval voyages (28).

6. Royster discusses Ishmael's pride in the whaling industry, his comic, ironic resignation toward labor, and Melville's supposedly tepid critique of capitalism in *Moby-Dick*. Dimock analyzes prophecy in the novel as imperialistic and adhering to the tenets Manifest Destiny.

7. For typologies of cannibalism, see Arens (17–18) and Goldman (1–26).

8. Melville owned a copy of Montaigne in 1848 (Howard 115). Beauchamp illustrates many similarities between Montaigne and Melville, as evidenced in Melville's early novels.

9. For an account of the Washingtonians and other temperance activities of this period, see Hampel.

10. For a detailed discussion of Queequeg as exemplifying Lockean ideals of life and liberty, see Markels. Fredricks' analysis of the politics of inclusion is typical of these uplifting readings of Melville's democratic tendencies: "They seal their bond by equally distributing Queequeg's money between them, pledging mutual devotion, and worshipping Queequeg's black idol together. Melville's subversion of the typology of covenant theology allows for a vision of democracy beyond the radical individualism of the Puritans: a vision of a democracy of multiculturalism and egalitarianism" (48–49).

11. Heimert proposes the Benton connection in his well-known and useful essay on *Moby-Dick*. Wallace draws some intriguing conclusions about Melville's appreciation for Turner; moreover, Wallace associates Melville's language in this short epitaph of a chapter to Turner's sea storm paintings, particularly *Fishermen upon a Lee-Shore* (1802) and *Waves Breaking on a Lee Shore* (1835). In this reading of "The Lee Shore," Wallace, however, neglects Turner's *The Slave Ship* (1840), which depicts horrible cruelty toward the slaves on the slavetrader *Zong*, as Walker informs us: "When a epidemic broke out, the captain ordered the sick and dying to be thrown overboard so that he could say they were lost at sea and claim insurance" (110). In *The Slave Ship*, chattel slaves drown in a blood-red sea as large fish and sharks approach to devour the hapless victims.

12. Duban, who credits Heimert's scholarship on political rhetoric of the day, cites the remarks of Representative Kenneth Rayner of North Carolina in 1845: "Arguments ... addressed to our national cupidity and pride ... are the arguments with which Ahab reconciled to himself the seizing of Naboth's Vineyard" (88). Typical of typological readings from the text to the world, he incorporates phrases from political debates and sees them in the novel's symbolic and allegorical structure.

13. Bohrer presents Melville's doubling of sea and universe, man and shark, as consuming agents in *Moby-Dick*; in particular, Bohrer notes that the Narcissus passage of "Loomings" foreshadows the "pervasive system of linked 'consumptive' analogies" in the novel (84).

14. For a useful discussion on the types of cannibalism confronting Queequeg and of Ishmael's view of Western culture, see Sanborn (148–56).

15. Berthold provides a comparative analysis of the rhetorical correspondences between *Moby-Dick* and slave narratives.

16. Kaufman offers invaluable and exhaustive analyses of complex economic arguments of antebellum America, particularly his chapters "Daniel Raymond on Protecting

the Republic from Slave Capital" and "Thomas Roderick Dew on Black Slavery as the Republic's Check on the Working Class."

17. For a full account of the Latimer case and the furor it caused among abolitionists in Massachusetts, see Quarles (193–95).

18. Douglass took Latimer on lecture tours immediately following his purchased freedom, and continued to lecture about this case for years, until 1854 when he learned that Latimer was arrested for pickpocketing and confessed to the crime (*The Frederick Douglass Papers* 230).

19. See the opening of Walker's Appeal which draws distinctions between subjugated men and animalized African Americans: "The Indians of North and South American—the Greeks—the Irish, subjected under the king of Great Britain—the Jews, that ancient people of the Lord—the inhabitants of the islands of the sea—in fine, all the inhabitants of the earth, (except however, the sons of Africa) are called men, and of course are, and ought to be free. But we, coloured people and our children are *brutes*!!" (9). Of course, Walker's rhetoric relies upon conventional arguments of historical and contemporary enslavement, all too familiar to the abolitionist cause.

20. Of note, White provides an analysis of the caption for a 1505 engraving of natives of America that reveals five principal taboos to Europeans: "nakedness, community of property, lawlessness, sexual promiscuity, and cannibalism" (187). Many of these traits can be observed among the crew aboard the *Pequod*.

21. Wish comments upon Fitzhugh's rhetorical appropriations from Carlyle's virulent racist polemics: "Especially valuable as propaganda material to Fitzhugh and the pro-slavery school were Carlyle's attacks on the West Indian experiment of emancipation. In December 1849, the Scot had published 'The Negro Question' in Fraser's, excoriating the results of freeing the blacks in the British Caribbean possessions" (74–75).

22. For a discussion of Melville holding the "minority position" in his indictment of the new economics of industrialism, see Thomas Bender (60).

WORKS CITED

Anbinder, Tyler. *Nativism & Slavery: The Northern Know Nothings & the Politics of the 1850s.* New York: Oxford University Press, 1992.

Arens, W. *The Man-Eating Myth: Anthropology & Anthropophagy.* New York: Oxford University Press, 1979.

Beauchamp, Gorman. "Montaigne, Melville, and the Cannibals." *Arizona Quarterly* 37 (1981): 293–309.

Bender, Thomas. *Toward An Urban Vision: Ideas and Institutions in Nineteenth Century America.* Baltimore: The Johns Hopkins University Press, 1975.

Berthold, Michael C. "*Moby-Dick* and American Slave Narrative." *Massachusetts Review* 35.1 (1994) 135–48.

Bohrer, Randall. "Melville's New Witness: Cannibalism and the Microcosm–Macrocosm Cosmology of *Moby-Dick*." *Studies in Romanticism* 22.1 (1983): 65–91.

Certeau, Michel de. "Montaigne's 'Of Cannibals': The Savage 'I.'" *Heterologies: Discourse on the Other.* Trans. Brian Massumi. Minneapolis: University of Minnesota Press, 1986. 67–79.

Crain, Caleb. "Lovers of Human Flesh: Homosexuality and Cannibalism in Melville's Novels." *American Literature* 66 (1994) 25–53.

Dimock, Wai-chee. *Empire of Liberty: Melville and the Poetics of Individualism*. Princeton: Princeton University Press, 1989.

Douglass, Frederick. *The Frederick Douglass Papers, Series One: Speeches, Debates, and Interviews*, Vol. 1, *1814–46*. Ed. John W. Blassingame. New Haven: Yale University Press, 1979.

———. *Liberator* (November 18, 1842). *Abolition and Social Justice in the Era of Reform*. Ed. Louis Filler. New York: Harper & Row, 1972. 156–60.

Dryden, Edgar A. *Melville's Thematics of Form: The Great Art of Telling the Truth*. Baltimore: The Johns Hopkins University Press, 1968.

Duban, James. *Melville's Major Fiction: Politics, Theology, and Imagination*. Dekalb: Northern Illinois University Press, 1983.

Fickes, Michael L. "'They Could Not Endure That Yoke': The Captivity of Pequot Women and Children after the War of 1637." *The New England Quarterly* 73.1 (2000): 58–81.

Filler, Louis. *The Crusade Against Slavery: 1830–1860*. New York: Harper & Brothers, 1960.

Fitzhugh, George. *Cannibals All! or, Slaves Without Masters*. Ed. C. Vann Woodward. Cambridge: Harvard University Press, 1982.

Fredricks, Nancy. *Melville's Art of Democracy*. Athens: University of Georgia Press, 1995.

Goldman, Laurence R. "From Pot to Polemic: Uses and Abuses of Cannibalism." *The Anthropology of Cannibalism*. Ed. Goldman. Westport, CT: Bergin & Garvey, 1999. 1–26.

Hampel, Robert L. *Temperance and Prohibition in Massachusetts, 1813–1852*. Ann Arbor: UMI Research Press, 1982.

Heimert, Alan. "*Moby-Dick* and American Political Symbolism." *American Quarterly* 15 (1963): 498–534.

Hodgen, Margaret T. *Early Anthropology in the Sixteenth and Seventeenth Centuries*. Philadelphia: University of Pennsylvania Press, 1964.

Howard, Leon. *Herman Melville, A Biography*. Berkeley: University of California Press, 1951.

Hutchinson, Thomas. *The History of the Colony of Massachusetts-Bay*. Vol. 1. New York: Arno Press, 1972.

Johnson, Eric S. "Uncas and the Politics of Contact." *Northeastern Indian Lives, 1632–1816*. Ed. Robert S. Grumet. Amherst: University of Massachusetts Press, 1996. 29–47.

Johnson, Reinhard O. "The Liberty Party in Massachusetts, 1840–1848: Antislavery Third Party Politics in the Bay State." *Civil War History* 28.3 (1982): 237–65.

Kaufman. Allen. *Capitalism, Slavery, and Republican Values: Antebellum Political Economists, 1819–1848*. Austin: University of Texas Press, 1982.

Keyssar, Alexander. *Out of Work: The First Century of Unemployment in Massachusetts*. Cambridge: Cambridge University Press, 1986.

Klarer, Mario. "Cannibalism and Carnivalesque: Incorporation as Utopia in the Early Image of America." *New Literary History* 30 (1999): 385–410:

Laurie, Bruce. "The 'Fair Field' of the 'Middle Ground': Abolitionism, Labor Reform, and the Making of an Antislavery Bloc in Antebellum Massachusetts." *Labor Histories: Class, Politics, and the Working-Class Experience*. Ed. Eric Arnesen, Julie Greene, and Bruce Laurie. Urbana: University of Illinois Press, 1998. 45–70.

Leach, Douglas Edward. *Flintlock and Tomahawk: New England in King Philip's War*. New York: W.W. Norton, 1966.

Leavitt, Joshua. "Financial Power of Slavery." *Boston Free American* (August 19, 184 1). Johnson, Reinhard.

Levy, Leonard W. *The Law of the Commonwealth and Chief Justice Shaw*. Cambridge: Harvard University Press, 1957.

Lewis, I. M. *Religion in Context: Cults and Charisma*. Cambridge: Cambridge University Press, 1986.

Markels, Julian. *Melville and the Politics of Identity: From King Lear to Moby-Dick*. Urbana: University of Illinois Press, 1993.

Mather, Cotton. *Magnalia Christi Americana*. Books 1 and 2. Ed. Kenneth B. Murdock. Cambridge: Harvard University Press, 1977.

———. *Selected Letters of Cotton Mather*. Comp. Kenneth Silverman. Baton Rouge: Louisiana State University Press, 1971.

Melville, Herman. *Moby-Dick*. Ed. Harrison Hayford and Hershel Parker. New York: W.W. Norton, 1967.

———. "The Paradise of Bachelors and the Tartarus of Maids." *The Piazza Tales and Other Prose Pieces, 1839–1860*. Ed. Harrison Hayford, Alma A. MacDougall, and G. Thomas Tanselle. Evanston: Northwestern University Press, 1987. 316–35.

Milton, John. *The Poetical Works of John Milton*. Ed. H. C. Beeching. Oxford: Oxford University Press, 1925.

Montaigne. "Of Cannibals." *The Complete Essays of Montaigne*. Trans. Donald M. Frame. Stanford: Stanford University Press, 1958. 150–59.

Otter, Samuel. *Melville's Anatomies*. Berkeley: University of California Press, 1999.

Pagden, Anthony. *The Fall of Natural Man: The American Indian and the Origins of Comparative Ethnology*. Cambridge: Cambridge University Press, 1986.

Quarles, Benjamin. *Black Abolitionists*. New York: Oxford University Press, 1969.

Rawson, Claude. "'Indians' and Irish: Montaigne, Swift, and the Cannibal Question." *Modern Language Quarterly* 53 (1992): 299–363.

Royster, Paul. "Melville's Economy of Language." *Ideology and Classic American Literature*. Ed. Sacvan Bercovitch and Myra Jehlen. Cambridge: Cambridge University Press, 1986. 313–36.

Sanborn, Geoffrey. *The Sign of the Cannibal: Melville and the Making of a Postcolonial Reader*. Durham: Duke University Press, 1998.

Schneidau, Herbert N. Sacred *Discontent: The Bible and Western Tradition*. Baton Rouge: Louisiana State University Press, 1976.

Shore, Laurence. *Southern Capitalists: The Ideological Leadership of an Elite, 1832–1855*. Chapel Hill: University of North Carolina Press, 1986.

Shuffelton, Frank. *Thomas Hooker, 1586–1647*. Princeton: Princeton University Press, 1977.

Simpson, Eleanor E. "Melville and the Negro: From *Typee* to Benito Cereno." *American Literature* 41 (1969): 19–38.

Sollers, Werner. *Beyond Ethnicity: Consent and Descent in American Culture*. New York: Oxford University Press, 1986.

Spanos, William V. *The Errant Art of Moby-Dick: The Canon, The Cold War, and the Struggle of American Studies*. Durham: Duke University Press, 1995.

Walker, David. *Appeal to the Coloured Citizens of the World*. Ed. Peter P Hinks. University Park: Pennsylvania State University Press, 2000.

Walker, John. *Joseph Mallord William Turner*. New York: Harry N. Abrams, 1983.

Wallace, Robert K. "Bulkington, J. M. W. Turner, and 'The Lee Shore.'" *Savage Eye: Melville and the Visual Arts*. Ed. Christopher Sten. Kent, OH: Kent State University Press, 1991. 55–76.

Westenbroek, Anthony. "Ishmael." *A Dictionary of Biblical Tradition in English Literature*. Ed. David Lyle Jeffrey. Grand Rapids, MI: William B. Eerdmans, 1992. 382–83.

White, Hayden. *Tropics of Discourse: Essays in Cultural Criticism*. Baltimore: The Johns Hopkins University Press, 1978.

Winthrop, John. *The Journal of John Winthrop, 1630–1649*. Ed. Richard S. Dunn, James Savage, and Laetitia Yeandle. Cambridge: Harvard University Press, 1996.

Wish, Harvey. *George Fitzhugh: Propagandist of the Old South*. Gloucester, MA: Peter Smith, 1962.

Woodward, C. Vann. "George Fitzhugh, *Sui Generis*." *Cannibals All! or, Slaves Without Masters*. Ed. Woodward. Cambridge: Harvard University Press, 1982.

FRED V. BERNARD

The Question of Race in Moby-Dick

Currently, Melvillean studies are awash with racial and ethnic interpretations. Except, however, for some nibbling at its edges, these efforts largely exclude *Moby-Dick*, perhaps because its surface seems unsupportive of racial arguments. But since the *Pequod* is a floating Babel of racial types, the novel may still have surprises that Melville makes us dive deep to identify.

Among the names of the crew, none is stranger than Ishmael's self-chosen name. When we address his race, we discover that because Melville nowhere says he is white we have supposed him to be so, since we also assume that Melville will do our work for us and tell us what he is. When Melville doesn't tell us, we assume that a white novelist would intend his narrator to be white. But doubt begins because Ishmael, as W. Jeffrey Bolster notes, is an occasionally encountered slave name[1] and because Biblical Ishmael's mother is a "bondservant" (*Genesis*, 21:10–13). Ishmael's choice of name for himself, in 1851, the year after the Fugitive Slave Law, makes possible his being a mulatto.

Ishmael is interested in the subject of slavery. Offhandedly, he identifies himself with bondsmen in colloquially asking, "Who aint a slave?" (*NN* 6). Ashore and at sea, he is closest to Queequeg and Pip, the black cabin boy, and his love and concern for them is as undying as the novel itself. He watches Stubb observing Pip taking a moment before the doubloon for conjugating

---

From *The Massachusetts Review* 43, no. 3 (Autumn 2002): 384–404. © 2002 by *The Massachusetts Review*.

look and *"getting it by heart"* (*NN* 434. My italics). This hint at Pip's doing "homework" to reinforce a recent lesson. Among the few literate seamen aboard the *Pequod*, who besides Ishmael and Ahab, a schoolteacher and a protector, would teach Pip to read and write, in order to calm his mind and free it from intellectual bondage through the gift of the mental worlds that English accesses?

Ishmael's interest in slavery is highlighted by the attempted segregation he and Queequeg experience aboard the New Bedford to Nantucket ferry, which was celebrated far its segregation. In the *Liberator* David Ruggles attacked this ferry for denying him equal rights, as did Frederick Douglass in the same issue and "H.S.", in the *Anti-Slavery Standard*, 26 August, 1841, p. 46. Captain Lot Phinney refused Ruggles a first-class ticket, "became furious [with him], commenced an assault and battery on my person, [and] took from me by force my private papers" (*Liberator*, 9 Judy, 1841, p. 110).

Three months later Douglass, along with Garrison and forty other Abolitionists, black and white, experienced segregation on this route when Phinney denied them equal treatment and accommodations and forced them to "occupy their proper place" (*Daily Evening Transcript*, 11 August, 1841, p. 2). "Forty-one abolitionists" aboard this ferry suffered segregation that Douglas and Garrison quickly attacked in powerful speeches, according to "H.S."'s account. Since Ishmael's and Douglass's route of New York, New Bedford, and Nantucket is the identical one of two men in search of work on whaling ships, each man experiencing racial segregation aboard his vessel, Melville appears to draw upon the experience of Douglass, Ruggles, and Garrison for his own fictional account aboard the *Moss*. Queequeg and Ishmael suffer the abuse of passengers and Captain, who appear to mistake Ishmael for a white man consorting with a runaway, since Queequeg's beaver hat and filed teeth (*NN* 27, 60) give him an appearance that John Hope Franklin and Loren Schweninger identify as characteristic of some fugitive slaves.[2] The episode adopts not only abolitionist arguments, as Carolyn Karcher finds Melville doing in Father Mapple's sermon,[3] but their route, dress, mutilation, and sufferings, too.

Ishmael associates atrocities with whiteness and finds something lurking "in the innermost idea of this hue [whiteness], which strikes more panic to the soul than fat redness which affrights in blood" (*NN* 1139). As the experiential backbone of black life, this is more likely a black than a white comment. Blacks quite comfortably make such statements, as the notation of white violence against blacks in the writing of Douglass, DuBois, Malcolm X, and Baldwin amply illustrates. The observation also undergirds the basic tenet of black aesthetics, that black is creative and beautiful. Ishmael affirms this very modern idea in stating that "there is an aesthetic in all things" (*NN*

278). And his terror over whiteness reflects a black psychological insight born of an experience apparently alien to much of the white population, for most empowered whites were and are prone to identify themselves as a peaceful, benevolent majority.

Ishmael's wages show that he is paid as a black and does not participate in white benefits. American pay scales having long been an accurate identifier of race and gender, Bildad's first offer of a seven hundred and seventy-seventh lay (*NN* 76) is impossibly extreme if Ishmael is white. Even his final three hundredth lay reflects the much inferior pay of blacks vs. whites aboard, for example, the *Lion*, of Nantucket, in 1807. On the *Lion*, black lays ran from 1/80 to 1/90.[4] In 1807, even the Boy's lay of 1/120 was more than two and a half times what Ishmael was to be paid in 1851.

Marginalization and hence race is also indicated by a life of odd jobs. Unlike educated whites, "unlettered Ishmael" (*NN* 347) is a drifter, as his diverse jobs suggest—"I have been ... a great digger of ditches, canals, and wells" (*NN* 456), labor, according to Franklin and Schweninger, left to blacks in the United States.[5] Indeed, few whites were *great* diggers of ditches, canals, and wells. Such hints, reflecting Ishmael's poverty, make his subtle account racially illuminating. Even Ishmael's self-identification seems to glance at his racial status, for Bolster notes that "just as the first generation of freed slaves were given the power to define themselves by selecting their own first and last names, so black seamen took advantage of sailors' anonymity to name themselves at will ... [I]t is clear that multiple identities and nicknames were common among slaves and free blacks before the Civil War."[6] Ishmael fits right in among the multiracial crew of the *Pequod* and he betrays his own color by references to "a story of a white man," "white seamen," and "the white sailor-savage" (*NN* 21, 242, 270), which contrast strongly, for example, with his neutral reference to an "oarsman" whom he singles out in a painting by Ambrose Louis Garneray (*NN* 266), an oarsman who is in fact a black. Moreover, when passengers give Ishmael and Queequeg "jeering glances" over their camaraderie and thus object to an assumed breach of the color barrier, Ishmael's snort, "as though a white man were anything more dignified than a whitewashed negro" (*NN* 60), offhandedly refers to himself as a whitewashed negro, i.e., a mulatto. Most subtly, on watch he imagines the separation of his body and soul, during which "my body continued to sway as a pendulum" (*NN* 282), as if from a lynching. Lynchings cause such separations, but so odd an image suggests a runaway's apprehension, and makes one wonder if he is one.

Like Ishmael, Ahab reveals subtle ethnic representation, despite our access to him being more limited. Even so, not once in the novel does Melville say that Ahab is white, though when he takes Pip by the hand (*NN*

522), Melville contrasts their colors. Everywhere else, Ishmael describes Ahab uncontrasted color as "solid bronze," his face as "tawny" (*NN* 123), and his torso as an "Egyptian chest" (*NN* 185), the latter image clearly associating him with Africa. Ishmael also describes him as "black terrific Ahab" (*NN* 152) and "dark Ahab" (*NN* 216). Since these metaphors can also allude to blood, they make him possibly double-blooded and suggest that he too is a mulatto. Moreover, because as Bolster points out, "African American mariners found few promotions outside whale ships and small coasters—especially after the 1830s."[7] Ahab's captaincy of a whaler financed by Quakers makes it possible that he too is a part-African American. In fact, Massachusetts' Paul Cuffe was a well-known black whaler-captain who, like Ahab, had business ventures with Quakers.

Although we will never prove that Ishmael and Ahab are either black or white, the evidence suggests they are mulattos. If he is half black, Ahab's tragedy is deeper than is commonly understood. Henry James helps us by pointing out that once a writer has identified his theme—and like Melville James insisted on using only strong ones—he should neglect "none of those [related states between certain figures] that directly minister to interest ..."[8] A black theme will minister to more interest if a tragic character is the very thing he is trying to destroy. Ahab, in short, becomes more tragic if he too is of mingled color and, like Ishmael, ambivalent about it—if his is the struggle of a self-loathing victim needing to kill what he is. Unclear of course is the part of Moby Dick's double identity, his whiteness or his blackness, that Ahab is trying to annihilate. This uncertainty bears strongly on Ahab's curse of a double identity, which is reflected in his trying to make the "white world his own," but "finding himself in a world where he does not belong."[9] Whichever part of himself Ahab is trying to destroy, Melville theme may involve a self-victimizing victim. Melville seems to owe Ahab's hempen death to the *Liberator*, which reports, 21 Sept., 1849, p. 151, that the bark *Janet* lost its "captain and five of the crew ... [when] the captain's boat, having been made fast to a whale ... is supposed to have been carried down by the line becoming foul." Like Ishmael Ahab suffers, as it were, a lynching and, like uncounted American blacks, dies a virtually predictable hempen death, a black man lynched by a white enemy, the rope catching him "round the neck" (*NN* 572). (Their parallel and symmetrical sufferings suggest that the two men as a set of mulattos are another instance of Harrison Hayford's celebrated, but not unnecessary, duplicates: they create symmetry.) And there are more hints that Ahab may be half black.

Early on, because Melville likens Ahab to "a man cut away from the stake, when the fire had ... wasted all the limbs without consuming them" (*NN* 123), and later invokes the stake again for another of his injuries (*NN*

463), Ahab's race becomes an open question. In 1851 America, a white man would not likely have been compared to a person burned at the stake, for this torture was not meted out to whites. It was, however, notoriously inflicted on many blacks, as the *Liberator* repeatedly reported, including Francis Macintosh, a deckhand aboard the *Flora*, who was burned to death at the stake in St Louis in the 1830s, in an event that attracted the attention of one of Melville's favorite writers, Charles Dickens, who recorded his outrage during his American tour.[10] On a different occasion, Ishmael records Ahab's rage, who "piled upon the whale's white hump the sum of all the general rage and hate felt by his whole race from Adam down" (*NN* 184), Adam of course (ordinarily painted as white) being the father of every black as well. Ahab also appears to be black because Melville likens him to Perseus (*NN* 261), who gained Andromeda's hand from her Ethiopian father for slaying a sea monster off the Ethiopian shore.

But perhaps Melville's most interesting hint at Ahab's race involves psychology. When Ahab's thumping whalebone leg keeps Stubb awake, the mate comes up on deck to ask that Ahab deaden the sound of the bone with tow. Ahab orders him below, "'Down, dog, and kennel!'" and gives him a second direct order, "'Avast!'" (*NN* 127). But Stubb hotheadedly refuses to stop, and Ahab must face him down. Stubb's foolhardy behavior may be neatly explained as his enjoyment of intimidating blacks. He intimidates Fleece, forcing him to preach to sharks; he intimidates Pip, abandoning him to the ocean; and he imagines intimidating a black on Negro Hill (*NN* 432), by exchanging imagined gold for some (sexual?) favor. Unable to tolerate black defiance, he seems to be responding to Ahab as to a defiant racial inferior who can be bullied by a naturally "superior" white.

Ahab's defiance of God also bears on his race, for he speaks as if he is the object of Divine hate. Many pre-Emancipation blacks felt that God was not a God of love and that slaveholders and slave-condoning churches were pleasing to him. The Abolitionist version of the Lord's Prayer began, "Our Father who art in *Hell*" (*Liberator*, 8 Sept. 1848, p. 144), and it produced the natural if equally spectacular corollary that "the slaveholders' God is the slaves' *devil*" (*Liberator*, 11 Aug. 1848, p. 126). Ahab has similar thoughts, for in "The Forge," he uses black blood to impart the "true death-temper" to his harpoon barbs with a pure Abolitionist-inspired blood-baptism sanctified by the prayer, "Ego non baptizo te in nomine patris, sed in nomine diaboli!" (*NN* 489)—I do not baptize you in the name of the Father but in the name of the devil; and in "The Candles" he proclaims the pure Garrisonian doctrine that the right worship of the God who brands him, mutilates him, and terrorizes with fire him and his crew is defiance. The moral energy animating Ahab's great verbal defiances is doubly dramatic if it is the expression of a powerless black man demanding respect and acknowledgment from a white Christian creator. And Melville had to be impervious to the potential point of his own Ahabian images of the man as solid bronze, dark, and black not to realize this. In any case, Ahab's defiance bears out the slave overtone in his name, the Biblical Ahab having scorned God and chosen Baal as his lord, *master*, and *owner*. But most important, because the Christian God-creator of the whiteness that mutilated Ahab will not grant his black prayer against whiteness, an apparently half-black Ahab baptizes his barbs with black blood in the name of the prince of darkness.

Ahab's pity is reserved for Starbuck and Pip, persons of color. Pip's loss of sanity makes Ahab protective: he even shares his cabin with him. This act presents the anomaly of a supposedly white captain sharing his quarters with not only a black, but an insane black. When Pip possesses the two greatest objects of mid-Nineteenth-century aversion, blackness and insanity, Ahab takes his hand and brings him into his own cabin. A white captain could hardly overcome racial antipathy, but a captain who himself is growing insane and who may have black blood would be drawn to a brother sufferer and could do it. Melville may have gotten the idea for this conjunction from a famous story about William Lloyd Garrison, whose Abolitionist-feared forces, so alarming to the South, turned out to be, by the report of the Mayor of Boston to the Governor of Virginia, only "a negro boy" (*Liberator* 8 Feb, 1850, p. 24). The prime example of monomania available to Melville's age was that of Garrison's abolitionist fervor, which has been noted as an influencing analogue for Ahab's hatred of Moby Dick.[11] It becomes all the more interesting because Garrison was also called a nigger, a slur that he reprinted (*Liberator*, 17 May, 1850, p. 77), and because his father, also a ship captain, bore a vivid scar on his neck. Garrison's life and work, some aspects of which concern blacks, seem to have influenced Melville.

We should note that a mulatto status for Ahab adds greater drama to the novel than does a white one. A mulatto Ahab will also explain a good measure of Ishmael's intense interest in the man. And a mulatto Ishmael becomes symmetrical when joined, through a lynching image, with a mulatto Ahab, the pair duplicating each other, like the sperm and right whale heads that act as balancing weights to keep the ship on an even keel. The human and psychological opposite weights in the novel are these two men, who create great strength and beauty throughout the book and, in turn, balance their prey.

These various black matters reflect one further well-known influence on Melville. In 1841, aboard the *Acushnet*, he gammed with young Owen Chase, son of the first mate of the *Essex* sunk by a whale in 1820, the father having survived the tragedy that reduced the white Nantucketers to eat all but one of the bodies of the black sailors who had died of malnutrition in the whaleboats.

Only recently has the racial issue in the cannibalism of the *Essex* survivors come to light. Nathaniel Philbrick, the latest writer to deal with the matter, notes that Owen Chase's 1821 account, which the son gave to Melville during their meeting, was partial and didn't tell the whole story: "It would be difficult for any reader of Chase's book alone to appreciate the true scope of the disaster. In particular, the fact that five out of the first six men to die were black is never commented on by Chase. By keeping many of the most disturbing and problematic aspects of the disaster offstage, Chase transforms the story of the *Essex* into a personal tale of trial and triumph."

Even more interesting is Philbrick's statement that "Only Nantucketers [i.e., whites] had emerged from Pollard's and Chase's whaleboats alive."[12] Of great interest then is the question whether, along with the sinking, the tragedy befalling the blacks influenced Melville. Was his interest confined to the ramming of their ill-fated ship, which was common knowledge, or did it include the cannibalism, which an otherwise abolitionist stronghold wanted hushed up? Put differently, would an American novelist of his eye for recording suffering, misery, and injustice, a novelist who held that the truths of life are too horrible for telling or acceptance, fail to be struck by the bitter irony that the white sailors who were willing to sleep and dine apart from their black mates were also content to eat most of those blacks when dead, and even jealously to horde and gnaw their bones? Does *Moby-Dick*, along with its many other fine, documented subjects, also deal with ethnicity and racial injustice, and did the *Essex* serve in Melville's awakening to it? This study, identifying Ishmael and Ahab as possible mulattos, suggests that the answer to these questions is yes.

And better yet, Melville seems to agree. For in "The Ship," as Mary Beth McDaniel has pointed out to me, Ishmael describes the *Pequod* as a bone-gnawer, "A cannibal of a ship, tricking herself forth in the chased bones of her enemies" (*NN* 70). The image suggests teeth-embossed bones used for insulting ornament; it punningly hints at Chase himself; and it implies double adversariality between ship and prey and whites and blacks.

This image of the *Pequod*, then, points us straight to an even larger matter. A white, killing ship; owned and provisioned by pacific Quakers— even Aunt Charity carries aboard a killing lance (*NN* 96)—commanded by a possibly mulatto captain, whose fate is narrated by a likely mulatto seaman, pursuing black victims northward at the time of the 1850 Fugitive Slave Act, opens directly onto the possibility, which does much more than merely nibble at the edges of the novel, that black whales heading northward, in the bloodied and unpeaceful Pacific ocean, are Melville's metaphor for or parallel to fugitive slaves, that the violence done to the whales reflects the violence done to slaves, that the hated white whale suggests a black who can pass for white, and that in short Melville is faithful to his black theme and has further surprises in store that bring us to the great heart at the center of that theme.

The novel itself takes us straight to that heart by producing the following sketch: on various whaling grounds, the whalemen, for sizeable financial gain, pursue big, black, brutish creatures (with fight-scarred backs and bodies) on their run northward, capturing and killing a few from among many others that escape, chaining the captured victims, beheading them and hanging the heads, skinning the bodies, cutting them up, and burning them in their own "fritters," while all the time seeking vengeance on a huge, albino monster, Moby Dick, who is sighted off southern Africa and followed far to the north, and whose retaliation against his attackers causes the deaths of all but one of them—of all but two really, when we remember the unnamed sailor who falls to his death in Chapter 126.

The work of a writer experienced in seeing one thing metaphorically in terms of another, the heart of this 1851 narrative accurately reflect, inferentially, and with paradigmatic simplicity, the fate of many back-scarred black fugitives, pursued northward by relentless hunters, for sizeable financial gain, and often captured, chained, hanged, beheaded, and sometimes burned alive. Writers recognize adaptable gifts, and the Fugitive Slave Law was such a gift to any writer interested in a great social theme. As my parallel suggests, Melville took advantage of it, helped perhaps by the antecedent *Essex* tragedy when two streams of thought, each involving the great sufferings of black creatures, coalesced for him in his 1841 encounter with Chase's son. Other transforming poetic analogues show the paradigm involved in the outline also at work in the episodes, the whole encouraging us to read the work along racial lines, especially since Melville appears to have drawn freely on the *Liberator* for ideas.

Some of Melville's incidents have details that strikingly match events described in Garrison's contemporary accounts. For example, Garrison reports that the whaler *Portsmouth* encountered a dense cloud that produced "many balls of fire. One ... struck the cutting pendants at the mainmast head, and *fell in fragments on the deck*, setting fire to the mast-head and rigging" ("Phenomenon at Sea," 15 June, 1849, p. 95. Garrison's italics). This episode became Melville's spectacular description of the corposant balls burning the *Pequod*'s masts like tapers in "The Candles." Another episode concerns Queequeg's coffin stocked with his cherished treasures, which is based on another *Liberator* news item, for 16 November, 1849, in which a Louisiana slave owner "had his coffin made before his death, of rough unhewed plank, [holding his treasure of] some two or three thousand dollars in gold" (p. 184). One final item appeared in the *Liberator* for 1 August 1851: "The quantity of cigars imported into the United States per annum, from Havana, is said to be Seven Hundred Millions, averaging in value twenty dollars per thousand, making the enormous sum of fourteen millions of dollars, which we pay for principally in specie" (p. 124). Melville uses this when Flask estimates the doubloon as worth "nine hundred and sixty cigars" (*NN* 433), giving the passages the unique signature of expensing the value of certain amounts of gold by certain numbers of cigars. These three sets of similarities go well beyond coincidence (as do others involving Frederick Douglass and Theodore Dwight Weld, which we will shortly encounter). Such passages illustrate the important (and doubted) influence on *Moby-Dick* of the most important abolitionist paper in the country, and they add to the hundreds of duplicates that Harrison Hayford assumes are functionless (*NN* 656). All of them can function as Melville's nudging us to see that the novel has also a duplicate subject, the pursuit and occasional slaughter of whales metaphorically duplicating the pursuit, capture, and occasional slaughter of fugitive blacks.

Melville suggests one method for reading *Moby-Dick* when Ahab notes the "'linked analogies'" of nature and the soul of man, in which "'not the smallest atom stirs or lives in matter, but has its cunning duplicate in mind'" (*NN* 312). Since, as the paradigm shows, the narrative metaphorically duplicates the pursuit of slaves, it encourages recognition of other implied correspondences, such as "cetolgy [linked] with ethnology" in Samuel Otter's phrase.[13] Paradigmatic "linked analogies," or implied correspondences, function as a poetic device and help the reader to dive deep. Concealing a subtext, they achieve a high degree of art—and keep his family, especially his father-in-law, Lemuel Shaw (who as Chief Justice of Massachusetts' Supreme Court was the only northern judge to return a slave to the South), from embarrassing associations with a work arguably favoring abolition.

One linked analogy appears as soon as we read that "blackness is the rule among almost all whales" [*NN* 141] (it is likewise the rule among almost all blacks), which rule gives a racial *and* a possible mixed-racial dimension to the novel, and to Ishmael and Ahab as well, and which places before us the novel's leviathanic theme—a theme of great interest to Frederick Douglass, who writes that "we [blacks] are navigating ships at sea." and that "we are pursuing the huge leviathans of the Pacific" (*Liberator*, 20 April, 1849, p. 62), and who also identifies with the stricken whale in a powerful harpoon metaphor: "the iron of slavery has pierced and rankled in my heart" (*Liberator*, 1 Dec. 1848, p. [189]). These statements would have greatly helped Melville's theme involving black creatures (and one not entirely black creature) heading north while pursued for capture by a captain and narrator who were half black.

In developing this theme, Melville then can describe a sperm whale's "broad, glossy back of an Ethiopian hue, glistening in the sun's rays like a mirror" (*NN* 283), and suggest the analogue of the sweating back of a black worker, poetically assisted by the African association. Further, the swelling black water the *Pequod* meets on the middle passage off the African coast moves Ishmael elegiacally: "And heaved and heaved, still unrestingly heaved the black sea, as if its vast tides were a conscience; and the great mundane soul were in anguish and remorse for the long sin and suffering it had bred" (*NN* 234). Melville's investing the black sea with a soul seeming to mourn its complicity in the huge traffic of coffled, Americas-bound slaves, who were sometimes pushed overboard during interceptive pursuits, or who often died and were thrown to the sharks, gives the passage its power. Upon entering those waters, Ishmael mournfully identifies with, and would have special reasons to identify with, as a likely mulatto aboard a ship captained by another possible mulatto, both men bred to suffering, the soul of the black sea.

The *Pequod*'s whaling occurs largely in the southern Pacific, as it drives north from the Cape to the Sea of Japan, which occupies almost the same northern latitude as Philadelphia. The whalers' hunt is stressed by various references to "southern whalesmen," "Southern whale-fishers," and "Southern fishers" (*NN* 156–58). When the magnitude of the slaughter grows depressingly clear, Ishmael raises the question of survival and says that the whales "can at last resort to their Polar citadels... among icy fields... and in a charmed circle of everlasting December, bid defiance to all pursuit from man" (*NN* 461). These matters offer a paradigm that links them by ready analogy with fugitive slaves being pursued north as they too seek freedom from southern hunters.

Important to the capture of runaways were their various identifying marks, some natural, others inflicted. Theodore Weld offers five and Charles Dickens three pages of advertisements describing distinguishing deformities, such as sears, missing teeth, or body parts that make identification easier. Whales, too, bear "bodily peculiarities" (*NN* 203), as Melville notes: "Not a few are captured having the deep scars of [amorous fights],—furrowed heads, broken teeth, scolloped fins, and in some instances, wrenched and dislocated mouths" (*NN* 392), along with the whalemen scars that Ishmael reports. One whale "marked like an old tortoise with mystic hieroglyphics upon the back" (*NN* 205) poetically suggests a famous daguerreotype of the scarred back of a severely flogged slave.[14]

In a novel drawing energy from the theme of slavery, one expects it to be comprehensively treated. Melville doesn't disappoint us. Slavery offered any number of notorious social implications. To establish one such analogue, Melville speaks of the segregation on "English railways [which are] at the expense of a separate car, specially reserved for the accommodation of royalty" (*NN* 399). The linked analogy here is plainly to the American Jim Crow nil car unroyally separating blacks from what, after Douglas, became an abolitionist commonplace called the aristocracy of skin,[15] thereby segregating white "royalty" from black "inferiors."

Melville accomplishes subtle paradigmatic linking by means of the analogy in the shared metaphors of *master* and *driver*—words with the double meanings that Sanford E. Marovitz believes George J. Adler inspired Melville to see.[16] If whales can be fish and can represent blacks, then *masters* can not only be captains of whalers, but can represent slave owners. *Drivers* can represent overseers "compelling the labor of slaves and cattle"[17] *and* hunter-mate-drivers "driving these leviathans before us" (*NN* 383). Franklin and Schweninger add the important detail that the infamous patrols pursuing fugitive slaves "consist[ed] of an officer and six men," a complement virtually matching a whaleboat's officer and five men. They also point out slave masters' networking to locate escapees: "Related by marriage and kinship, the families of the planter aristocracy communicated often with one another... [especially about] possible destinations" to which their slave might flee.[18] Readers will recognize the parallel here to Ahab speaking to other passing masters as to Moby Dick's heading.

In a pursuit, the crews, back-breakingly driven like brutalized slaves, chase whales that suffer the unrelenting miseries of the pursued and captured runaways. A whale's "tormented body rolling not in brine but in blood" (*NN* 285), would be tormented by the salt sea washing its wounds, much as slaves were tormented by masters who had them flogged—a practice Melville especially hated—and their lacerated backs washed with brine or salt.[19] In his sections addressing the argument that slave masters are not cruel to their slaves, Weld writes, in 1839, that the cruelty occurs unseen, except to overseers and other slaves. Weld's analysis shows the financial reason leading the slave master to kill certain groups of slaves, slaves who were old, worn out, infirm, maimed or deformed, blind, and "slaves under overseers whose wages are proportioned to the crop which they raise."[20] Death to such persons represents cruelty inflicted on helplessness.

Melville illustrates this cruelty in "The Virgin," where he narrates the horrific death of an old whale that matches Weld's classes point for point, it being worn out, infirm, diseased, maimed, deformed, blind, and worth an easy lay-divided three thousand dollars" (*NN* 354) to the hunters. It is an easy prey because it is maimed "in the unnatural stump of his starboard fin" (*NN* 353). (In their chapter "On the Run," Franklin and Schweninger note that "physical handicaps did not dissuade slaves from attempting to escape.")[21] Pursuing this hapless victim, the mates verbally whip their crews, like an overseer forcing renewed effort from slaves. Finally, for maximum speed, pulling "'like god-dam,'" the crewmen are urged to "'burst a blood-vessel'" and to "'snap your spine in two-and-twenty places'" (*NN* 353, 354). This back-breaking labor suggests an analogue to slaves exhausted in the chase after a fellow slave. But inhuman as such labor is, its object here is largely barbarous. For eyes, the victim "protruded blind bulbs, horribly pitiable to see. But pity was there none" (*NN* 357). Flask can't resist torturing the dying bull with its "strangely discolored bunch or protuberance, the size of a bushel, low down on the flank. 'A nice spot; cried Flask. Just let me prick him there once'" (*NN* 357). Such whaling-ground's barbarity was unsuspected and unseen by the public, and it hints at genital mutilation because of Flask's verb *prick*. Literature possesses few deaths equally pathetic and needless, for the whale sinks while chained to the *Pequod*, which is nearly carried down with it. The killers, like overseers who tortured and killed slaves, thus end up having nothing for their cruelty but its infliction. Franklin and Schweninger remark that "What happened when [masters] caught up with their slaves usually went unsaid in the record, but it is difficult to believe they did not seek a harsh retribution ..."[22]

During a pursuit, Flask gives a further Southern dimension to the hunt by promising the room to "'sign over to you my Martha's Vineyard *plantation*, boys'" (*NN* 222. My italics), if they will beach him on the whale's back. This joke shows Melville working an important slavery term into his story. When captured, the black brute is chained to the ship and dismembered, beginning with the highly valuable head. On 1 Nov 1850, p. 173, Garrison reprinted, from the *Guilford Horn*, a slave owner's reward of $125.00 for the return of an escaped slave, but "One Hundred and Fifty Dollars will be given for his HEAD ..." Garrison also printed on 13 June 1851, p. 94, George Thompson's speech concerning a planter's "large reward for [his] slave's capture, and a larger reward to the man who should bring him *the slave's head*" (Garrison's italics). Tying this analogue to Melville is the fact that these slave heads, like those of the sperm whale and those hawked by Queequeg, were worth more money than the mere bodies of the victims.

With a whale slumped in its securing chains, the black Daggoo is ordered overboard to cut Stubb a supper steak "'from his small,'" for "Nantucketers ... relish ... that particular part, ... the tapering extremity of the body" (*NN* 292). Stubb means to follow his supper on the whale's genital organ with "Whale-balls for breakfast" (*NN* 397): only by taking this as a reference to testicles does it become duplicative with whale meatballs (*NN* 298). In any case, a black performs each operation, as well as the preparation of the items,

Fleece being roused from sleep to feed the victorious hunter (*NN* 294). The linking analogy is genital mutilation that befell some offending blacks in a timeless, emasculatory ritual, meant to transfer the victim's potency to his conqueror. A hundred and fifty years ago the *Liberator* veiled these practices: "'two men... *tied* and *whipped to death a negro man* .... The circumstances... were very exceedingly shocking—but we forbear detail'" (10 Aug, 1849, p. 128. Garrison's italics). So too does Melville, who hints at the whales incised penis and leaves us to see that Fleece expects Stubb's brutalizing blow to the groin (*NN* 297).

After beheading and stripping comes the trying out, an operation involving "the curious anomaly of the most solid masonry joining with oak and hemp... It is as if from the open field a brick-kiln were transported to [the *Pequod*'s] planks" (*NN* 421). The anomaly is that a firepit, not a brick-kiln, is found in a field near an oak overhung with a hemp rope.) Wood begins the burning, and fritters sustains it: "once ignited, the whale supplies his own fuel and burns by his own body" (*NN 422*). Melville veils a hated and resisted truth—that whites burned blacks to death—by means of the paradigmatically-linked subtext of a black being hemp-lynched from an oak, taken dawn, and burned to ashes, in a fire fed by his own fat. This processing is matched in Garrison's columns where we find many reports of white, Christian, gruesome mistreatment of blacks, including burnings—of a black burned by a slow fire (8 Dec. 1848 p. 194), of another whose owner "tortured him all day [and] burnt parts of his body off with fire" (9 Nov. 1849, p. 181), of two Negroes "tied ... to a tree and burned ... to death" (14 Dec. 1849 p. 200), and of Negroes "burn[ed] at the stake" (14 Dec. 1849, p. 197). If Ahab is half black, accounts like these seem to have inspired the stake imagery that Melville associates with him.

In executions of blacks and slaves, the mutilational focus, intent on maximum humiliation and destruction of identity, fastened upon the three matters of decapitation, emasculation, and burning, i.e., skinning. The perfect symbol of the altered black is the peeled, beheaded, emasculated ghostly white corpse of the processed whale floating away and being stripped by sharks below and birds above (*NN* 308)—perfect because cut down to size, rendered harmlessly dead, turned mainstream white, and utterly isolated.

Burned, scarred and isolated, Ahab still has great pity for Pip, who seems to have suffered from another notorious white injustice against blacks. This one, which raised much disgust, was the infamous practice of kidnapping northern blacks, often children, for sale into southern slavery. Because of a mystery in his life, Pip seems to have known this fate. Melville forces us to explain the anomaly of Alabama figuring in the life of a boy brought up in Connecticut. Melville may explain this mystery with another one, that of

Pip's emphatic calling himself a craw: "'I'm a Crow ... Caw! caw! caw! caw! caw! caw! Ain't I a crow?'" (*NN* 434). Since both Pip's race and mental state are already well established, this emphasis is best explained by recognizing Pip as a black bird, and black birds as the prey of *blackbirders*—kidnappers who stole free northern blacks, often children, according to Carol Wilson,[23] and sold them south into slavery, beginning in 1829.

Melville used his opportunities to treat the great aspects of his potent theme. One thematic topic involves the still argued claim that blacks are mentally inferior to whites. Moby Dick himself is the analogical embodiment of the notion that the preeminence of whiteness "applies to the human race itself, giving the white man ideal mastership over every dusky tribe" (*NN* 189). But Ishmael has no tender illusions about whiteness, for it panicked blacks and galled whales, and the panic suggests black fear of violent whites. Whites rationalized the enslavement and killing of blacks by a dehumanizing argument that Ishmael ironically echoes as justifying the slaughter of whales, it being "very hard really to believe that such bulky manses of overgrowth can possibly be instinct, in all parts, with the name sort of life that lives in a dog or a horse" (*NN* 273). This passage reflects the typical psychology in Southern descriptions of the "mental limitations" of slaves (often by persons denying slaves access to the education that would improve them). One old American racist joke involves the brawny black so dumb that he cannot be killed by blows to the head, the one place also where the sperm whale is unkillable: its forehead seems "paved with horses' hoofs" (*NN* 337). (The head is presented as a weapon for ramming and bludgeoning its opponents, just as blacks were forced to butt heads with each other in the Navy (*White-Jacket NN* 275).

The sperm whale's head is "impregnable, uninjurable," and behind it swims "a mass of tremendous life, only to be adequately estimated as piled wood is—by the cord, and all obedient to one volition, as the smallest insect." From such a creature come the "inconsiderable braining feats" (*NN* 337–38) of this monster, who sounds similar to black hewers of wood and drawers of water—ox-dumb but potent (*NN* 337–38). Small wonder, then, that such a monstrous brute has so small a brain—really only "A Nut," and fit to make the creature a placid worker for the mowing of fields. Indeed the skull-case so resembles man's that looking at it prompts Ishmael's thought," "This *man* [my italics] had no self-esteem, and no veneration. And by these negations, considered along with the affirmative fact of his prodigious bulk and power, you can best form to yourself the truest, though not the most exhilarating conception of what the most exalted potency is" (*NN* 349). Both whales and slaves can be regarded, mistakenly, as potent sexual predators, instead of as the exquisite creations they really are. For the whale, and thus the black, is a creature of God, and invested with an "august dignity" that "is not the dignity of kings and robes, but that abounding dignity which has no robed investiture. Thou shalt see a shining in the arm that wields a pick or drives a spike [and pickaxe and sledgehammer were commonly wielded by our John Henrys], that democratic dignity which, on all hands, radiates without end from God Himself! The centre and circumference of all democracy! His omnipresence, our divine equality!" (*NN* 117) the fatherhood of God producing the brotherhood of man.

Finally, linked analogies bring us to the white whale itself. Moby Dick appears to analogize a black passing for white, who, in part, is all the more intensely pursued for that reason. Melville's alchemies, turning the *Liberator*'s lead into *Moby-Dick*'s gold, reveal the transformation of a whaling story into a virulent, non-paternalistic subtext inspired by Chase, Douglass, Weld, and Garrison: who first told Melville about the *Essex* crew eating its blacks may never be known. In the transformation, Melville affirms that the "common decency of human recognition is the meanest slave's right" (*NN* 244), which undercuts slavery's rationale and makes its justification virtually impossible. In *Moby-Dick*, and before Walt Whitman and Mark Twain, Melville celebrates in an unmatched story the unsung, faceless, nameless strugglers of our country, a crew "chiefly made up of mongrel renegades, and cutaways, and cannibals" (*NN* 186). If Ishmael and Ahab are mulattos, they represent the South's feared mongrelization of the white race. But for Melville they embody the courage and nobility of an oppressed race, and *Moby-Dick* is a tribute and an epitaph that will outshine and outlast the merely marble and gilded monuments of princes and presidents. Our most accepted notion of blacks concerns their "simple intelligence," fitting them for hewing, carrying, field work, law wages, and therefore slavery. How better for Melville to explode this idea than to have a mulatto *Pequod* captain almost circumnavigate the globe to find a single whale in the Pacific ocean on a voyage that a mulatto seaman brilliantly chronicles, while presenting the classical background, general history, and a nearly encyclopedic exposition of the intricacies of so complex a profession? "Unlettered Ishmael"'s (*NN* 347) narrative is to this day our earliest literary account of two major American industries, whaling and slavery, the whole of the account being thematic, arguably not digressional, and worthy of a new and fresh discussion concerning the novel and the novelist.

NOTES

I have worked into my text two sets of citations, those to newspapers and those to the Northwestern-Newberry edition, ed. by Harrison Hayford, Hershel Parker, and Thomas Tanselle, Evanston and Chicago, 1968–91. Drs. Sterling Stuckey, Sally Hoople,

John Bryant, and Leo W. Graf, Jr., along with Nicole Squires and John Hayes, have made important contributions to this paper, for the ideas of which I alone am responsible.

1. W. Jeffrey Bolster, *Black Jacks: African American Seamen in the Age of Sail* (Cambridge, Mass., and London: Harvard University Press, 1997). 25. Hereafter cited as Bolster.

2. John Hope Franklin and Loren Schweninger, *Runaway Slaves: Rebels on the Plantation* (New York/Oxford: Oxford University Press, 1999), 222, 232. Hereafter cited as Franklin and Schweninger.

3. Carolyn L. Karcher, *Shadow over the Promised Land: Slavery, Race and Violence in Melville's America* (Baton Rouge and London: Louisiana State University Press, 1980), 10.

4. Alexander Starbuck, *History of the American Whaling Fishery* (Secaucus, N.J.: Castle, 1989). 51.

5. Franklin and Schweninger, 135.

6. Bolster. 216.

7. Bolster, 176.

8. *The Novels and Tales of Henry James* (New York: Charles Scribner's Sons, 1907), I, vii.

9. Edgar A. Dryden, *Melville's Thematics of Form: The Great Art of Telling the Truth* (Baltimore and London: The Johns Hopkins University Press, 1981), 104.

10. Charles Dickens, *American Notes: A Journey* (New York: Fromme International Publishing Corporation, 1985), 230.

11. David S. Reynolds, *Beneath the American Renaissance: Subversive Imagination in the Age of Emerson and Melville* (New York: Alfred A. Knopf, 1988), 156.

12. Nathaniel Philbrick, *In the Heart of the Sea: The Tragedy of the Whaleship Essex* (New York: Viking, 2000), 204, 192.

13. Samuel Otter, *Melville's Anatomics* (Berkeley: University of California Press, 1999), 2.

14. Kwame Anthony Appiah and Henry Louis Gates, Jr., eds., *Africana* (New York: Basic Civitas Books, 1999), 1731.

15. John W. Blassingame, et al., eds. *The Frederick Douglass Papers / Series One: Speeches, Debates, and Interviews, Volume 2: 1847–54* (New Haven and London: Yale University Press, 1982), II, 3.

16. Sanford E. Marovitz, "More Chartless Voyaging: Melville and Adler at Sea," in *Studies in the American Renaissance*, ed. Joel Myerson (Charlottesville: University Press of Virginia, 1986), 301.

17. Timothy (sic.) Dwight Weld, *American Slavery As It Is: Testimony of a Thousand Witnesses* (New York: Arno Press and The New York Times, 1969), 110. Hereafter cited as Weld.

18. Franklin and Schweninger, 154, 165.

19. Weld, 46, 49, 50, 60 ff; Franklin and Schweninger, 45.

20. Weld, 133.

21. Franklin and Schweninger, 39

22. Franklin and Schweninger, 170.

23. Carol Wilson, *Freedom at Risk: The Kidnapping of Free Blacks in America, 1780–1865* (Louisville: The University Press of Kentucky, 1994), 113–114.

CAROLYN L. KARCHER

A Jonah's Warning to America in Moby-Dick

Centering his allegorical indictment of slavery on the experience of men abused and demeaned beyond the uttermost limits of human endurance, as Melville did in *White-Jacket* and "The Town-Ho's Story," inevitably led him to concentrate on the moral issue of whether men in such circumstances may justifiably resort to violence to overthrow their oppressors. This literary exploration in turn confronted Melville with his own unresolved conflict between submitting to and rebelling against repressive authority, be it parental, societal, religious, or political. Since he envisioned both alternatives as self-destructive, he seems to have been unable to sustain the tension of openly identifying with the slave. Instead, he retreated to the safer emotional vantage point from which, in *Mardi*, he had first begun exploring the moral problems that slavery posed. Displacing his personal conflict over defying authority onto the nation at large, Melville concerned himself increasingly with the political dilemma of ending slavery in time to avert an interracial bloodbath, yet in such a way as not to court the destruction of the Union. This shift of focus also entailed a more global assessment of slavery as an institution that different peoples had imposed on each other from time immemorial and that deformed both its perpetrators and its victims, generating an endless cycle of vengeance.

From *Shadow Over the Promised Land: Slavery, Race, and Violence in Melville's America*, pp. 62–91.
© 1980 Louisiana State University Press.

The watershed in Melville's approach to slavery occurs in *Moby-Dick*, where he views the problem of slavery from many angles, including the metaphysical. As Ishmael muses ironically: "Who aint a slave? Tell me that. Well, then, however the old sea-captains may order me about—however they may thump and punch me about, I have the satisfaction of knowing that it is all right; that everybody else is one way or other served in much the same way—either in a physical or metaphysical point of view, that is; and so the universal thump is passed round, and all hands should rub each other's shoulder-blades, and be content" (MD, 15).

In *Moby-Dick*, Melville envisages several possible dénouements to the American crisis over slavery, along with various answers to the question of whether individuals (and nations) help to weave their own destiny into the warp of necessity or are entirely caught in the threads of Fate's loom.[1] "The Town-Ho's Story" offers Steelkilt's rebellion and its successful issue as one such dénouement.[2] The main narrative of *Moby-Dick* offers another alternative to Ahab's destructive polity and the retribution it brings on the *Pequod*; for Ishmael, buoyed up by the coffin his friend Queequeg had ordered for himself and subsequently turned into a life buoy for the *Pequod*, miraculously escapes the cataclysm that overtakes his shipmates. As the means of Ishmael's escape betokens, his freely chosen friendship with Queequeg plays a conspicuous part in modifying his destiny, even though "those stage managers, the Fates," may have had the first and last word in sending him on this ill-starred voyage and ordaining its ending.[3] Ishmael's friendship with Queequeg dramatizes the conclusions about racial prejudice that Melville had reached in *Redburn* and suggests that by embracing the Negro as an equal partner, American citizens might still avert the tempest that threatened to engulf their ship of state.

But before we can be sure of these racial implications, we must first determine whether Melville meant to identify Queequeg with the Negro—a question that has elicited lively debate among critics interested in Melville's racial attitudes. Those who credit Melville with enlightened racial views cite the cannibal as a fully developed and complimentary negroid characterization and emphasize the unprecedented egalitarianism of picturing a white man sharing a bed with a dark-skinned savage. Conversely, those who accuse Melville of racism point out that Queequeg is not an American Negro and theorize that Melville's deeply felt Marquesan experience might have led to a "deification of Polynesians" without affecting his prejudices toward Africans or, for that matter, American Indians.[4] What both sides seem to have missed—despite recognition of the way Queequeg telescopes Polynesian, American Indian, African, Islamic, and even Christian features and customs—is how deliberately Melville has blurred racial lines in portraying the savage, and how explicitly he has related Queequeg's ambiguously perceived racial identity to the issue of anti-Negro prejudice.

The most obvious sign that Melville intended to endow Queequeg with African attributes is the series of allusions that initially provoked the controversy. As critics of both schools have noted, Queequeg, though a native of the South Sea islands, incongruously worships a "little deformed image ... exactly the color of a three days' old Congo baby," prompting Ishmael to call it his "Negro idol" (MD, 30, 51). Furthermore, Queequeg and Ishmael later attract from passersby some of the hostile notice that Redburn imagines his ship's black steward would have received had he walked arm in arm with a white woman in the streets of New York. Since Ishmael and Queequeg are of the same sex, they are not mobbed, but they are greeted with stares and jeers. Ishmael pointedly comments that these taunts are due not to the outlandish figure Queequeg cuts—the citizens of New Bedford being "used to seeing cannibals like him in their streets"—but to the sight of two racially diverse "fellow beings" on such "companionable" terms. Underscoring the parallel with black–white relations in America, he drops the word "cannibal" to moralize outright: "as though a white man were anything more dignified than a whitewashed Negro" (MD, 58–60).[5]

Hence it should be clear that Queequeg represents yet another of the composite racial figures that Melville created to undermine racial categories and to inculcate the lessons in racial tolerance and cultural relativism that he himself had learned in *Typee*. Through Ishmael's encounter with Queequeg, Melville shows how an educated young man of respectable social background learns to overcome his provincial bigotry and racial prejudices, just as he had earlier shown Redburn learning to overcome his anti-Negro feelings. With Ishmael, however, Melville takes the reader further than with Redburn, since he also calls into question for the first time the reality of the racial differences to which prejudice was generally ascribed in his day.

Even before Ishmael actually meets Queequeg, he confronts the problem of whether he "might be cherishing unwarrantable prejudices against this unknown harpooneer," with whom the landlord has proposed that he share the only remaining bed in the inn (MD, 25). The joke is that the well-defined prejudices Ishmael holds do not prevent the racial identity of his bedfellow from eluding him for the better part of a long chapter. Thus when Ishmael learns that the mysterious harpooneer "is actually engaged this blessed Saturday night, or rather Sunday morning, in peddling his head around this town," he does not connect this "cannibal business" with the previous revelation that the harpooneer is "a dark complexioned chap" who "eats nothing but steaks, and likes 'em rare" (MD, 22, 25, 27). Instead, Ishmael expostulates with the landlord, unconsciously basing his claim to sagacity on color: "you'd better stop spinning that yarn to me—I'm not green." Accentuating the racial implications of this pun, the landlord's answering pun—"May be not ... but I rayther guess you'll be done *brown* if that ere harpooneer hears you a slanderin' his head" (MD, 26)—hints at the first lessons Ishmael will learn on being thrown together with Queequeg: that color prejudice is a two-way street and color itself a treacherous criterion on which to predicate anyone's identity, let alone his worth. Ishmael's continued obtuseness regarding Queequeg's racial identity becomes more significant when the very sight of the cannibal fails to enlighten him. At the first view of Queequeg's "dark, purplish, yellow" face, "here and there stuck over with large, blackish looking squares," Ishmael supposes that "he's been in a fight, got dreadfully cut, and here he is, just from the surgeon" (MD, 28). On perceiving that the black squares on Queequeg's cheeks are not "sticking-plasters," but "stains of some sort or other," Ishmael takes Queequeg for a "white man ... who, falling among the cannibals, had been tattooed by them" (MD, 29). He moralizes: "And what is it, thought I, after all! It's only his outside; a man can be honest in any sort of skin." Ironically, Ishmael has not meant to articulate a protest against color-consciousness.

Still under the misapprehension that Queequeg is a "white man," Ishmael struggles to explain how a white could have acquired such an "unearthly complexion." Echoing the scientific debates about whether racial features resulted from the influence of climate or from primordial biological differences, he wavers between two theories—that "the sun ... produced these extraordinary effects upon the skin," or alternatively, that the stranger's distinctive skin color might arise from some deeper cause than climate: "I never heard of a hot sun's tanning a white man into a purplish yellow one." The "bald purplish head" that the stranger reveals on taking off his beaver hat frightens Ishmael more than his discolored tattooed skin, perhaps because it looks "for all the world like a mildewed skull"—just such a mildewed skull, in fact, as American archaeologists and ethnologists were currently disinterring from Indian burial grounds as a means of determining the racial character of America's aboriginal population.[6] Hitherto curious enough to master his alarm, Ishmael now feels ready to bolt from the room. He accounts for his terror by remarking, "Ignorance is the parent of fear, and being completely nonplussed and confounded about the stranger, I confess I was now as much afraid of him as if it was the devil himself" (MD, 29).

Once again, however, this broad-minded interpretation of racial prejudice ironically precedes Ishmael's realization that Queequeg is not a white man gone native, but an "abominable savage" from the South Seas—a fact that only becomes "quite plain" to him after Queequeg has completely undressed, disclosing a body tattooed from head to foot. Not until Queequeg has sprung upon him crying "Who-e debel you?", bringing the landlord to the rescue, does Ishmael belatedly digest the intuitions he has had about how irrelevant a man's skin color is to his character, and why people of different skin color fear each other as devils: "What's all this fuss I have been making about, thought I to myself—the man's a human being just as I am: he has just as much reason to fear me, as I have to be afraid of him" (MD, 31).

Overcoming color prejudice is but the initial stage of the transformation Ishmael undergoes. Once he removes his racial coloring glasses, Ishmael begins to see his savage bedfellow in another light, which in turn affects his perceptions of his white countrymen. The first breakthrough, occurs when Ishmael realizes that the cannibal is in fact behaving "in not only a civil but a really kind and charitable way" toward him. By the next morning, Ishmael has also become aware of the unflattering contrast between his own "great rudeness" in staring at Queequeg and "watching all his toilette motions" as if he were an animal in the zoo, and Queequeg's "civility and consideration" in offering to leave the room so that Ishmael can dress in privacy. This leads Ishmael to question the appropriateness of the terms "savage" and "civilized" and to conclude that savages may be more "civilized" in certain respects than so-called "civilized" peoples: "Thinks I, Queequeg ... this is a very civilized overture; but, the truth is, these savages have an innate sense of delicacy, say what you will; it is marvellous how essentially polite they are" (MD, 34). Although Ishmael proceeds to regale the reader with a description of how Queequeg commences "dressing at top by donning his beaver hat" and then, "minus his trowsers," crushes himself "boots in hand, and hat on—under the bed ... to be private when putting on his boots," his sense of Queequeg's idiosyncracies soon gives way to a growing appreciation of the savage's human qualities.

On joining the other sailors at breakfast, Ishmael already views the difference between them and Queequeg as one of degree, rather than kind. Whereas earlier he had tried to classify Queequeg as "white" or "savage," he now foregoes these racial categories altogether and distinguishes among the sailors only on the basis of their sun tans:

> This young fellow's healthy cheek is like a sun-toasted pear in hue, and would seem to smell almost as musky; he cannot have been three days landed from his Indian voyage. That man next him looks a few shades lighter; you might say a touch of satin wood is in him. In the complexion of a third still lingers a tropic tawn, but slightly bleached withal; *he* doubtless has tarried whole weeks ashore. But who could show a cheek like Queequeg?

which, barred with various tints, seemed like the Andes' western
slope, to show forth in one array, contrasting climates, zone by
zone. (MD, 36)

Queequeg's uniqueness, in other words, consists not in being "colored," as
opposed to white (or purplish yellow, as opposed to another shade), but in
being a compendium of the colors produced by various climates (apparently
Ishmael has opted for the climatic explanation of racial differences).

Similarly, when Ishmael goes on to compare Queequeg's bearing and
manners with those of his compeers, he no longer dwells on "Queequeg's
peculiarities here; how he eschewed coffee and hot rolls, and applied
his undivided attention to beefsteaks, done rare," serving himself with
his harpoon. Instead, what impresses Ishmael is how much more poised
Queequeg looks than the American sailors. They, in their native land, sit "at
a social breakfast table—all of the same calling, all of kindred tastes—looking
round as sheepishly at each other as though they had never been out of
sight of some sheepfold among the Green Mountains." Queequeg, twenty
thousand miles away from home and amid people whose language he can
barely speak, presides "at the head of the table ... as cool as an icicle" (MD,
36–37).

In the next chapter, where Ishmael confronts the cross section of
nations and races thronging the streets of New Bedford, his astonishment
"at first catching a glimpse of so outlandish an individual as Queequeg
circulating among the polite society of a civilized town" entirely evaporates.
He remarks:

> In thoroughfares nigh the docks, any considerable seaport will
> frequently offer to view the queerest looking nondescripts
> from foreign parts. Even in Broadway and Chestnut streets,
> Mediterranean mariners will sometimes jostle the affrighted
> ladies. Regent street is not unknown to Lascars and Malays; and
> at Bombay, in the Apollo Green, live Yankees have often scared
> the natives.... In New Bedford, actual cannibals stand chatting at
> street corners; savages outright; many of whom yet carry on their
> bones unholy flesh. It makes a stranger stare. (MD, 37)

Lumping Mediterranean mariners and Yankees with Lascars and Malays,
Ishmael jolts us into realizing, as *he* now does, that we are as anomalous to
foreign peoples as they are to us—indeed perhaps more so, since the Lascars
and Malays in London seem to attract no notice from the British, and the
savages in jaded New Bedford go unheeded except by strangers, whereas in

Bombay "live Yankees have often scared the natives." He also implies that no set of racial traits is inherently stranger than any other; that the strangeness, in short, is in the eye of the beholder. Thus a white seaman from Spain or Italy can seem more fearsome to an American lady who has never seen one than a cannibal does to a native of New Bedford. Ishmael delivers the final blow to his countrymen's ethnocentrism and color consciousness by asserting that what the reader will find "still more curious, certainly more comical" than all the dark-skinned "Feegeeans, Tongatabooans, Erromanggoans, Pannangians, and Brighggians" he will run across in New Bedford, is the spectacle of the "green Vermonters and New Hampshire men" who descend on the town by the score "all athirst for gain and glory" in the untried career of whaling: "Many are as green as the Green Mountains whence they come.... Look there! that chap strutting round the corner. He wears a beaver hat and swallow-tailed coat, girdled with a sailor-belt and sheath-knife. Here comes another with a sou'wester and a bombazine cloak" (MD, 37–38). The analogy with Queequeg in his beaver hat is unmistakable, as is the moral, driven home in the following paragraph, that the South Sea savage who dons his boots under the bed is intrinsically no more ludicrous than the homegrown "bumpkin dandy" who mows his native acres "in buckskin gloves" during the dog days, "for fear of tanning his hands" (MD, 38).

The change in Ishmael's perceptions, resulting in this sophisticated cultural relativism, culminates when he is able to discern the nobility of character underlying Queequeg's bizarre exterior:

> Savage though he was, and hideously marred about the face—at least to my taste—his countenance yet had a something in it which was by no means disagreeable. You cannot hide the soul. Through all his unearthly tattooings, I thought I saw the traces of a simple honest heart; and in his large, deep eyes, fiery black and bold, there seemed tokens of a spirit that would dare a thousand devils. And besides all this, there was a certain lofty bearing about the Pagan, which even his uncouthness could not altogether maim. He looked like a man who had never cringed and never had had a creditor. (MD, 51–52)

Not only does Ishmael overlook the disfigurements that had previously repelled him; he has also come to realize that his own distaste for tattooing is as ethnocentric as Queequeg's preference for it. But Ishmael's most radical departure from the racial prejudice that had originally distorted Queequeg into a devil in his eyes consists in ascribing phrenological excellence to Queequeg's negroid cranial conformation, with its retreating forehead and projecting brow, and identifying it with George Washington's: "certain it was his head was phrenologically an excellent one. It may seem ridiculous, but it reminded me of General Washington's head, as seen in the popular busts of him. It had the same long regularly graded retreating slope from above the brows, which were likewise very projecting, like two long promontories thickly wooded on top. Queequeg was George Washington cannibalistically developed" (MD, 52). We need only recall that nineteenth-century Americans placed Washington side by side with Shakespeare at the pinnacle of human evolution—and consigned the African cannibal to its nadir—to measure the distance Ishmael has traveled.[7]

Paralleling Ishmael's intellectual growth is the maturation of his acquaintance with Queequeg into a friendship destined to alter the course of his life. When Ishmael accepts Queequeg as his bedfellow with the famous words, "Better sleep with a sober cannibal than a drunken Christian," he carries the principles of racial tolerance and egalitarianism to what Redburn had recognized as their logical conclusion—vindicating "amalgamation." Ishmael, however, goes a step beyond Redburn; for he actually practices what he preaches and contracts a "marriage" with someone of another race symbolically associated with America's twin pariahs, the Negro and the Indian.

The insistent matrimonial imagery describing Ishmael's budding friendship with his new bedfellow has drawn much comment, both for its homosexual and its racial overtones.[8] Whatever sexual predilections it may indicate in Melville, he knew he could get away with dramatizing a happy interracial marriage by disguising it as a male comradeship which his public would not dare interpret as homosexual. The crucial fact about Melville's imagery, after all, is that it elevates the taboo relationship between a white and a nonwhite to the plane of a legal marriage between equals—and a love marriage at that. Except when Ishmael, under the influence of his "unwarrantable prejudices," worries about having a strange harpooneer "tumble in upon me at midnight" with no way of knowing "from what vile hole he had been coming" (MD, 24), Melville's jokes about the relationship are never merely bawdy. On the contrary, Ishmael and Queequeg consummate their friendship in the landlord's own conjugal bed, where their union issues in a "hatchet-faced baby" (Queequeg's tomahawk-calumet); Queequeg holds Ishmael in a "bridegroom clasp ... as though naught but death should part us twain" (which indeed proves to be the case); Queequeg pronounces himself "married" to Ishmael, according to "his country's phrase"; Queequeg and Ishmael lie abed chatting in their "hearts' honeymoon" like "some old couples"; and Ishmael at last sees "how elastic our stiff prejudices grow when love once comes to bend them" (MD, 27, 33, 53–55).

Beyond its propagandistic function of vindicating interracial marriage, the narrative significance of Ishmael's friendship with Queequeg lies in symbolizing the commitment that Ishmael makes, through Queequeg, to loving his fellow man and acknowledging the tie that binds him to the rest of humanity. This commitment, which will later protect Ishmael against succumbing entirely to Ahab's hate-driven pursuit of the white whale, initially rescues him from the mood of misanthropic despair that had impelled him to go to sea as an antidote to "methodically knocking people's hats off" and a "substitute for pistol and ball" (MD, 12).[9]

On Ishmael's second day with Queequeg, as he sits in the bedroom watching the savage, he begins "to be sensible of strange feelings": "I felt a melting in me. No more my splintered heart and maddened hand were turned against the wolfish world. This soothing savage had redeemed it. There he sat, his very indifference speaking a nature in which there lurked no civilized hypocrisies and bland deceits" (MD, 53). The scene that follows evokes the historical encounter between white settlers and American Indians and offers a moving alternative to the mutual hostilities that had ensued when whites had seized Indian lands, anathemized the Indians' way of life, and set out to destroy the Indians themselves in wars like the one that had left the Pequots—the "celebrated tribe of Massachusetts Indians" for whom the *Pequod* is named—"extinct as the ancient Medes" (MD, 67). Queequeg responds warmly to Ishmael's overtures, and the two seal their friendship over that hoary Indian symbol, the peace pipe.[10] Thereupon Queequeg embraces Ishmael, declares that they are henceforth "married" and that "he would gladly die for me, if need should be," and divides his belongings equally with Ishmael while Ishmael remonstrates against his generosity. Climaxing this ritual, which suggests an egalitarian marriage of the races on the American continent and their sharing of America's resources in a conjugal spirit, Queequeg invites Ishmael to join him in worshipping his negro idol—a reversal of the traditional roles of white missionary and savage proselyte. Ishmael's acquiescence and his use of the golden rule to justify it represent Melville's crowning affirmation that the essence of religion is a love for one's fellow man that transcends all barriers of race and creed and precludes all forms of intolerance:

> I was a good Christian; born and bred in the bosom of the infallible Presbyterian Church. How then could I unite with this wild idolator in worshipping his piece of wood? But what is worship? thought I. Do you suppose now, Ishmael, that the magnanimous God of heaven and earth—pagans and all included—can possibly be jealous of an insignificant bit of black wood? Impossible!

But what is worship?—to do the will of God—that is worship.
And what is the will of God?—to do to my fellow man what I
would have my fellow man to do to me—that is the will of God.
Now, Queequeg is my fellow man. And what do I wish that this
Queequeg would do to me? Why, unite with me in my particular
Presbyterian form of worship. Consequently, I must then unite
with him in his; ergo, I must turn idolator. So I kindled the shav-
ings; helped prop up the innocent little idol; offered him burnt
biscuit with Queequeg; salaamed before him twice or thrice;
kissed his nose; and that done, we undressed and went to bed, at
peace with our own consciences and all the world. (MD, 54)

Ishmael is not simply saying that the true spirit of the golden rule is contrary
to the letter of Christianity, or that his "particular Presbyterian form of
worship" is intrinsically no more faithful to the religion Jesus preached
through the golden rule than Queequeg's idolatry. On the profoundest level,
he is asserting that loving one's fellow man means wishing to overcome
human separateness by sharing whatever is precious in one's own eyes with
one's fellow, and that the union made possible by respecting this wish is more
sacred than the most sacred institutions of any culture.

Ishmael's surrender to Queequeg is the first of the quasi-mystical
experiences of human solidarity that eventuate in freeing him from Ahab's
obsession with the "subtle demonisms of life and thought ... personified ... in
Moby Dick" (MD, 160). The second experience occurs in the chapter called
"The Monkey-Rope," where Ishmael, bound to Queequeg by a rope attached
to both their belts during the precarious blubber-stripping operation, so as
to ensure that Ishmael will pay with his own life for any failure to guard
Queequeg's, has an appalling insight into the "dangerous liabilities" of being
"wedded" to his fellow man "for better or for worse":

So strongly and metaphysically did I conceive of my situation
then, that while earnestly watching his [Queequeg's] motions,
I seemed distinctly to perceive that my own individuality was
now merged in a joint stock company of two: that my free will
had received a mortal wound; and that another's mistake or misfortune might plunge innocent me into unmerited disaster and
death.... I saw that this situation of mine was the precise situation
of every mortal that breathes; only, in most cases, he, one way
or other, has this Siamese connexion with a plurality of other
mortals. If your banker breaks, you snap; if your apothecary by
mistake sends you poison in your pills, you die. True, you may say

that, by exceeding caution, you may possibly escape these and the multitudinous other evil chances of life. But handle Queequeg's monkey-rope heedfully as I would, sometimes he jerked it so, that I came very near sliding overboard. Nor could I possibly forget that, do what I would, I only had the management of one end of it. (MD, 271)

In short, Ishmael apprehends on a metaphysical level the same truth that Melville dramatized through Redburn's subjection to social discrimination in England—that he must indeed be his brother's keeper, since no misfortune befalling his brother is without peril to himself, however innocent he may be of causing it.

Ishmael's third major experience of human solidarity reaffirms the more positive aspect of the "Siamese ligature" binding him to the rest of mankind, which his marriage with Queequeg originally expressed. As Ishmael sits with other sailors at the task of squeezing crystallized lumps of spermaceti back into liquid, he is transported into a state of ecstatic good will toward humanity in which he forgets "all about our horrible oath" to hunt Moby Dick to his death and purges his hands and heart of it:

> Squeeze! squeeze! squeeze! all the morning long; I squeezed that sperm till I myself almost melted into it; I squeezed that sperm till a strange sort of insanity came over me; and I found myself unwittingly squeezing my co-laborers' hands in it, mistaking their hands for the gentle globules. Such an abounding, affectionate, friendly, loving feeling did this avocation beget; that at last I was continually squeezing their hands, and looking up into their eyes sentimentally; as much as to say,—Oh! my dear fellow beings, why should we longer cherish any social acerbities, or know the slightest ill-humor or envy! Come; let us squeeze hands all round; nay, let us all squeeze ourselves into each other; let us squeeze ourselves universally into the very milk and sperm of kindness. (MD, 348–49)

Despite the comic homoerotic spirit of this passage,[11] it serves as serious a purpose as the comic account of the friendship with Queequeg that reaches its consummation in the landlord's conjugal bed. Like the earlier episode in which Ishmael discovers "how elastic our stiff prejudices grow when love once comes to bend them" (MD, 55), Ishmael's rhapsodic description of being fused into loving oneness with his compeers calls upon the reader to renounce the "social acerbities" that alienate him from his "fellow beings" and to give himself up instead to the barrier-dissolving power of love.

Two chapters later, in "The Try-Works," Ishmael shows the reader the antithesis of this ideal and invites him to join in choosing once and for all between saving himself and his fellow men by acknowledging the "Siamese ligature" that binds them together, or destroying himself and them by denying their common humanity to pursue a phantasm. Steering the ship while whale blubber is being boiled down into oil, Ishmael finds himself possessed for the last time by Ahab's infernal vision of the world. As Ishmael gazes into the flaming try-works, his friend Queequeg and the other pagan harpooneers, whose task is to pitch the "hissing masses of blubber into the scalding pots" with their "huge pronged poles," begin to look to him like devils stoking the flames of hell. At the same time, the "capricious emblazonings" of the try-works transform the lounging sailors of the night watch, with some of whom Ishmael has been blissfully squeezing sperm only a few hours before, into "tawny," smoke-begrimed barbarians. Interpreting their venial sailor yarns now as "tales of terror" about "unholy adventures," Ishmael fancies that their "uncivilized laughter forked upwards out of them, like the flames from the furnace" (MD, 353). In this state of mind, he perceives the "rushing *Pequod*, freighted with savages, and laden with fire, and burning a corpse, and plunging into that blackness of darkness," as the "material counterpart of her monomaniac commander's soul" (MD, 354).

The mental aberration Ishmael comes to share with Ahab in "The Try-Works" consists in focusing so exclusively on the dark side of life that he no longer sees anything but evil. As Ishmael explains: "Wrapped, for that interval, in darkness myself, I but the better saw the redness, the madness, the ghastliness of others." The moral price of such an obsession with evil, Ishmael discovers, is that his soul becomes deadened to good until it is perverted into a mirror of the evil he sees in others: "The continual sight of the fiend shapes before me, capering half in smoke and half in fire, these at last begat kindred visions in my soul" (MD, 354). But as Ishmael has already become aware while holding Queequeg by the monkey-rope, no man can endanger himself without the risk of likewise plunging others into "unmerited disaster and death" (MD, 271). Thus Ishmael almost capsizes the ship when, in the midst of his hallucination at the helm, he unwittingly turns his back on the tiller and compass in accordance with his inverted moral perceptions. Unlike Ahab, however, whose ultimate shipwreck he prefigures, Ishmael awakens from his hallucination in time to right the ship and rescue her crew from the consequences of his madness. The moral he draws from this experience marks the parting of his way from Ahab's:

Look not too long in the face of the fire, O man! Never dream with thy hand on the helm! Turn not thy back to the compass; accept the first hint of the hitching tiller; believe not the artificial fire, when its redness makes all things look ghastly. To-morrow, in the natural sun, the skies will be bright; those who glared like devils in the forking flames, the morn will show in far other, at least gentler, relief; the glorious, golden, glad sun, the only true lamp—all others but liars! (MD, 354)

If Ishmael refuses to credit the hellish view of his fellow men disclosed by firelight, it is not because he would overlook the evil in people; rather, it is because he would not lose sight of their humanity in contemplating their flaws. The natural light of the sun, Ishmael concludes, reveals evil enough to afflict a wise man without his needing to intensify it: "The sun hides not Virginia's Dismal Swamp, nor Rome's accursed Campagna, nor wide Sahara, nor all the millions of miles of deserts and of griefs beneath the moon. The sun hides not the ocean, which is the dark side of this earth, and which is two thirds of this earth. So, therefore, that mortal man who hath more of joy than sorrow in him, that mortal man cannot be true–not true, or undeveloped" (MD, 354–55).

The ultimate difference between Ishmael and Ahab—tested and sealed by the choice Ishmael makes in turning away from the fire to save the ship—is that Ishmael's marriage with Queequeg has made it possible for him to retain his human values and his allegiance to his fellow man in the face of the overwhelming evil and woe he sees in the world. Although Ishmael's commitment to preserving the *Pequod* and her crew cannot prevail against Ahab's monomania, he does survive to warn his compatriots away from the debacle toward which their ship of state is heading, and to seduce them into the marriage with their dark-complexioned fellow man and the consummation of their union with all mankind which, he has learned, constitute their sole hope of changing their disastrous course.

So far we have been considering the alternatives Melville offers in *Moby-Dick* to Ahab's polity and the shipwreck in which it culminates: the mutiny Steelkilt enacts in "The Town-Ho's Story" and the friendship with Queequeg through which Ishmael dissociates himself from Ahab's monomaniacal pursuit of a phantasm. Now we must confront the disaster Ishmael escapes and attempt to define more precisely the political meaning with which Melville invests it.

As early as the second chapter of *Moby-Dick*, Melville hints that the fateful whaling voyage on which Ishmael has set out, scheduled in the "grand programme of Providence" between a *"Grand Contested Election for the Presidency of the United States"* and a "BLOODY BATTLE IN AFFGHANISTAN," symbolizes the apocalyptic judgment that threatens America for her continued enslavement of the Negro. Heading toward the waterfront in quest of cheap lodgings in New Bedford, Ishmael stumbles over the ash-box of a Negro church which he mistakes for an inn and which he forebodingly dubs "the sign of 'The Trap'" (MD, 18). On entering, he is greeted by an assembly of black faces that reminds him of "the great Black Parliament sitting in Tophet," and he hears a Negro preacher, whom he recognizes intuitively for "a black Angel of Doom," warn of "the blackness of darkness, and the weeping and wailing and teeth-gnashing there" (MD, 18). This Negro preacher, whose message Ishmael heeds by backing out muttering, "Wretched entertainment at the sign of 'The Trap!'", is the first of the black characters in *Moby-Dick* who prophesy of the retribution overtaking their white oppressors.

But the next warning Ishmael hears is delivered by a white preacher in a chapel whose black-bordered marble tablets, dedicated to whalemen killed in the chase, starkly admonish Ishmael that he has embarked on a deadly career. Father Mapple's sermon, as Charles H. Foster and Alan Heimert have shown, resounds with the abolitionist rhetoric of the momentous years 1850–1851, when the Compromise of 1850 and the implementation of its infamous Fugitive Slave Law were polarizing the country.[12] Like the abolitionists, who called upon Americans to obey "a higher law than the Constitution," Father Mapple promises "Delight,—top-gallant delight ... to him, who acknowledges no law or lord, but the Lord his God, and is only a patriot to heaven" (MD, 51). Echoing the denunciations abolitionists thundered against the two Massachusetts dignitaries responsible for legislating and executing the Fugitive Slave Law—Senator Daniel Webster and Melville's own father-in-law, Judge Lemuel Shaw—Father Mapple also preaches "Woe to him who seeks to pour oil upon the waters when God has brewed them into a gale!" and condemns "all sin though he pluck it out from under the robes of Senators and Judges" (MD, 50–51).

The document Foster cites as bearing the closest resemblance to Father Mapple's sermon, however, is not an abolitionist tract, but the celebrated letter Melville wrote to Hawthorne while working on *Moby-Dick*—the letter in which he complained: "Try to get a living by the Truth—and go to the Soup Societies. Heavens! Let any clergyman try to preach the Truth from its very stronghold, the pulpit, and they would ride him out of his church on his own pulpit bannister."[13] The association clearly reveals that Melville felt his own truth-telling mission to be akin to a clergyman's. Indeed, in the next paragraph of his letter, Melville ruefully confesses to Hawthorne that he has been preaching "an endless sermon." Hence we can conclude that the "awful lesson which Jonah teaches" Father Mapple as "an anointed pilot-prophet"—"To preach the Truth to the face of Falsehood!"—is one that Melville considered equally applicable to himself and which, in *Moby-Dick*, is addressed specifically to his narrator Ishmael. Ishmael, in fact, will undergo a near-fatal encounter with a whale analogous to Jonah's and, like Jonah, will escape to prophesy of the doom that awaits an unrepentant people. The very purpose of his narrative, Ishmael implies in the epigraph that prefaces the account of his rescue, is to make the chastising experience he has undergone serve as a warning to his readers: "AND I ONLY AM ESCAPED ALONE TO *TELL THEE*" (italics added).[14] By identifying Ishmael with Jonah, Melville may also have been inviting his readers to learn a lesson from the portion of Jonah's story that Father Mapple does not discuss in his sermon. Just as the citizens of Nineveh, to whom Jonah had been assigned to prophesy the destruction of their city, ultimately repented of their wickedness and thus turned God's wrath into mercy, so the epilogue of *Moby-Dick* suggests that Ishmael's fellow citizens may perhaps avert the apocalyptic doom the *Pequod's* fate augurs, if they heed his message in time and choose to follow his example rather than Ahab's.[15]

After Father Mapple, Ishmael will hear a number of white voices warn of impending judgment in the fanatical accents of the sectarian millennialists who, concurrently with the abolitionists, were deluging the country with Old and New Testament apocalyptic prophecies, literally applied to the contemporary American scene.[16] The first of these is the mercenary, pharisaical owner of the *Pequod*, Captain Bildad, who presses on Queequeg a tract entitled, "The Latter Day Coming; or No Time to Lose," and admonishes him: "Son of darkness, I must do my duty by thee; I am part owner of this ship, and feel concerned for the souls of all its crew; if thou still clingest to thy Pagan ways, which I sadly fear, I beseech thee, remain not for aye a Belial bondsman. Spurn the idol Bel, and the hideous dragon; turn from the wrath to come" (MD, 85).

In the next chapter, Ishmael and Queequeg are accosted by a second crier of doom, a ragged prophet calling himself Elijah, after the Old Testament prophet who denounced King Ahab's wickedness and foretold his downfall, and who, as many millennialists believed, was to return to earth to herald "the great and dreadful day of the LORD" (Mal. 4:5). Although Ishmael dismisses Elijah as "nothing but a humbug, trying to be a bugbear," the stranger's oracular pronouncements correctly warn that in the *Pequod's* voyage the crew's "souls" are at stake; and his crazy ruminations formulate a philosophical problem central to *Moby-Dick*—that of predetermination versus free will: "Well, well, what's signed, is signed; and what's to be, will be; and then again, perhaps it wont be, after all" (MD, 87–88).

The last of these unlikely augurs of the *Pequod's* fate is the delirious Shaker prophet aboard the whaler *Jeroboam*, who calls himself the archangel Gabriel and claims to carry in his vest-pocket the terrible "seventh vial" of the Apocalypse. Categorically branded a fanatic whose "measureless self-deception" is only surpassed by "his measureless power of deceiving and bedevilling so many others," Gabriel nevertheless proves right in predicting "speedy doom to the sacrilegious assailants" of Moby Dick and in telling Ahab that he is soon to go the way of the *Jeroboam's* mate, struck down by Moby Dick in the chase. Further enhancing his prophetic stature, the "crazy sea" itself appears to be "leagued with" Gabriel: waves rock the *Jeroboam's* whale boat and interrupt her captain's story whenever he attempts to reprimand or discredit the self-styled archangel (MD, 266–68). Although all of these apocalyptic alarmists are stigmatized as zealots or lunatics, the eventual fulfillment of their prognostications forces us to take them more seriously than Ishmael does. Perhaps Melville means to suggest that among the critics of America's polity, even those who represented the lunatic fringe were "bottomed upon the truth, more or less" (as Melville's "endless sermon" to Hawthorne asserts of "Reformers" in general),[17] in sensing that the nation was rushing headlong toward an apocalyptic holocaust.

The chapter in which Melville envisions this holocaust most explicitly as an interracial and fratricidal conflict over slavery is one in which the angels of doom are once again black. Significantly, neither Ishmael nor Queequeg participates in this scene, entitled "Midnight, Forecastle," where the crew's "federated" unity breaks down into local particularisms as sailors from "all the isles of the sea, and all the ends of the earth" (MD, 108) riot in their distinctive ways after sealing their commitment to Ahab's feud. Paralleling the onset of a storm at sea, the undercurrent of racial antagonisms expressed through these revels at length erupts in a row between the African harpooneer Daggoo and a Spanish sailor. The row is touched off when Daggoo's hypersensitivity to racist slurs makes him bristle at an old Manxman's warning that the "pitch black" sky, shot through with "lurid-like" lightning flashes, presages danger for the ship. "What of that?" parries the African; "Who's afraid of black's afraid of me! I'm quarried out of it!" (MD, 153).

Daggoo, whom Ishmael has earlier described as "a gigantic, coal-black negro-savage, with a lion-like tread—an Ahasuerus to behold" (MD, 107), is the very embodiment of the "erect, lofty-minded African" Melville had imagined in *White-Jacket*. Like Queequeg, whose free spirit he shares, Daggoo has "voluntarily shipped on board of a whaler" and has "retained all his barbaric virtues," never having been exposed to slavery or second-class citizenship. Even more than Queequeg, Daggoo towers over his white shipmates in physique and dignity: "There was a corporeal humility in looking up at him; and a white man standing before him seemed a white flag come to beg truce of a fortress" (MD, 108). Daggoo also resembles that noble white primitive, Steelkilt, in his striking superiority to his commanding officer, the third mate Flask. "Curious to tell," remarks Ishmael, "this imperial negro, Ahasuerus Daggoo, was the Squire of little Flask, who looked like a chess-man beside him"—a contrast that becomes more uncomplimentary to Flask than ever during the chase, when Flask finds himself too "small and short" to satisfy the "large and tall ambition" that he can fulfill only by climbing onto his black harpooneer's "lofty shoulders":

> But the sight of little Flask mounted upon gigantic Daggoo was yet more curious; for sustaining himself with a cool, indifferent, easy, unthought of, barbaric majesty, the noble negro to every roll of the sea harmoniously rolled his fine form. On his broad back, flaxen-haired Flask seemed a snow-flake. The bearer looked nobler than the rider. Though, truly, vivacious, tumultuous, ostentatious little Flask would now and then stamp with impa-tience; but not one added heave did he thereby give to the negro's lordly chest. (MD, 191)

Interestingly, just as Ahasuerus Daggoo corresponds to Charlemagne Steelkilt, the "pugnacious" Flask has equally strong affinities with Steelkilt's mate Radney, likewise a Vineyarder and "full of social quarrel" (MD, 106, 210). Thus Alan Heimert has linked Flask, as well as Radney, with the "'fiery and intractable race' which Melville discovered in the south of Vivenza" and has interpreted the picture of "Flask, perched precariously on Daggoo's shoulders," as an icon of "the southern economy itself," precariously based on the Negro.[18]

Notwithstanding these analogies, the interracial row Melville stages in "Midnight, Forecastle" differs considerably from the paradigmatic slave revolt dramatized in "The Town-Ho's Story." To begin with, the Spanish sailor ranged against Daggoo is not his commanding officer, but a regular seaman who technically ranks below Daggoo in the hierarchy of a whaling crew, where a harpooneer enjoys the status of a petty officer. Daggoo's and the Spaniard's relative positions aboard the *Pequod* appropriately reflect a period in history when the Spaniards were subjugated by the Moors, an African people who ruled Spain for more than five centuries. Evidently the Spanish sailor remembers this. "Ah!—the old grudge makes me touchy," he mutters on hearing Daggoo flaunt his blackness, and he immediately assumes that the African "wants to bully." His response to fear is the same that elicited Queequeg's cry, "Who-e debel you?" and Ishmael's confession, "I was now as much afraid of [the stranger] as if it was the devil himself" (MD, 29, 31): "Aye, harpooneer," he tells Daggoo, as the Spanish colonists of the New World and their Anglo-Saxon successors told their Indian and African captives, "thy race is the undeniable dark side of mankind—devilish dark at that." He adds, as if to imply that he is merely stating a fact rather than casting an aspersion, "No offence." But Daggoo, whose pride in his African heritage has not been crushed by a white supremacist society, is proof against this attempt to sap his self-esteem by injecting him with his enemy's prejudices. "White skin, white liver!" he retorts in kind, meeting further provocation with his fists. Meanwhile, the Spaniard tries to knife the unarmed Daggoo, prompting the reader to wonder whether the white race, rather than the black, might not incarnate the devilish side of mankind.

Once again, however, Melville's obvious sympathy with Daggoo's reaction to the Spaniard's insults does not prevail against his horror of violence, and he brings this racial row to an abortive end. As the threatened storm at last bursts, forestalling the consummation of these racial hatreds and reuniting the crew in the ship's defense, Daggoo cedes his place as a black angel of doom to a less menacing figure—"Black Little Pip," the "poor Alabama boy" who shrinks from his violent shipmates and is "called a coward here," though destined to be "hailed a hero" in heaven (MD, 108). Chorus-like, Pip speaks the last lines in this theatrical chapter, commenting on the scene he has witnessed and the tempest in which it has culminated, and articulating Melville's premonitions about the storm brewing over black slavery on the American continent:

> Jimmini, what a squall! But those chaps there are worse yet—
> they are your white squalls, they. White squalls? white whale,
> shirr! shirr! Here have I heard all their chat just now, and the
> white whale—shirr! shirr!—but spoken of once! and only this
> evening—it makes me jingle all over like my tambourine—that
> anaconda of an old man swore 'em in to hunt him! Oh, thou big
> white God aloft there somewhere in yon darkness, have mercy on
> this small black boy down here; preserve him from all men that
> have no bowels to feel fear! (MD, 154–55)

Whatever the metaphysical meaning of Ahab's fiery hunt, the association Pip makes between the white whale and the "white squalls" personified by the crew gives the hunt political connotations and suggests that civil war was one of the consequences Melville apprehended from his nation's pursuit of a white phantasm. Indeed, he seems to imply here that civil war, as a storm that ultimately imperils the whole crew, constitutes a worse danger for his ship of state than even an interracial conflict. At the same time, Melville offers the hope that the very threat of such a cataclysm might somehow serve to bring about a union of expedience, if not a love marriage, among the hostile members of his nation's crew. In this respect, "Midnight, Forecastle" ends more optimistically than Ishmael's narrative. It also ends more optimistically than a later narrative that it foreshadows—"Benito Cereno"—which restages the confrontation between the two parties Melville saw as historical prototypes of the southern slaveholder and his slave: the Spaniards who introduced African slavery into the New World and the full-blooded Africans who embodied the cultural heritage of American blacks and thus impressed Melville as the most fitting vindicators of black pride and black manhood.[19]

Although the way in which Pip's alarm succeeds Daggoo's militancy in "Midnight, Forecastle" expresses Melville's recoil from violent solutions to the slavery problem, it in no sense implies that Melville would ever embrace the stereotype of the happy slave as an alternative to facing America's black nemesis. Pip no less than Daggoo incarnates Melville's conviction that the Negro held the key to America's destiny. Throughout *Moby-Dick*, Melville makes his three principal black characters—Daggoo, Pip, and the ship's cook Fleece—serve as angels of doom, warning the *Pequod* of her fate and sometimes actually lifting up their voices against whites. Of the three, Pip is most explicitly cast as a prophet, especially after an event befalls him "which ended in providing the sometimes madly merry and predestinated craft with a living and ever accompanying prophecy of whatever shattered sequel might prove her own" (MD, 344). This event, which Charles H. Foster and Alan Heimert have likened to the northern abandonment of the Negro betokened by Judge Shaw's remanding of the fugitive slave Thomas Sims, is Stubb's abandonment of Pip when the latter jumps from a whale boat in the midst of the chase.[20] "A whale would sell for thirty times what you would, Pip, in Alabama," Stubb tells Pip in admonishing him not to jump, thereby indirectly hinting, according to Ishmael, "that though man loves his fellow, yet man is a money-making animal, which propensity too often interferes with his benevolence" (MD, 346).

Before his tragic mishap, Pip seems to epitomize the Negro's proverbial gaiety: "Pip, though over tender-hearted, was at bottom very bright, with that pleasant, genial, jolly brightness peculiar to his tribe; a tribe, which ever enjoy all holidays and festivities with finer, freer relish than any other race. For blacks, the year's calendar should show naught but three hundred and

sixty-five Fourth of Julys and New Year's Days" (MD, 345). In asserting that
Pip and his fellow blacks are capable of an uninhibited enjoyment of life's
pleasures that eludes other races, Melville verges on romantic racialism. Yet
he pointedly refrains from claiming that the calendar does show "naught
but three hundred and sixty-five Fourth of Julys and New Year's Days" for
blacks, which would amount to endorsing the popular notion that the Negro
was less susceptible to sorrow or pain than other races. On the contrary, he
observes, Pip's love of life and "all life's peaceable securities" has made him
suffer hardships all the more keenly, "so that the panic-striking business in
which he had somehow unaccountably become entrapped, had most sadly
blurred his brightness" (MD, 345). Just as the "healthful glow" of a diamond
worn on a "blue-veined neck" in the clear light of day acquires an evil blaze
when set against a "gloomy ground" and illuminated by "unnatural gases,"
so, intimates Melville, does the air of joviality the Negro wears turn sinister
against the backdrop of slavery, where song and dance function to deaden
pain rather than to express happiness. Thus Pip's clouded brightness is
"destined to be luridly illumined by strange wild fires" after the injury the
"panic-striking business" of whaling inflicts on him.

   Left floating for hours in the ocean with no assurance of being
rescued, Pip experiences an "intense concentration of self in the middle of
such a heartless immensity" that permanently affects his sanity (MD, 347).
Thereafter he becomes an oracular voice reproaching his shipmates for
their callousness and echoing the heartlessness of a God who allows evil and
does not intervene to prevent his creatures from destroying each other and
themselves. "Pip! Pip! Pip! One hundred pounds of clay reward for Pip; five
feet high—looks cowardly—quickest known by that!" (MD, 427), he calls
out, in what Alan Heimert has characterized as a "tragic parody of a fugitive-
slave handbill."[21] Pip watches and sums up his shipmates' deluded attempts
to decipher the cryptic signs of their destiny engraved on Ahab's doubloon:
"I look, you look, he looks; we look, ye look, they look." His chorus-like
commentary ends in weird apocalyptic accents:

> Here's the ship's navel, this doubloon here, and they are all on
> fire to unscrew it. But, unscrew your navel, and what's the con-
> sequence? Then again, if it stays here, that is ugly, too, for when
> aught's nailed to the mast it's a sign that things grow desperate.
> Ha, ha! old Ahab! the White Whale; he'll nail ye! This is a pine
> tree. My father, in old Tolland county, cut down a pine tree once,
> and found a silver ring grown over in it; some old darkey's wed-
> ding ring. How did it get there? And so they'll say in the resur-
> rection, when they come to fish up this old mast, and find a dou-

bloon lodged in it, with bedded oysters for the shaggy bark. Oh, the gold! the precious, precious gold!—the green miser'll hoard ye soon! Hish! hish! God goes 'mong the worlds blackberrying. Cook! ho, cook! and cook us! (MD, 363)

Pip's "crazy-witty" language, though as undecipherable as the doubloon, heralds the *Pequod*'s watery end and links it to the fires of hell, the general resurrection to follow, and the casual indifference of a "blackberrying" (black burying?) reaper god, treading the grapes of wrath on a pleasure party. At the same time, Pip's tale of the "old darkey's wedding ring" that his father found embedded in a pine tree seems to hark back obscurely to Ishmael's wedding imagery and the alternative to apocalyptic destruction that it offers the reader.

Indeed, Pip and Ishmael have many affinities with each other, as Edgar A. Dryden has pointed out.[22] Not only does Pip's experience of being a "castaway" prefigure Ishmael's at the end of the book, but it gives Pip insights much like those at which Ishmael arrives in contemplating the whiteness of the whale. Pip perceives in the infinite ocean where he has been abandoned the same "heartless voids and immensities of the universe" that Ishmael apprehends in the "indefiniteness" of whiteness (MD, 169, 347). Similarly, Pip sees "God's foot upon the treadle of the loom" in the "wondrous depths" to which he is transported and feels God's indifference, as Ishmael does when he comes face to face with the world's "weaver-god" in a "wondrous" bower in the Arsacides and finds him so "deafened" by his weaving "that he hears no mortal voice" (MD, 374).

Pip also holds out to Ahab the same promise of redemption through love that Queequeg holds out to Ishmael. He attracts Ahab's attention on the heels of one more ill omen that the monomaniacal captain has stubbornly refused to heed—the snapping of the log-line. Troubled by Pip's madness, Ahab reproaches the gods for having begotten this helpless black boy only to abandon him. "There can be no hearts above the snow-line," he exclaims (MD, 428). In identifying the "frozen heavens" with the North, as Alan Heimert has noticed, Ahab echoes the southern apologists' "ringing indictment of northern hypocrisy and indifference to the Negro's welfare."[23] Yet when he vows that "Ahab's cabin shall be Pip's home henceforth, while Ahab lives," the captain ironically overlooks the problem of what will happen to Pip afterwards. He thus follows the example of both the gods he denounces and the numerous southern masters whose deaths plunged favorite slaves into the worst horrors of slavery.

Ultimately, of course, Ahab will forsake Pip to pursue the fanatic chase he has never considered giving up. But for the moment, he seems to be feeling the "Siamese ligature" with Pip that Ishmael learns to acknowledge toward all mankind. "Thou touchest my inmost centre, boy; thou art tied to me by cords woven of my heart-strings," he tells Pip. Pip likewise seizes Ahab's hand "as a man-rope; something that weak souls may hold by," recalling the monkey-rope through which Ishmael is "wedded" to Queequeg "for better or for worse." Like Ishmael and Queequeg, Ahab and Pip even contract a symbolic marriage. Claiming that "had poor Pip but felt so kind a thing" as the "velvet shark-skin" of Ahab's hand, he might never have been lost, Pip summons the blacksmith to "rivet these two hands together; the black one with the white, for I will not let this go" (MD, 428). Ahab, on his part, characteristically turns the ritual into a histrionic gesture meant to vindicate his quarrel with God: "Lo! ye believers in gods all goodness, and in man all ill, to you! see the omniscient gods oblivious of suffering man; and man, though idiotic, and knowing not what he does, yet full of the sweet things of love and gratitude. Come! I feel prouder leading thee by thy black hand, than though I grasped an Emperor's!" (MD, 428). It is no accident, however, that Ahab's union with Pip takes place in the chapter "The Log and Line," where it is framed by the snapping of the log-line and by the old Manxman's complaints that the line is too "rotten" to mend. The same is evidently true of the cords woven of Ahab's heart-strings, which prove too fragile to hold him to Pip when he feels Moby Dick's pull. Thus Pip's description of Ahab's hand as "velvet shark-skin" may express a crazy intuition of the irredeemable sharkishness underlying Ahab's kindness towards him. Ahab, unlike Ishmael, is not saved by his marriage with his fellow man, since he does not truly commit himself to it as the alternative to the phantasmic hunt through which he carries his shipmates to their doom.

In his role as a prophet, Pip acts both as a harbinger of doom and as a potential savior. The other two blacks whose voices we hear aboard the *Pequod* speak mainly in the stern accents of the former. Daggoo, besides championing the dignity of blackness and physically attacking a white man who dares to deny it, literally becomes an apocalyptic "angel of doom": on the first day Moby Dick is sighted, he rouses his sleeping shipmates "with such judgment claps that they seemed to exhale from the scuttle, so instantaneously did they appear with their clothes in their hands" (MD, 446).

Still more ominous is the role played by old Fleece, the ship's cook, whose sermon to the sharks (a cynical parody of St. Francis' sermon to the birds)[24] ends on a note that recalls "the blackness of darkness, and the weeping and wailing and teeth-gnashing there," of which the black clergyman encountered by Ishmael in New Bedford had warned. Fleece is the only black character in *Moby-Dick* to speak in dialect and to exhibit the mannerisms of a slave, yet his sullen pretense of following orders is as subversive as Daggoo's militancy and shows how aware Melville was of the artful sabotage that represented the slave's chief weapon against his master.[25] Awakened by Stubb at midnight to cook him a whale steak, Fleece is subsequently charged with the task of exhorting the sharks to cease their din over the dead whale's body so that Stubb can enjoy his whale steak in peace. The parallel between the sharks—"invariable outriders," Melville tells us, "of all slave ships crossing the Atlantic"—and "Massa Stubb," who treats this crippled old black like a slave, is unmistakable, and Fleece subtly underscores it in the "benediction" he delivers to the sharks at the conclusion of his unheeded sermon about "gobern[ing] de shark in you": "Cussed fellow-critters! Kick up de damndest row as ever you can; fill your dam' bellies till dey bust—and den die" (MD, 249, 251–52). Stubb continues to bedevil the old man, criticizing his cooking, making fun of his religious hopes, and calling him back twice more to order various other whale delicacies for breakfast and supper, but Fleece has the last word, and a baleful word it is: "'Wish, by gor! whale eat him, 'stead of him eat whale. I'm bressed if he ain't more of shark dan Massa Shark hisself,' muttered the old man, limping away; with which sage ejaculation he went to his hammock" (MD, 254). Whether curse or prophecy, Fleece's "sage ejaculation" is destined to be dramatically borne out; for Stubb is indeed eaten by a whale in the end, though not without Fleece's sharing his fate. As Ishmael has learned, men cannot escape the "dangerous liabilities," however unjust, of being bound together, so that like the *Pequod*'s shipwreck, an apocalyptic shipwreck over slavery would engulf all Americans—guilty or innocent, white or black, southern or northern. Appropriately, the *Pequod* goes down with that primal American, Tashtego the Indian, nailing her flag to the mast and capturing in its folds the bird that symbolized America's expansive ambitions—the skyhawk, or eagle.[26]

To end our examination of *Moby-Dick* with the somber judgment that America's black avenging angels invoke on her would, however, be untrue to the spirit of Melville's epilogue—an epilogue reaffirming, through Ishmael's miraculous escape on Queequeg's coffin, the hope of salvation that a love marriage between the races promises. That hope may appear slight at best—and almost a mockery in view of Queequeg's own death—until we recall the parallel between Ishmael and Jonah that redefines Ishmael as not merely the sole survivor of an apocalyptic cataclysm, but the prophet of a future cataclysm that may yet be averted by timely repentance. Ishmael's role as a Jonah also puts Queequeg's otherwise morally inexplicable death in another light; for shortly after offering to die for Ishmael "if need should be," Queequeg, it will be remembered, sends Ishmael out at the behest of his "negro idol" Yojo to select the ship on which they will both sail, while he himself spends the day—characterized by Ishmael as "some sort of Lent or Ramadan"—closeted with Yojo in "fasting, humiliation, and prayer" (MD, 66), as if to intercede for Ishmael. The fruit of both Queequeg's intercession and Yojo's alleged effort to befriend Ishmael and Queequeg is that Ishmael chooses the *Pequod* in preference to two other ships whose names suggest damnation and the devil's proverbial fondness for "that good dish, man"[27]—the *Devil-Dam* and the *Tit-bit*. In short, it is possible to read *Moby-Dick* as a morality play staged for an American Nineveh, in which *Yojo* acts as the chastising yet ultimately merciful God who commissions Ishmael/ Jonah to prophesy of the retribution overtaking an unregenerate nation, and Queequeg as a Christlike redeemer whose life inculcates the message of love, and whose death propitiates divine justice for the sins of his fellow men.[28]

Yet one feels that such a reading is not altogether honest in the face of the cruel irony of being asked to accept the fate meted out to Ishmael and Queequeg as a mark of Yojo's favor, not to mention the equivocal syntax describing Yojo as "a rather good sort of god, who perhaps meant well enough upon the whole, but in all cases did not succeed in his benevolent designs" (MD, 66)—both typifying Melville's wry vision of the deity. It is symptomatic of the far bleaker view Melville would soon come to take of the slavery dilemma and its probable outcome that the metaphysical implications of *Moby-Dick*, most strikingly embodied in the appalling white whale himself, are nowhere near as hopeful as the political or humanistic implications of Ishmael's friendship with Queequeg. Nor has this paradox failed to trouble other interpreters of the book's political symbolism.[29] As it happens, Melville's greatest statement of the democratic faith that animates all his early works was also his last. No sooner was *Moby-Dick* off his hands than Melville found himself "plunged ... into certain silly thoughts and wayward speculations," as he wrote to a sympathetic Pittsfield neighbor,[30] that led him to his next book, the desperately cynical *Pierre*.

NOTES

1. *Moby-Dick*, Chaps. 1, 47, 93, 102, 134, epilogue.

2. Heimert, "*Moby-Dick* and American Political Symbolism," 530, suggests that Melville may have originally conceived the tale "as something other than a mere interlude" in a more hopeful political allegory that he did not "imagine ... as ending in disaster."

3. In Chapter 1, Ishmael asserts that "those stage managers, the Fates," impelled him to go on a whaling voyage while "cajoling me into the delusion that it was a choice resulting from my own unbiased freewill," and he identifies the whale, and specifically the "phantom" of Moby Dick, as one of the chief inducements (MD, 16). In the epilogue, Ishmael is "he whom the Fates ordained to take the place of Ahab's bowsman" and thus

to escape going down with the *Pequod*. But as Edgar A. Dryden has shown (*Melville's Thematics of Form*, 104–13), Ishmael also recognizes the possibility of "weaving his own destiny" by telling his tale.

4. In the first camp, see Simpson, "Melville and the Negro," 27–29; Zirker, "Slavery Dilemma in *White-Jacket*," 480; and Grejda, *Common Continent of Men*, 86–97. In the second, see Widmer, *The Ways of Nihilism*, 69–70, n. 11; and James Baird, *Ishmael: A Study of the Symbolic Mode in Primitivism* (New York, 1960), 118–20, 297–40.

5. Kaplan, "Melville and the American National Sin," 325, 330–31; Simpson, "Melville and the Negro," 28; Baird, *Ishmael*, 237–40.

6. On the scientific debates over race and climate, see Winthrop D. Jordan, *White Over Black: American Attitudes Toward the Negro, 1550–1812* (Baltimore, 1969), 512–41; also Stanton, *The Leopard's Spots*, 1–44, 82–89.

7. See "Is Man One or Many?" 5.

8. On its homosexual overtones, see Arvin, *Herman Melville*, 27–28, 174; Daniel G. Hoffman, *Form and Fable in American Fiction* (New York, 1861), 264–68; Leslie A. Fiedler, *Love and Death in the American Novel* (rev. ed.; New York, 1966), 366–90; and Miller, *Melville*, 200–201. On its racial overtones, see Simpson, "Melville and the Negro," 28–29; Zirker, "Slavery Dilemma in *White-Jacket*," 480; and Grejda, *Common Continent of Men*, 96–97.

9. Among the many critics who have pointed this out are William Ellery Sedgwick, *Herman Melville: The Tragedy of Mind* (Cambridge, Mass., 1944), 119–26, reprinted in the Norton Critical Edition of *Moby-Dick*, 643–48; Arvin, *Herman Melville*, 170–71, 174–82; Baird, *Ishmael*, 233–51; Hoffman, *Form and Fable*, 235, 262–71; William Rosenfeld, "Uncertain Faith: Queequeg's Coffin and Melville's Use of the Bible," *Texas Studies in Literature and Language*, VII (1966), 320–22; Carl F. Strauch, "Ishmael: Time and Personality in *Moby-Dick*," *Studies in the Novel*, 1 (1969), 468, 476, 480–81; Robert Zoellner, *The Salt-Sea Mastodon: A Reading of "Moby-Dick"* (Berkeley, 1973), Chap. 11; Grejda, *Common Continent of Men*, 95–96.

10. See Hennig Cohen, "Melville's Tomahawk Pipe: Artifact and Symbol," *Studies in the Novel*, 1 (1969), 397–400.

11. See Fiedler, *Love and Death*, 371–72.

12. Foster, "Something in Emblems," 11–20; Heimert, "*Moby-Dick* and American Political Symbolism," 508–12.

13. Foster, "Something in Emblems," 8–11, 17; Davis and Gilman (eds.), *Letters of Melville*, 128–31.

14. Dryden, *Melville's Thematics of Form*, 105, emphasizes the significance that the epigraph gives to Ishmael's telling of his experience.

15. For interpretations of Father Mapple's sermon antithetical to mine, see Nathalia Wright, *Melville's Use of the Bible* (New York, 1969), 82–84; Hoffman, *Form and Fable*, 236, 257–62; and Zoellner, *Salt-Sea Mastodon*, Chap. 4.

16. Among the sects predicting an imminent fulfillment of apocalyptic prophecy were the Shakers, the Mormons, and the Millerites (followers of William Miller, who had predicted that the end of the world would occur in 1843–1844). I do not agree with Heimert, "*Moby-Dick* and American Political Symbolism," 514–15, that Melville is identifying these enthusiastic sectarians with the abolitionists.

17. Davis and Gilman (eds.), *Letters of Melville*, 127.

18. Heimert, "*Moby-Dick* and American Political Symbolism," 502. See also Kaplan, "Melville and the American National Sin," 24, 327–28; and Simpson, "Melville and the Negro," 29–30, on the antiracist implications of this icon.

19. Other critics who have noted the relationship between "Midnight, Forecastle" and "Benito Cereno" are Kaplan, "Melville and the American National Sin," 22, n. 21, 329; Simpson, "Melville and the Negro," 90; and Charles Nicol, "The Iconography of Evil and Ideal in 'Benito Cereno,'" in Raymona E. Hull (ed.), *Studies in the Minor and Later Works of Melville* (Hartford, 1970), 28–29.

20. Foster, "Something in Emblems," 25; Heimert, "*Moby-Dick* and American Political Symbolism," 513.

21. Heimert, "*Moby-Dick* and American Political Symbolism," 513.

22. Dryden, *Melville's Thematics of Form*, 104–105.

23. Heimert, "*Moby-Dick* and American Political Symbolism," 513.

24. Noted by Tyrus Hillway, "In Defense of Melville's 'Fleece,'" *Extracts*, XIX (1974), 10; also Zoellner, *Salt-Sea Mastodon*, 223.

25. Fleece has been the subject of another critical controversy over Melville's racial attitudes. Among those who see him as a racist stereotype are Simpson, "Melville and the Negro," 32; Zoellner, *Salt-Sea Mastodon*, 220; and Edward Stone, "The Whiteness of the Whale," *CLA Journal*, XVIII (1975), 355–59, 362. Among those who see Fleece as a covert rebel are Kaplan, "Melville and the American National Sin," 330; Hillway, "In Defense of 'Fleece,'" 10–11; Grejda, *Common Continent of Men*, 106–107; and Stuart C. Woodruff, "Stubb's Supper," *Emerson Society Quarterly*, XLIII (1966), 46–48.

26. This symbolism is discussed by Foster, "Something in Emblems," 33; and Heimert, "*Moby-Dick* and American Political Symbolism," 504, 507–508.

27. From Herman Melville, *The Confidence-Man: His Masquerade*, ed. H. Bruce Franklin, 187.

28. For similar interpretations, see Rosenfeld, "Uncertain Faith," 320–22; and Strauch, "Ishmael: Time and Personality," 480. Other critics who stress Yojo's and Queequeg's redemptiveness, though in different terms, are Zoellner, *Salt-Sea Mastodon*, 69–71 and Chap. 11; and Hoffman, *Form and Fable*, 270–71.

29. See, for examples, Heimert, "*Moby-Dick* and American Political Symbolism," 532–33; and Milton R. Stern, "*Moby-Dick*, Millennial Attitudes, and Politics," *Emerson Society Quarterly*, LIV (1969), 52–53, 60. The crux of the problem is that if, like the vast majority of critics, one views the white whale as embodying either "the heartless voids and immensities" of a godless natural universe, or a supernatural power capriciously indifferent and perhaps outright inimical to man, one is forced to recognize a certain grandeur in Ahab's defiance of Moby Dick—a grandeur transcending his role as a political demagogue. Joyce Sparer Adler's brilliant reading of *Moby-Dick* in her forthcoming book on Melville's attitude toward war may resolve this seeming contradiction.

30. Davis and Gilman (eds.), *Letters of Melville*, 138.

DAVID S. REYNOLDS

"Its wood could only be American!": Moby-Dick and Antebellum Popular Culture

Despite growing interest in the historical dimensions of *Moby-Dick*, it has been difficult for scholars to dispel the longstanding myth that Melville was alienated from his contemporary popular culture. Ever since Raymond Weaver portrayed him as the isolated, rebellious "Devil's Advocate," Melville has been generally viewed as an uncharacteristic nay-sayer in an age of progressivist optimism, a mythic stylist exiled from a Philistine culture of utilitarianism and literal-mindedness.

This notion of Melville's distance from his literary and social culture contravenes his own convictions about the symbiotic relationship between art and society. "Great geniuses are parts of the times," he proclaimed in his essay on Hawthorne; "they themselves are the times, and possess a correspondent coloring."[1] He appears to have been particularly responsive to the ephemeral literature of his time and culture. In his semiautobiographical portrait of Pierre Glendinning, he explained that even apparently trivial literature contributed to his author-hero's creativity: "A varied scope of reading, little suspected by his friends, and randomly acquired by a random but lynx-eyed mind ... poured one considerable contributary stream into that bottomless spring of original thought which the occasion and time had caused to burst out in himself."[2] Melville himself was a lynx-eyed reader quick to discover literary possibilities in randomly acquired minor literature.

From *Critical Essays on Herman Melville's* Moby-Dick, Brian Higgins and Hershel Parker, ed., pp. 523–544. © 1992, G.K. Hall.

His reading seems to have been done in the spirit of a character in *White-Jacket* who says that "public libraries have an imposing air, and doubtless contain invaluable volumes, yet, somehow, the books that prove most agreeable, grateful, and companionable, are those we pick up by chance here and there; ... those which pretend to little, but abound in much."[3]

In fact, it was precisely Melville's *openness* to images from various contemporary cultural arenas—not, as is commonly thought, his *alienation* from his culture—that accounts for the special complexity of *Moby-Dick*. Melville's narrative art was one of wide-ranging assimilation and literary transformation. It reflected his statement in "Hawthorne and His Mosses" that the American writer was "bound to carry republican progressiveness into Literature, as well as into Life."[4] A principal misconception about *Moby-Dick* is that its ambiguities stood in opposition to a popular culture that was uniformly tame and moralistic. Actually, antebellum popular culture was full of contradictions and paradoxes that became textually inscribed in Melville's most capacious novel.

The main types of popular writing Melville drew from in *Moby-Dick* were Romantic Adventure fiction, dark reform literature, radical-democrat fiction, and subversive humor.[5] Melville had learned key images and stereotypes from each of these modes by immersing himself in American popular culture as a writer for the mass market earlier in his career. Melville knew that his first two novels were, as he wrote his publisher about *Omoo*, "calculated for popular reading."[6] After soaring to allegorical and philosophical heights in *Mardi*, he again wrote unabashedly for the popular audience in *Redburn* and *White-Jacket*, which he called "two *jobs*, which I have done for money."[7] As dismissive as Melville was about some of this early fiction, he learned much from his forays into popular culture. Taken together, Melville's early works show him to have been a daring experimenter with popular images. The breadth of his experimentation placed him in an ideal position to produce a novel of full cultural representativeness. When Melville is studied in terms of his popular cultural backgrounds, we see the validity of a contemporary reviewer's remark that in *Moby-Dick* he seemed "resolved to combine all his popular characteristics."[8]

In the most basic sense, *Moby-Dick* falls in the category of Romantic Adventure, by far the most popular type of fiction published in America during the two decades immediately prior to the publication of the novel.[9] When Melville described *Moby-Dick* to his British publisher as "a romance of adventure, founded upon certain wild legends in the Southern Sperm Whale Fisheries" (*Letters*, 109), he was placing the novel in the Romantic Adventure category. Despite the twentieth-century reputation of *Moby-Dick* as a premodern metaphysical fiction unusual for its day, it should be noted that contemporary reviews of the novel, which were predominantly favorable, emphasized its divertingly adventurous aspects.

It is understandable that many contemporary reviewers felt comfortable with *Moby-Dick*, because Melville was drawing off a well-established convention of adventurous sea novels. A good amount of fiction about destructive whales or other monstrous creatures had appeared during the 1830s and 1840s. J. N. Reynolds's "Mocha Dick, or The White Whale of the Pacific," a story in the May 1839 issue of the New York *Knickerbocker*, is full of analogies to *Moby-Dick*: both works center on a dramatic chase for a white sperm whale legendary for its indestructibility; both reproduce the salty dialect of whalemen engaged in dangerous pursuit of the white whale; and both utilize this fearless pursuit as a means of illustrating the inherent democratic dignity of the unfavored trade of whaling.[10] Another work that strikingly prefigures *Moby-Dick* is "Whaling in the Pacific. Encounter with a White Whale," a tale published 8 October 1842 in the popular Boston weekly *Uncle Sam*. This story features a dauntless Captain Coffin and his mates (one of them named Starbuck) who one day lower for a white whale that is harpooned but then crushes two whale boats with his jaws and kills several seamen in bloody revenge.

Moby-Dick was also presaged by three popular sea novels quoted in the prefatory "Extracts" to Melville's novel: Joseph C. Hart's *Miriam Coffin* (1834), William Comstock's *The Life of Samuel Comstock, the Terrible Whaleman* (1840), and Harry Halyard's pulp novel *Wharton the Whale-Killer!* (1848). Hart's *Miriam Coffin*, like *Moby-Dick*, is climaxed by a dramatic sequence in which a mace named Starbuck resists his captain's orders to join the chase for a ferocious sperm whale, for he feels the chase is doomed to end in death for all. As it turns out, the whale kills Starbuck and then smashes into the whale ship, causing it to sink and the sailors to flee to lifeboats until they are rescued. *The Life of Samuel Comstock* is a Dark Adventure pamphlet novel—that is, a popular novel that intersperses adventure and philosophical gloom—about a fiercely independent Nantucket lad who, rather like Melville's Ishmael, first is subjected to hypocritical Quakers and later serves under a whale-ship captain described as "passionate, violent, and sometimes tyrannical," always threatening "to nail the men to the deck, if they do not hasten to their duty."[11] *Wharton the Whale-Killer!*, by the popular novelist Harry Halyard, includes a vivid sequence in which a ship's captain offers a reward to the first sailor who can raise a whale; his wager is met when a greenhorn sights a whale from a masthead, initiating a long whale chase, made lively by a swearing mate who grins in the face of destruction, a sequence that culminates in the whale being killed and drawn alongside the ship for cutting in. Also in the novel is an interpolated story of a whale that rams a ship. Since Melville quotes from *Wharton the Whale-Killer!* in his "Extracts," it seems likely that he knew of another Halyard novel, *The Doom of the Dolphin* (also 1848), which featured a grim engraving of huge whale flukes cracking apart splintered boats with terrified sailors flying through the air and other whales hovering near a ship in the background. The scene on which the engraving was based involves several boats that fail in their attempt to kill a sperm whale described as "a regular old white-headed eighty barrel fellow."[12] Another pre-Melvillian Dark Adventure pamphlet novel was Life *in a Whale Ship* (1841), an episodic novel narrated by an old philosophical salt named Romanta. Like *Moby-Dick*, *Life in a Whale Ship* contains detailed anecdotes about gams and ill-fated whale chases, often interspersed with dark philosophical reflections. Melville's images of face and the Spirit Spout are strikingly anticipated in Romanta's account of a whaling crew who felt that "their doom and every incident attending it was writ out at length previous to that eventful day—that it was revealed to them the moment they struck their whale—that its phantom voice urged them on, and that they had not the desire or the power to disobey," suggesting that our final fate is revealed to us through its spirit-agent."[13]

Melville's emphasis upon the unparalleled immensity and destructiveness of his white whale can be viewed as part of a growing fascination with monsters of all varieties. There had arisen a wild one-upmanship among popular adventure writers competing against each other to see who could produce the most savage, freakish beast. In *The Raven and the Whale* Perry Miller suggests as a source for Melville's white whale the terrific antediluvian beast described in *Behemoth* (1839), a novel by Melville's New York literary associate Cornelius Mathews. Mathews's monster, however, was only one of several tremendous creatures in popular literature of Melville's day. For example, strange encounters between humans and sea monsters were standard fare in grotesque humor periodicals such as the Crockett almanacs. The 1838 Crockett almanac included a sketch, "Colonel Crockett and the Sea Sarpint," in which Davy Crockett battles a kraken said to be long enough to twist the hair of an angel who straddles the land and the sea. The 1849 Crockett almanac contained a story, "Crockett and the Great Prairie Serpent," about a huge snake, said to be larger than any kraken, whom Crockett wrestles and lashes to death. In the Crockett almanac for 1850, Crockett's nautical friend Ben Harding tells a violent story about a time he and a sailor friend harpooned a whale, climbed aboard a whale's back, and went for a dizzying ride until at last the whale vindictively rammed against their ship, which was saved only when the whale was killed by a lance. The largest monster in antebellum literature was the kraken depicted in Eugene Batchelder's *Romance of the Sea-Serpent, or The Ichthyosaurus* (1849), a bizarre narrative poem about a sea serpent that terrorizes the coast of Massachusetts, destroys a huge ship in mid-ocean, repasts on human remains gruesomely with sharks and whales, attends a Harvard commencement (where he has been asked to speak), shocks partygoers by appearing at a Newport ball, and at last is hunted and killed by a fleet of Newport sailors.

To mention such possible antecedents of *Moby-Dick*, however, is to underscore the originality of Melville's novel. All the above works share a common trait of most Romantic Adventure novels of the day: they trivialize a topic that Melville treats with seriousness and artistic care. In *Miriam Coffin*, *Samuel Comstock*, *Life in a Whale Ship*, and Harry Halyard's novels, whaling adventure is included rather arbitrarily as part of meandering narratives that also describe other lively topics such as piracy, doomsaying, battles with South Sea natives, and murder. Even the two works that might seem closest to Melville, "Mocha Dick" and "Encounter with a White Whale," have a flat, neutral quality. As for humorous writings like the Crockett almanacs and Batchelder's *Romance of the Sea-Serpent*, they show just how devoid of probability or significance huge creatures could be when treated by authors interested solely in purveying freaks for antebellum sensation-lovers.

Melville's whale is at once more realistic and more mythic than the monsters of popular literature. On the one hand, Melville includes an unprecedented amount of factual information about the whale in order to counteract what Ishmael calls the "curious imaginary portraits of him which even down to the present day confidently challenge the faith of the landsman" (260). The "plain facts" about whaling are designed to prevent us from dismissing Moby Dick, in Ishmael's words, as merely "a monstrous fable" or "a hideous and intolerable allegory" (205). Even though factual sections of *Moby-Dick* like the "Cetology" chapter are partly tongue-in-cheek, there is clearly a serious intent behind Ishmael's statement that "the various species of whales need some sort of popular comprehensive classification" (136). While this cetological factuality is Melville's rhetorical answer to the haphazard, often inane treatment of monsters in popular culture, his contrasting emphasis on the final indecipherability of sea creatures succeeds in summoning up a sense of mystery he felt was also needed since, as Ishmael laments, "man has lost that sense of the full awfulness of the sea which aboriginally belongs to it" (273). Any rare or mysterious sea phenomenon— squid, sharks, brit—assumes momentous import in the novel, and, as for whales, "the great Leviathan is that one creature in the world which must remain unpainted to the last" (264). The whale's facticity and his ultimate unreadability—both insisted upon with equal vigor in the novel—are crucial to Melville's mission of bringing both solidity and suggestiveness to a topic, the pursuit of monstrous creatures, that had been widely trivialized in popular culture.

The factual side of whaling, as we know, was known to Melville as a result of his experience aboard whale ships and his reading of contemporary whaling books such as Thomas Beale's *The Natural History of the Sperm Whale* and William Scoresby, Jr.'s *Northern Whale-Fishery*.[14] But Melville's means of achieving what Robert Richardson calls "mythic investiture"—the infusion of natural objects, especially the whale, with mystic otherness[15]—have remained largely unexplained. To find cultural roots for the mythic, richly ambiguous quality of *Moby-Dick* we must look not to Romantic Adventure fiction, which we saw to be generally nonsymbolic and merely adventurous, but to other areas of antebellum popular culture, particularly dark-reform literature and radical-democrat fiction. A principal distinction between *Moby-Dick* and other adventure fiction was Melville's assimilation of a full range of zestful, paradoxical images from such dark popular literature.

The capacity for a richly imagistic work such as *Moby-Dick* had been inherent in American popular culture since the early 1830s, when vehement reformers began coining larger-than-life, mythic metaphors for the social vices they fiercely denounced. Virtually every reform movement of the day—temperance, antislavery, antiprostitution, naval reform, utopian socialism—became notably sensationalized in the hands of popular reformers competing for the attention of an American public increasingly taken with Dark Adventure novels and crime-filled penny newspapers. The "dark" or "immoral" reformers, as I call them, righteously proclaimed that they were wallowing in foul moral sewers only to scour them clean; but their seamy writings prove that they were more powerfully drawn to wallowing than to cleaning. They scandalized conservatives with their emphasis upon the perverse results rather than the moral remedies of social vice. Some immoral reformers, such as the notorious antiprostitution reformer John McDowall and the dramatic temperance orator John B. Gough, were publicly exposed as opportunistic frauds; others, such as the uncompromising abolitionist William Lloyd Garrison and the labor advocate Mike Walsh, were regularly denounced as "ultraists" who exaggerated the horrific aspects of social ills.

The dark reformers introduced a fierce new rhetoric that featured veil-lifting imagery, mythic metaphors, and post-Calvinist gloom. In popular reform newspapers and pamphlets, vice was regularly described as a "monster" stalking over mountains and rivers, or a "whirlpool" sucking helpless victims to destruction, or an "ocean" threatening to engulf the world, or an all-controlling "fate." Often such analogies had a distinctly pre-Melvillian ring, as when a writer for Garrison's *Liberator*, alarmed by the rise of various social vices in America, wrote: "The whale which swallowed up the recreant prophet [Jonah] may be likened to the many monsters which swallow up the aberrant sinner of our own days," except that "the whales of this latter day are much more voracious than that of old; inasmuch as the whale which swallowed up the prophet Jonah cast him forth again after the third day. But, in our days, when a hapless mortal once gets within the jaws of the monster, he is lost forever; he is not so fortunate as to be vomited forth on dry land."[16] In the dark-reform imagination, modern "whales"—moral vices like drinking and prostitution as well as social injustices such as slavery, poverty, and upper-class hypocrisy—were far deadlier than the biblical one because they seemed ubiquitous and inescapable.

By the time he wrote *Moby-Dick* Melville had gained full exposure to popular reforms, for he had experimented broadly with reform themes and images in his first five novels. In *Typee* and *Omoo* he had assumed a standard reform stance in his exposure of hypocrisy among white Christians on South Sea islands; other reforms he utilized were antiprostitution, temperance, peace reform, and utopian socialism, all of which had been widely debated in the popular press. In *Mardi* such reforms as temperance, socialism, and antislavery provide a backdrop to Melville's pondering of moral paradoxes and social conflict. The popular-oriented *Redburn* is filled with dark-temperance and city-mysteries images of the crassest variety, such as the picture of frivolous rich people and huge dens of sin in the modern city or a sailor's horrid suicide after heavy drinking or the sensational account of another sailor burned alive in flames produced by spontaneous combustion produced by cheap liquor he has drunk. In *White-Jacket* Melville used naval reform as a vehicle for diving into the mire of nineteenth-century social vices and for probing deep ironies in human nature and society.

Having experimented with so many different reform voices in his early novels, Melville had reached a level of stylization whereby reform content was abandoned but reform images and subversive spirit were retained. He wished to fully utilize reform images in the pursuit of truth but, simultaneously, to detach himself from specific reform programs—probably because he realized that in an age of immoral reformers, the reform mode was widely held suspect. As he wrote in a June 1851 letter to Hawthorne: "It can hardly be doubted that all Reformers are bottomed upon the truth, more or less; and to the world at large are not reformers almost universally laughing-stocks?" (*Letters*, 127) Poised between the intensely reformist *White-Jacket* and the ambiguous later novels, *Moby-Dick* shows the reform impulse at last fully divested of didacticism.

Since *Moby-Dick* can be viewed as the culmination of Melville's early permutations of the dark-reform mode, it is understandable that the novel has far more direct references to popular reform movements than even the most reform-minded of his previous novels. Temperance, antislavery, socialism, anti-Catholicism, antiwar—these and other popular reforms provide a wealth of images to Melville in *Moby-Dick*. Ironically, however, the novel does not seem reformist at all. This is because reform imagery has eventually become for Melville a colorful shell, largely devoid of political or didactic content, that can be arranged at will in the overall mosaic of a subversive novel.

This stylization of reform runs throughout the novel. It is visible, for example, in Melville's creative adaptation of dark-temperance imagery. Such imagery abounds in the early scene in which Ishmael witnesses the *Grampus* crew, just home from a three years' voyage, rushing straight into the Spouter-Inn's bar (the entrance to which is a huge whale jaw) and getting drunk on drinks poured by the bartender Jonah, while the temperate Bulkington watches aloof and then disappears. Just as popular reformers had regularly described alcohol as an all-devouring "whale" or all-consuming "poison," so Melville described the *Grampus* crew entering through "jaws of swift destruction" to be served "deliriums and death" by a prophetically named bartender (14). Just as reformers had emphasized the illusoriness of alcohol's pleasures, so Melville writes: "Abominable are the tumblers into which he pours his poison. Though true cylinders without—within, the green goggling glasses deceitfully tapered downward to a cheating bottom" (14). The Spouter-Inn barroom scene shows Melville typically adopting a popular mode as a preparatory literary exercise: just as the bartender pours poisonous drinks to rambunctious sailors who are inside symbolic whale's jaws, so in a sense the dark-temperance mode "pours" *Moby-Dick* by providing Melville with various subversive images.

Melville is now so sensitively attuned to all possible permutations of the dark-temperance mode that he can shift with ease between antitemperance and protemperance stances, giving full moral credence to no single viewpoint and always seeking the rhetorical potentialities of whatever stance he assumes. He sounds antitemperance when he has the comical mate Stubb, a boisterous advocate of grog, snicker at Dough-Boy for giving someone ginger-water; Stubb declares, "There is some sneaking Temperance Society movement about this business" (322). Melville also strikes antitemperance notes when he gives an updated sketch of the biblical rich man Dives, who, "a president of a temperance society ... only drinks the tepid tears of orphans" (11), and when he ironically depicts Jack Bunger, the captain of the *Samuel Enderby*, as a self-avowed "strict total abstinence man" who nevertheless gets drunk on the sly (440). On the other hand, Melville sounds protemperance in his portrait of the wretched Perth, the blacksmith who had been driven to sea after alcohol had shattered his family and who is now the lonely forger of harpoons for Ahab. Retracing how the insidious "Bottle Conjuror" had torn apart Perth's happy home, Melville calls death "the only desirable sequel for a career like this," and death "is but the first salutation to the possibilities of the immense Remote, the Wild, the Watery, the Unshored"—and so Perth commits a kind of suicide by going to sea on the *Pequod*, where he is left a stolid relic, a man "past scorching," well suited to forge the harpoon that Ahab will baptize in the devil's name and hurl at the white whale (485, 486).

It would be easy enough to run through the entire novel and suggest specific reform influences for other scenes as well. The city-mysteries mode (as popularized in antebellum novels that portrayed crime and desolation in American cities) enhances the gloom of Ishmael's opening entrance into New Bedford, as he stumbles over an ashbox and asks, "[A]re these ashes from that destroyed city, Gomorrah?" (9). Ishmael's ironic query "Who aint a slave?" (6) would seem to owe much to the fiery New York radical Mike Walsh, who in the late 1840s famously universalized the notion of slavery by stressing that *both* Northern wage slaves and Southern chattel slaves were equally oppressed. Sensational anti-Catholic imagery sometimes adds color or irreverence, as when Ishmael asks why a Midwestern Protestant is terrified by the mention of "a White Friar or a White Nun," or when the account of the mincer who wears the whale's cassock (i.e., penis skin), leads to the bawdy pun: "what a candidate for an archbishoprick, what a lad for a Pope, this mincer!" (192, 420). A particularly concentrated grouping of popular reform images occurs in Ishmael's discussion of "fast fish" (things that are considered personal property merely because they happen to be in one's possession): in listing examples of fast fish, Melville brings together typical ironic imagery from antislavery agitation ("Republican slaves"), property-law reform (the widow in the hands of a "rapacious landlord"), socialist and city-mysteries writings (a poor family cheated by a banker; laborers exploited by a rich churchman) (397).

Such individual sources, however, are less important than the overall dark-reform *écriture* that governs the novel. Scholars have long sought historical prototypes for several scenes and characters, but the results have often proven contradictory. Ahab, for instance, has been variously associated with the radical abolitionist Garrison, with Garrison's arch-opponent Calhoun, and with the moderate politician Daniel Webster! Such historical source-study can be constricting, for in fact *Moby-Dick* moves beyond slavery or antislavery, protemperance or antitemperance, to a literary realm in which subversive reform energy and rhetoric, rather than reform message, become the literary artist's central concern. The many explicit reform devices in *Moby-Dick* are pushed toward literariness by Melville's devotion to the subversive images that formed a rhetorical sub-basis of all dark-reform writings. Ultimately, Melville in *Moby-Dick* is a gigantic dark reformer, towering above all reform programs but driven by his age's powerful reform impulse. If other reformers (and Melville himself in his earlier fiction) had "lifted the veil" off social corruption or lamented the "pasteboard" artificiality of certain people, Melville has Ahab describe all visible objects as "pasteboard masks" and declare that man's highest goal is to "strike through the mask" (164). In this sense, the object of Ahab's quest is the ultimate dark-reform mythic image, which now has been granted an independent life and an alluringly malevolent will of its own. The white whale brings together all the "whales" swimming in all the turbulent "oceans" of the image-fashioning ultraists. If popular reformers had seen society as a "whited sepulchre" hiding submerged evil, so the white whale is invested with the most apparently benign but most ultimately subversive qualities, suggesting to Ishmael that "all deified Nature absolutely paints like the harlot, whose allurements cover nothing but the charnel-house within" (195). If popular reformers regularly used post-Calvinist images, Melville secularly enacts the Calvinist God itself, as the whole novel culminates in the destruction of Ahab and his crew by the "predestinating head" of Moby Dick, which is alive with "retribution, swift vengeance, eternal malice" (571).

If reform literature supplied Melville with potent, often disturbing images, the allied mode of radical-democrat fiction contributed various paradoxical character types. The group of popular writers I am calling radical *democrats*—most notably George Lippard, A. J. H. Duganne, George G. Foster, and George Thompson—in the 1840s carried both social protest and literary irrationalism to new extremes. Alarmed by widening class divisions and all forms of social oppression, the radical democrats used every degree of literary invective to expose what they regarded as the prevailing depravity of America's ruling class. They translated into nightmarish fiction the prevailing metaphors of dark reform. America in their eyes was no more than a whited sepulchre with rottenness within, a place of appalling "city mysteries." Their exaggerated impulse to "tear away veils" or "strike through masks" produced militant declarations like this one in a Duganne novel: "Terrible, terrible will be the reaction, when the veil is torn aside, when the sepulchres, no longer whited, burst forth in their own horror and loathsomeness."[17] Best-selling novels such as Lippard's *The Quaker City* (1844–45), Duganne's *The Knights of the Seal* (1845), Thompson's *New York Life* (1849), and Ned Buntline's *The G'hals of New York* (1850) depicted a topsy-turvy world in which justified outcasts and likable criminals actually seemed more worthy than conventionally virtuous characters, whose probity was held suspect because it reflected an inherently unjust social system. The great conflict in radical-democrat fiction was between the smirking justified criminal and what may be called the oxymoronic oppressor: the outwardly respectable but inwardly corrupt social leader who variously appeared as the churchgoing capitalist, the religious slaveholder, the unctuous reverend rake, and so on. The hero of this fiction was a mixed figure known as the "b'hoy" (street slang for "boy"), the crude yet acute, wicked yet thoroughly likable city youth who had arisen in the street gangs of the Eastern cities and then was mythologized in pamphlet novels and melodramas. These radical-democrat stereotypes reflected deep working-class aggressions and fantasies in the turbulent decade following the crushing economic panic of 1837.

In time, however, radical-democrat literature became notably vulgarized when it was taken up by opportunistic authors who exaggerated gross sensationalism but left behind serious political goals. In the late 1840s, a sudden explosion of cheap pamphlet novels, stimulated mainly by mass publishers' adoption of the new cylinder press, brought about a cheapening of the radical-democrat mode. In the countless pamphlet novels by now forgotten authors like Benjamin Barker, Charles E. Averill, Maturin Murray Ballou, Osgood Bradbury, and George Thompson, the fiery rhetoric and revolutionary themes of radical-democrat fiction became mechanically mass-produced, giving rise to a grisly formula fiction about likable criminals warring against secretly corrupt social rulers, with the b'hoy now presented as merely a punchy, cocksure swaggerer with few vestiges of his former earnestness. Mingled with these grotesque caricatures of radical-democrat types were scenes of almost unparalleled atrocity and perversity, involving lively topics such as blood-drinking, whippings, devilish baptisms, cannibalism, and delirium tremens. How popular was this sensational pamphlet fiction? In 1850 Melville's friend Evert A. Duyckinck ran an article on crime-filled pamphlet novels in the *Literary World* containing the assertion that "the reader who sets out to master all the yellow cover literature of the day, works very hard for a living."[18] Similarly, the Boston critic Edwin P. Whipple lamented that the rage of the hour was "the Romance of Rascality." "According to the philosophy obtaining among the romancers of rascality," Whipple wrote, "the fact that an object creates physical disgust, is the reason why we should take it to our arms; the fact that a man excites moral reprobation, is his claim upon our sympathy."[19]

By the time he wrote *Moby-Dick* Melville's imagination was bristling with the polarities of American radical democracy. He himself had become a kind of likable criminal, one who could write in his June 1851 letter to Hawthorne: "When you see or hear of my ruthless democracy on all sides, you may possibly feel a touch of a shrink, or something of that sort. It is but nature to be shy of a mortal who boldly declares that a thief in jail is

as honorable a personage as Gen. George Washington" (*Letters*, 126–27).
He had become a fully American metaphysical outlaw who could place a
thief on the same level as George Washington. He could proclaim himself
simultaneously the greatest democrat and the greatest misanthrope. He had
arrived at the very core of the popular paradox that fused criminality and
goodness, iconoclasm and patriotism.

Melville's transformation of popular strategies in *Moby-Dick* is revealed
in his willed *fusion* of the justified criminal and the oxymoronic oppressor.
True, sometimes he is quite close to the popular radical democrats, as
in his satirical portrait of the oxymoronic Captain Bildad, the querulous
Quaker and penny-pinching Christian. Because he had immersed himself so
completely in the inverted value system of radical democracy, he could now
deal convincingly only with paradoxical characters. Throughout *Moby-Dick*,
conventionally virtuous figures (the "pious, good man" Starbuck [79], the
noble Bulkington, Aunt Charity, Dough-Boy) are doomed to impotency,
while richly paradoxical figures (the "swearing good man" Ahab [79], the
likable outcast Ishmael, the humane cannibal Queequeg, the whole rollicking
Pequod crew) control the narrative. But Melville departs from the popular
radical democrats by bringing together stereotypes that in popular fiction
remain uncompromisingly opposed. Captain Ahab is his central fusing agent.
As we have seen, Ahab is the gargantuan immoral reformer tearing away
"pasteboard masks." At the same time, he is the sympathetic criminal who is
on a seemingly justified vindictive quest and who reflects the inversions of
radical-democrat fiction. These inversions in popular fiction had been aptly
summed up by an essayist for the *Knickerbocker*: "The heroes of many of the
novelists of the present day have almost converted us to the belief that there
is no moral incompatibility between a criminal and a judge, and that a series
of violations of the law is no obstacle to a man attaining fame, fortune, and
honor."[20] Ahab, recognizing the deep moral implications of the sympathetic
criminal, uses a similar metaphor when he cries to Starbuck: "Where do
murderers go, man! Who's to doom, when the judge himself is dragged to the
bar?" (545). Ahab is also the tyrannical oppressor who can only be described
oxymoronically as "a swearing good man" and "a grand, ungodly, god-like
man" (79). Although he embodies all the wildness and contradictions of
these varied popular characters, he does not have their extreme heartlessness.
The popular characters' haphazard aims are answered by his unprecedented
singleness of purpose; their horrid willingness to murder human beings
contrasts with his intent to hunt down a whale; their unmitigated inhumanity
differs from his capacity to display occasional "humanities," as when he
tearfully recalls his wife and child or when he befriends the hapless cabin-boy
Pip.

If Ahab represents a humanized version of the oxymoronic oppressor and the justified criminal, Ishmael is the transformed version of another radical-democrat stereotype: the b'hoy. A figure of both reality and legend, the b'hoy had been an appropriate hero of radical-democrat fiction, since he was a mixture of bad qualities (rebelliousness, egotism, indolence) and good ones (native intelligence, confidence, an inclination to adopt the manners of the upper-class). By 1850, widespread vulgarization of the b'hoy figure in the popular press made this figure seem a great ideal that had gone sour. George G. Foster, a New York journalist in Melville's circle, identified the b'hoy as a representative indigenous character who offered "a rich and certain harvest" for American authors, but he rightly noted that "only the coarser and more vulgar traits," the "faults, vices, and barbarisms" were now being drawn by popular writers who aimed at "enlisting the brutal sympathies and passions of their audiences."[21] In popular melodramas like Benjamin A. Baker's *A Glance at New York in 1848* and in countless pamphlet novels, the b'hoy was little more than a gangster whose amoral violence was a source of crude fun for the antebellum public.

In his portrait of Ishmael, Melville borrows from the b'hoy stereotype. In the opening pages of the novel Ishmael is established as the indigent, loafing, acute, brash, genial New Yorker who plays pranks, hates respectable jobs, and aches for adventure. Melville's contemporary readers surely saw signs of the b'hoy in an unconventional narrator who boasts that he travels not with commodores and who abominates "all honorable respectable toils, trials, and tribulations of every kind whatsoever" (5). Like the typical sensation-loving b'hoy, Ishmael feels "an everlasting itch for things remote" and is attracted by "the wild and distant seas" with their "undeliverable, nameless perils" (7). The images that surround him in the early chapters—images of suicide, funerals, coffins, cannibalism, the gallows, tombstones—place him in the blackly humorous domain familiar to the popular b'hoy. His entire voyage becomes a kind of popular culture text when he imagines "WHALING VOYAGE BY ONE ISHMAEL" squeezed as on a theater poster between sensational headlines about a hotly contested election and a bloody battle in Afghanistan (7).

But in the process of adopting the b'hoy Melville reconstructs him. Ishmael was not the first b'hoy narrator in American fiction, but he was the first pressed in the direction of the humane and the broadly tolerant. He is the b'hoy reconceived by a writer who recognized the universal, fully human potentialities of his own culture's popular images. Ishmael is not merely the "hose" or "Sikesey" of melodramas and pamphlet novels, the two-fisted b'hoy who mocks aristocrats and gets involved in comical pranks. He is also the flexible, loving youth who stirs our deepest democratic sympathies when he embraces Queequeg, a man he had previously feared as a bloodthirsty cannibal.

Through the developing Ishmael–Queequeg relationship, Melville enriches not only the b'hoy but another stereotype who had figured largely in radical-democrat fiction: the savage non-white. Radical democrats had regularly depicted even the most fierce oppressed peoples and minority groups as more noble than secretly corrupt social leaders. In his characterization of Queequeg, Melville may have been indebted to George Lippard, the most popular radical-democrat novelist of the day. Lippard's best-selling volumes *Blanche of Brandywine* (1846) and *Washington and His Generals* (1847) both had included memorable episodes involving a massive black soldier of the American Revolution, Black Sampson, who slashed through British lines with his tremendous scythe waving and his dog "Debbil" by his side. Radical-democrat egalitarianism had special import in the portrayal of Black Sampson, who is not only poor but also a Negro savage haunted by memories of his former noble stature as the son of the king of an African tribe. Although Lippard sympathetically portrays Sampson as one of the proudest and best soldiers of Washington's army, in typical fashion he permits the Black Sampson episode to degenerate into grotesque black humor. Sampson seizes his giant scythe and rushes into battle, decapitating and dismembering British soldiers with obvious love of gore. He screams to his dog: "We am gwain' mowin' today," and indeed he mows down every soldier in sight.[22] In *Blanche of Brandywine* Lippard writes that such violence exemplifies "the instinct of Carnage ... which makes a man thirst for blood, which makes him mad for joy, when he steeps his arms to the elbows in his foeman's gore, which makes him shout and halloo, and laugh, as he goes murdering on over piles of dead!"

In portraying Queequeg, Melville takes up where Lippard left off, beginning with violent images but then moving to a dissolution of violence and an affirmation of affectionate brotherhood. Lippard had concluded the Sampson episode with a fiendish picture of his warrior-savage mowing down humans with his tremendous scythe. Melville begins with the deadly scythe and then progresses through various darkly humorous scenes toward a consoling portrait of Queequeg's humaneness. When in Chapter 3 Ishmael enters the Spouter-Inn, he sees hanging on the wall several "heathenish" weapons, the most terrifying of which is "sickle-shaped, with a vast handle sweeping round like the segment made in the new-mown grass by a long-armed mower," making Ishmael wonder "what monstrous cannibal and savage could ever have gone a death-harvesting with such a hacking, horrifying implement" (13). Having initiated the Spouter-Inn sequence with this Lippardian image, Melville remains, through this and the following chapter, in the realm of radical-democrat sensationalism: Queequeg is reported to have trouble selling his heads because "the market's overstocked"; when Queequeg leaps into bed with Ishmael he screams, "Who-e debel you?," and Ishmael in turn yells for the landlord Peter Coffin (18, 23). To this point, the tone of Melville's episode is not distant from the end of Lippard's. The huge deadly sickle, the images of mowing and death-harvesting, the references to decapitation and dismemberment, the word "debel"—all of these images place Melville's episode in the familiar arena of radical-democrat fiction.

Melville, however, prevents the sequence from descending into the merely perverse. Rather than allow his savage character to become a grisly emblem of gleeful carnage, as does Lippard, Melville makes him an emblem of universal love. He is able to do so primarily because he is more open than Lippard to the *reconstructive* possibilities of the radical-democrat vision. Whereas Sampson goes to bloody extremes as a member of George Washington's army, Queequeg at first seems a sanguinary demon but soon is described as "George Washington cannibalistically developed," a pagan savage without "civilized hypocrisies and bland deceits" who becomes admirable because of his tenderness and generosity (50, 51). Melville is able to lift Queequeg out of the mire of sensationalism because he has him embraced by an enriched version of that flexible radical-democrat hero, the b'hoy. The "marriage" of Ishmael and Queequeg is Melville's rhetorical intermerging of two popular characters—the b'hoy and the oppressed non-white—on the ground of common humanity. Melville burrows through the cheapened radical democracy of popular culture to a genuine radical democracy signaled by deep affection between two good-hearted human beings of different races.

Another popular cultural phenomenon relevant to *Moby-Dick* was subversive humor, which appeared variously as Old Southwest humor, radical-democrat humor, and what I term urban humor. Old Southwest humor introduced irreverent outbursts and colloquial boasts by rascalish folk heroes such as Davy Crockett, Nimrod Wildfire, Roaring Ralph Stackpole, and other popular "screamers" or "ring-tailed roarers." Radical-democrat humor, popularized particularly by George Lippard and George Thompson, gave a black edge to American humor, as devilish, downtrodden heroes sneered at a society that always struck them, in their favorite word, as irredeemably "queer." Urban humor, a stylized brand of humor that arose in such periodicals as the *Yankee Doodle* and the *New York Picayune*, travestied all modes of antebellum popular writings—sermons, domestic fiction, Dark Adventure novels, immoral reform, sensational newspapers and pamphlets— with the effect of divesting these modes of any fixed meaning and casting them into the relativist, carnivalized realm of parody and absurdity.

Permeating urban humor was the spirit of the age's great master-showman, Phineas T. Barnum, for whom all aspects of American culture, moral or immoral, were equally objects of public display and manipulation. In the various types of native humor, the centrifugal discourse that characterized all American subversive literature reached a bizarre extreme. Mark Twain would later remark that the only truly indigenous American literary form was the tall tale: the exaggerated, virtually structureless string of improbable events related by a vernacular narrator. This kind of willed directionlessness was in fact a common denominator of several indigenous types of subversive humor, all of which featured a rapid succession of inconsequential and absurdly juxtaposed images.

Some of the humorous images in *Moby-Dick* are lifted directly from the pages of popular humor. For example, urban humor directly influenced the characterizations of the black cook Fleece and the crazed cabin-boy Pip. Both are variations upon the Negro preacher featured in William H. Levison's burlesque sermon series published in *The New York Picayune* from 1847 onward and later published in two popular volumes, *Julius Caesar Hannibal* and *Black Diamonds*. Fleece's comic sermon to the sharks in Chapter 64 is an adaptation of the burlesque sermons by Levison's Julius Caesar Hannibal, the pedantic, ill-spoken black preacher who regaled antebellum readers with his darkly humorous discourses (called "black diamonds") on varied topics.[23] Just as Levison's Hannibal inevitably began his sermons with blessings such as "Blubed Sinners" or "Helpluss Brutheren," so Fleece addresses his congregation as "Belubed fellow-critturs" (295). Melville's contemporary readers would have found familiar amusement in the fact that Fleece uses sharks as his text, because Levison's Hannibal had preached funny sermons about many strange animals: the crocodile, the lobster, the monkey, the hog, and the whale. Nor would they have been surprised by Fleece's ultimately cynical message—the horrifying voraciousness of the sharks, symbolizing the cannibalism of humankind and nature—for Hannibal often emphasized human savagery and universal mistrust.

Whereas Levison had popularized what he called "black diamonds"— the darkly humorous sayings of Julius Caesar Hannibal—Melville took the further step of actually creating a black diamond in Pip, a character who emerges from the ocean depths with a dark wisdom that can be best expressed in mad laughter. The connection between Melville's and Levison's characters would have been immediately apparent to antebellum readers, for when Pip is introduced he is compared at length to a diamond. Emphasizing that "this little black was brilliant, for even blackness has its brilliancy," Melville describes the increased brilliancy created by Pip's dreary nautical environment by noting: "When the cunning jeweler would show you the diamond in its most impressive lustre, he lays it against a gloomy ground, and then lights it up, not by the sun, but by some unnatural gases. Then come out those fiery effulgences, infernally superb; then the evil-blazing diamond, once the divinest symbol of the crystal skies, looks like some crown-jewel stolen from the King of Hell" (412). In time, Pip becomes a kind of living embodiment of the "black diamonds" Hannibal delivers, for the darkest of Hannibal's reflections, pertaining to the relativism of all human viewpoints, is metonymically expressed by the insane cabin-boy in his relativist outburst after conflicting interpretations of the doubloon: "I look, you look, he looks; we look, ye look, they look" (434). Melville has converted the "black diamonds" of one of his age's leading urban humorists, Levison, into a memorable fictional character whose insane wisdom shines luridly over the conclusion of his novel.

Melville's adaptations of Levison are part of a larger strategy in *Moby-Dick* of absorbing all the wilder elements of popular humor. The bizarre, volcanic oaths of Old Southwest humor are transcribed in Peleg's vow that he will "swallow a live goat with all his hair and horns on" and Stubb's boast that he will pull off the devil's tail and sell it as an ox whip (77, 327). The leering sarcasm and nightmarish imagery of popular humorists is captured in the portrayal of Stubb, who embodies the explosive forces of dark humor that fly quickly into the cynical and the chaotic as result of disillusion with perceived reality. Described as "one of those odd sort of humorists, whose jollity is sometimes so curiously ambiguous" (219), the comically churlish, grinning Stubb is particularly derivative of radical-democrat humor in its extreme form. The irony of the radical democrats often went beyond social criticism to dark generalizations about a world that suddenly seemed profoundly awry. The word "queer" had special prominence in the radical-democrat lexicon, for it summoned up the skewed reality that the dark humorists perceived. George Lippard again stands out as the main popularizer of this word, for his writings are filled with sarcastic comments about the "queer" arrangement of things. "Queer world this!" exclaims a character typically in Lippard's *The Quaker City*. "Don't know much about other worlds, but it strikes me that if a prize were offered somewhere by somebody, for the queerest world a-going, this world of ours might be rigged up nice, and sent in like a bit of show beef, as the premium queer world.[24] So significant was this word to Lippard that in 1849 his reform newspaper, *The Quaker City*, featured a regular weekly column, "It is a Queer World," which reported grotesque social injustices.

For Melville, too, the word "queer" became particularly descriptive of the world as seen from a humorous perspective. When he was in the final stages of *Moby-Dick* he wrote Hawthorne a letter in which he imagined them together in heaven, sipping champagne and singing "humorous, comic songs—'Oh, when I lived in that queer little hole called the world'" (*Letters*, 128). In *Moby-Dick*, this radical-democrat sarcasm surfaces in Ishmael's account of "certain queer times" when the universe seems "a vast practical joke" (226). It is particularly embodied in Stubb, whose favorite word is "queer." When Ahab strikes him and sends him below, Stubb mutters, "It's very queer.... It's queer; very queer; and he's queer too; aye, take him fore and aft, he's about the queerest old man Stubb ever sailed with.... Damn me, but all things are queer, come to think of 'em" (128). His response to the doubloon is a dismissive "Humph! in my poor, insignificant opinion, I regard this as queer" (432). The ship's carpenter sums up Stubb well when he comments that "Stubb always says [Ahab is] queer; says nothing but that one sufficient little word queer; he's queer, says Stubb; he's queer—queer, queer; and keeps dinning it into Mr. Starbuck all the time—queer, sir—queer, queer, very queer" (472). In addition to parroting the radical democrats' favorite word, Stubb is closely linked to the bizarre, nightmarish imagery of the popular subversive imagination. Two of the strangest moments in *Moby-Dick* pertain to Stubb's overactive, disordered imagination. In Chapter 31 he reports his "queer dream" in which he tries to kick Ahab, who, shockingly, turns into a pyramid, which Stubb pummels with his leg until he is approached by a humpbacked merman, who turns threateningly to show Stubb a back studded with marlinespikes and then, after advising Stubb not to kick the pyramid anymore, seems "in some queer fashion, to swim off into the air" (132). The second strange moment comes when Stubb tries to comment on the doubloon: his remarks are a tangle of shifting, circular astrological readings.

The centrifugal cultural forces embodied in Stubb are also visible in the *Pequod*'s crew, particularly in the picture in Chapter 40 of the crew's boisterous revel in the forecastle. The black humor of the radical democrats was often punctuated by scenes of orgies meant to reflect the wildness and savagery lurking below the civilized surfaces of life. In Lippard's *The Quaker City* there is the freakish scene in which drunken characters whip themselves into a frenzy manifested by incoherent exclamations, erotic oaths, and complete noncommunication. It is this kind of disorganized blasphemy that Melville recreates in the forecastle revel. Like much American subversive humor, it firmly dismisses sentimentality (the first Nantucket sailor exclaims, "Oh, boys, don't be sentimental; it's bad for the digestion!" [173]) and proceeds into an inconsequential succession of oaths and jests that include a Lippardian mixture of sexual and dark images, such as warm bosoms, lithe limbs, and dancing on graves. Like so many scenes in popular subversive texts, this one culminates in sadistic threats between bloodthirsty characters who engage in a terrible brawl.

Surveying the popular images and devices in *Moby-Dick*—from Romantic Adventure, reform literature, radical-democrat fiction, and subversive humor—it is safe to call the novel the most broadly absorptive fiction of the antebellum period. Indeed, besides the above connections between *Moby-Dick* and antebellum popular culture, there are other linkages that might be suggested. Melville's use of the tryworks as a symbol of hell, for instance, had been presaged in a *New England Magazine* article, "A Chapter on Whaling," which pointed out that the tryworks by night is "too like Dante's purgatory, to be neglected" by American authors.[25] Ahab's deterministic outcries—for example, "Fool! I am the Fates' lieutenant; I act under orders" (561) or "By heaven, man, we are turned round and round in this world, like yonder windlass, and Fate is the handspike" (545)—seem to echo similar outbursts by popular sea-captains like J. H. Ingraham's Lafitte, who declares: "Fate! Fate! I am the football of circumstances! How often have I been led by my destiny to do deeds at which my soul revolted!"[26] Ahab's devilish baptism of his crew followed a convention in Dark Adventure fiction of the day and in fact was mild when compared with the following typical moments in popular yellow fiction: in Augusta Franklin's *The Sea-Gull; or, The Pirates League!* (1846) initiates into a crime band are forced to gash open their arms with knives, let their blood flow freely into bowls, swear to follow the Evil One, and then kill a young woman; in Robert F. Greeley's *Old Cro' Nest; or, The Outlaws of the Hudson* (1846) a man joining a criminal band has to stab his own arm, write a red cross with blood, and be branded by a scalding iron; in *The Female Land Pirate* (1847) a woman being initiated into a murderers' league is forced to stab a man and write in his blood the oath that she will *"cling to every thing wicked, abjure every thing holy, deny God and the Bible."*[27] Given this popular-cultural background, Melville was actually meliorating horrid popular imagery when he had Ahab puncture the arms of his three harpooners and use their "baptismal blood" to consecrate their quest in the name of the Devil (489).

Melville's melioration of the devilish-ritual motif reflects his general strategy of transforming the merely perverse into the resonantly wicked and suggestively ambiguous. The most horrifying aspect of dark popular literature, especially crime-filled Dark Adventure fiction, is the flat indifference with which the most brutal deeds are performed. In this sense, *Moby-Dick* may be viewed as a rhetorical answer to a body of popular sensational novels that suddenly flooded the market in the late 1840s. One would have to look long in literary annals to find so purely disgusting a succession of popular novels as *The Female Land Pirate* (1847), *Amelia Sherwood; or, Bloody Scenes at the California Gold Miner* (1848), George Lippard's *The Empire City* (1849), Henri Foster's *Ellen Grafton, or the Den of Crime* (1850), and the many novels of the arch-sensationalist George Thompson, including *The House Breaker* (1848), *Venus in Boston* (1849), *The Countess* (1849), and *City Crimes* (1849). The blood that flows through the pages of these novels is always *human* blood, in scenes of murder, torture, cannibalism, and blood-drinking that have unthinkably perverse implications. Typical of the sensibility behind this fiction is the heroine of *The Female Land Pirate*, who kills and maims so many people that, in her words, "I soon learned to look upon a murder as indifferently as a butcher would look upon the death of an animal; so great is the force of habit."[28]

Bloodletting in *Moby-Dick*, in contrast, is carefully calibrated so that it is made meaningful rather than arbitrary or gratuitous. Given Ahab's overwhelming determination to kill Moby Dick, the bloody baptism of his harpoon seems justified. Elsewhere in the novel, Melville gives us potentially gory scenes—for example, Ishmael's night in bed with a hatchet-wielding cannibal, the scuffle after the forecastle revel, Starbuck's pointing the rifle at Ahab—but determinedly avoids bloody violence and in fact makes these scenes preparatory to alternate scenes of deep human togetherness (the "marriage" between Ishmael and Queequeg, the unified commitment of the crew to Ahab's quest, the momentary tearful affection between Ahab and Starbuck). Blood does flow through *Moby-Dick*, but it is the blood of purposefully hunted whales, not of arbitrarily maimed or murdered human beings. Melville provides an outlet for the sanguinary fantasies of his readers by describing gore spouting freely from wounded whales and by having all but one of his sailors killed in the end, but he does not step across the boundary into sadism and inhumanity, as do the popular sensationalists. In fact, the whale hunt is in several senses a deeply *humanizing* experience, since it draws crew members of all races together in a tight teamwork of pursuit, killing, cutting in, and trying out—all the duties of the whaling trade that demand expert individual skill but also constant interdependence. Thus, at key moments in his whaling activities Ishmael deeply senses his radical dependence on others (in "The Monkey-Rope") and his love of his fellow man (in "A Squeeze of the Hand").

Melville's overriding technique in *Moby-Dick* is to allow all the centrifugal, disorienting forces within the American popular mind to be fully released momentarily through structural "escape valves," usually a chapter or a small cluster of chapters, and then, having released some of the subversive steam, disperse its remaining energy through counterbalancing factual chapters or through the powerfully centripetal plot line, main characters, and symbols. Melville could incorporate all his culture's images, from the religious to the sensational, and yet rescue them from their native directionlessness by introducing a centripetal action (the quest for the white whale) with a centripetal object (the whale itself) through a centripetal agent (Ahab, and then the whole crew)—all driven by hope for a centripetal reward, the doubloon fixed to the mast.

Even in fashioning these centripetal images, Melville borrowed from popular culture. For instance, his use of the Biblical names Ishmael and Ahab lend depth and grandeur to common figures such as the b'hoy and the tyrannical captain; and this very fusion of sacrosanct Biblical archetypes with modern-day figures was made possible by a widespread secularization of popular religious culture in nineteenth-century America, a phenomenon also visible in Father Mapple's anecdotal sermon and in Ishmael's homely fantasy of "rows of angels in paradise, each with his hands in a jar of spermaceti" (416). This secularized reapplication of the religious imagery contributed as well to the supernatural overtones of Fedallah, often associated with the devil, and of the white whale itself, a magnificent combination of God and Satan. Another popular phenomenon that greatly aided Melville was pseudosciences such as mesmerism (mind control through what was seen as electrical, magnetic energy) and phrenology and physiognomy (the interpretation of character through the reading of physical characteristics). In the fluid atmosphere of antebellum popular culture, these pseudosciences were handled with unprecedented flexibility and creativity. The popular mesmerists' belief in mind control through electrical fluid was inventively reapplied by Melville to enhance the centripetal quality of his main plot and characters. Ahab is not merely a charismatic sea captain. In antebellum terms, he was one of very few individuals gifted with enough "odic force," or magnetic energy, to govern the wills of others. It was the popular acceptance of control through magnetic force that made possible such statements as "[Ahab] would fain have shocked into them the same fiery emotion accumulated within the Leyden jar of his own magnetic life" (165), or "Ahab kept his magnet at Starbuck's brain" (212), or "a certain magnetism shot into [the harpooners'] congenial hearts from inflexible Ahab's" (518). The popular notion that a mesmerist lost some electrical fluid during a session is reflected in Ahab's declaration, when the three mates look away from him, "'tis well. For did ye three but once take the full-forced shock, then mine own electric thing, *that* had perhaps expired from out of me" (166). Moby Dick, too, is invested with electrical attractiveness when Ahab explains his obsession with the white whale by crying: "He's all a magnet!" (441). As for physiognomy and phrenology, these popular pseudosciences allow Melville to do some fanciful character-reading through descriptions of the whale's face and head. "To scan the lines of his face, or feel the bumps on the head of this Leviathan," Melville writes; "this is a thing which no Physiognomist or Phrenologist has as yet undertaken" (345)—and so he devotes two detailed chapters to a pseudoscientific reading of the facial bumps and vertebra of the whale, aptly concluding that the sperm whale has an unusually large "organ of firmness or indomitableness" (350). Yet another cultural phenomenon that aided Melville's centripetal aims was the railroad, the new mode of transportation, and the factory, the increasingly important locus of economic production. Put to metaphorical use, they perfectly enforce Melville's centripetalism, for Ahab can declare, "The path to my fixed purpose is laid with iron rails, whereon my soul is grooved to run.... Naught's an obstacle, naught's an angle to the iron way!" (168). And Ahab's relationship with his crew is vivified by a factory metaphor when he says, "my one cogged circle fits into all their various wheels" (168).

Melville's broad-scale assimilation of popular images greatly complicates the longstanding issue of "meaning" in *Moby-Dick*. The issue becomes even more complex when we keep in mind not only Melville's reapplications of popular cultural phenomena but also his omnivorous gatherings from elite sources. Ahab is, as we have seen, a combination of many popular types; but he is also drawn, as various critics have suggested, from the wicked Ahab of I Kings, Prometheus, Faust, Lear, Milton's Satan, Captain Charles Wilkes, and other figures of fact and legend. Ishmael, likewise, is not merely a refashioned b'hoy but also derives from the old Testament outcast beloved of God, just as Pip resembles Lear's fool, and so on. The white whale is an especially ambiguous repository of popular and archetypal images.

But in all these cases, precise meaning matters less than the dazzling ability of Melville's characters and symbols to radiate meanings. Melville's comprehensive pillaging of classic religious and literary sources reveals his overarching interest in adding resonance and suggestiveness to popular cultural chronotopes that were formless, neutral, or contradictory in their native state. The *Pequod's* quest for the whale is ultimately self-destructive and the book's truth remains tantalizingly elusive; but this does not place *Moby-Dick* at odds with American culture, as is commonly believed. What distinguishes this novel from its many popular prototypes is that it absorbs numerous American images and treats them not frivolously or haphazardly, as did the popular texts, but instead takes them seriously, salvages them from the anarchically directionless and gives them new intensity and mythic reference. Melville's quest is dangerous, but it is also exhilarating and finally joyful. Upon completing the novel Melville could express his paradoxical feeling of danger and peace by writing to Hawthorne: "I have written a wicked book, and feel spotless as the lamb. Ineffable socialities are in me" (*Letters*, 142). Having written a novel that fully absorbed the subversive forces of his culture, Melville could nonetheless feel warmly calm because he had produced a lasting testament to the creative spirit.

NOTES

1. "Hawthorne and His Mosses," *The Piazza Tales and Other Prose Pieces, 1839–1860*, eds. Harrison Hayford, Alma A. MacDougall, G. Thomas Tanselle and others (Evanston and Chicago: Northwestern University Press and The Newberry Library, 1987), 246. "Mosses" first appeared in two installments in the New York *Literary World*, nos. 185–86 (17–24 August 1850). Citations for *Moby-Dick* are from *Moby-Dick; or, the Whale*, ed. Harrison Hayford, Hershel Parker, and G. Thomas Tanselle (Evanston and Chicago: Northwestern University Press and The Newberry Library, 1988), and will be cited parenthetically.

2. *Pierre; or, The Ambiguities*, ed. Harrison Hayford, Hershel Parker, and G. Thomas Tanselle (Evanston and Chicago: Northwestern University Press and The Newberry Library, 1971), 283.

3. *White-Jacket; or, The World in a Man-of-War*, ed. Harrison Hayford, Hershel Parker, and G. Thomas Tanselle (Evanston and Chicago: Northwestern University Press and The Newberry Library, 1970), 169.

4. *The Piazza Tales*, 245.

5. I discuss these and other types of popular antebellum literature at length in *Beneath the American Renaissance: The Subversive Imagination in the Age of Emerson and Melville* (New York: Alfred A. Knopf, 1988). The present article incorporates and expands upon arguments made in *Beneath the American Renaissance*.

6. Melville to John Murray, 29 January 1847, *The Letters of Herman Melville*, ed. Merrell R. Davis and William H. Gilman (New Haven: Yale University Press, 1960), 53; hereafter cited as *Letters*.

7. Herman Melville to Lemuel Shaw, 6 October 1849, *Letters*, 91.

8. New York *Home Journal*, 29 November 1851, reprinted in *MOBY-DICK as Doubloon: Essays and Extracts (1851–1870)*, ed. Hershel Parker and Harrison Hayford (New York: Norton, 1970), 56.

9. In a comprehensive survey of the volumes listed in Lyle Henry Wright's *American Fiction, 1774–1850: A Contribution toward a Bibliography* (San Marino: Huntington Library, 1957), I have found that the number of Romantic Adventure and Subversive novels published in America rose from about 20 percent before 1800 to about 55 percent for the 1841–1850 decade.

10. Reynolds's "Mocha Dick" is conveniently available in *Moby-Dick*, eds. Harrison Hayford and Hershel Parker (New York: Norton, 1967), 571–90.

11. William Comstock, *The Life of Samuel Comstock, the Terrible Whaleman, Containing an Account of the Mutiny, and Massacre of the Officers of the Ship Globe, of Nantucket* (Boston: James Fisher, 1840), 69.

12. *The Doom of the Dolphin; or, The Sorceress of the Sea* (Boston: F. Gleason, 1848), 83.

13. *Life in a Whale Ship* (1841), reprinted as *Romance of the Deep; or the Cruise of the Aeronaut ... During a Three Years' Voyage in an American Whale Ship* (Boston: Redding and Co., 1846), 25.

14. The most comprehensive discussion of Melville's use of whaling books remains Howard Vincent, *The Trying-Out of Moby-Dick* (Boston: Houghton Mifflin, 1949).

15. Robert D. Richardson, *Myth and Literature in the American Renaissance* (Bloomington: Indiana University Press, 1978), 212–13.

16. *The Liberator*, 22 January 1831.

17. A. J. H. Duganne, *The Knights of the Seal; or, The Mysteries of Three Cities* (Philadelphia: Colon and Adriance, 1845), 112.

18. *The Literary World*, 9 February 1850.

19. E. Whipple, "The Romance of Rascality" (1848), in *One Hundred Years Ago: American Writings* of 1848, ed. James Playstead Wood (New York: Funk and Wagnalls, 1948), 479.

20. *Knickerbocker Magazine*, 8 (October 1836), 619.

21. G. Foster, *New York by Gas-Light* (New York: DeWitt and Davenport, 1850), 109; *New York in Slices* (New York: William H. Graham, 1849), 44.

22. The Black Sampson episode from *Washington and His Generals* is reprinted in *George Lippard, Prophet of Protest: Writings of an American Radical*, ed. David S. Reynolds (New York: Peter Lang, 1986), 123–28. The following quotation from *Blanche of Brandywine* is in Reynolds, *George Lippard, Prophet of Protest*, 286.

23. Typical burlesque sermons are collected in W. H. Levison, *Black Diamonds; or, Humor, Satire, and Sentiment. Treated Scientifically by Professor Julius Caesar Hannibal: A Series of Burlesque Lectures, Darkly Colored. Originally Published in "The New York Picayune"* (New York: A. Ranney, 1855)

24. G. Lippard, *The Quaker City; or, The Monks of Monk Hall* (1845; rpt. New York: Odyssey, 1970), 34.

25. *New England Magazine*, June 1835, 449.

26. Joseph Holt Ingraham, *Lafitte, The Pirate of the Gulf* (New York: Harper & Bros., 1836), 62.

27. *The Female Land Pirate; or, Awful, Mysterious and Horrible Disclosure of Amanda Bannoris* (Cincinnati: E. E. Barclay, 1847), 18.

28. *The Female Land Pirate*, 20.

HENRY NASH SMITH

The Madness of Ahab

In the course of *Moby Dick*, Ishmael and other characters declare again and again that Ahab is insane. The Captain is said to be "crazy" or "mad" or "lunatic" or, most often, "monomaniac." On at least two occasions, Ahab calls himself "mad." Ahab's madness is of decisive importance because the voyage of the *Pequod* that provides a framework for the story originates in his quest for revenge on the White Whale, a quest that Starbuck, the first mate, tells Ahab to his face is not only "madness" but also "blasphemy." Ahab's violation of the moral and legal obligations imposed on him as captain brings about the sinking of the *Pequod* as well as his now death and the deaths of all the crew except Ishmael. Thus if we take into account only Ahab's observable behavior, he must be judged guilty of monstrous crimes. Yet Melville evidently considers him to be in many ways admirable, a "pageant creature, formed for noble tragedies." The combination of vast guilt with equally great virtues and capacities constituted, in Melville's eyes, tragic grandeur, as represented by the Prometheus of Aeschylus, or by Hamlet and Lear, or in lesser degree by Byron's Manfred and Cain. Hamlet and Lear were particularly significant models because Melville believed them to be insane.

The drastic reshaping of *Moby-Dick* that Melville undertook in the late summer of 1850, after he had believed the book to be far along toward completion, resulted from his decision to transform the character

From *The Critical Response to Herman Melville's* Moby-Dick, Kevin J. Hayes, ed., pp. 183–200. Originally published in *Yale Review* 66 (1976): 14–32. © 1976 by Henry Nash Smith.

of the Captain and to give him a major role in the story. The coarse, brutal commander who had figured in the early chapters of the first draft, resembling several skippers in Melville's earlier books, became the Ahab we know. In the process, the hint of arbitrariness and violence almost inevitably associated with such wielders of power in the microcosm of a ship at sea took on a portentous, even metaphysical, significance that Melville summed up by calling Ahab a madman.

The line of development in Melville's work culminating in Ahab is short. It first becomes clearly visible two years before the publication of *Moby-Dick*, in *Mardi* (1849). The narrator in the early part of this book is a young extrovert seaman not unlike Tommo in *Typee* or the anonymous narrator of *Omoo*. When Melville shifts from the straightforward account of a South Sea voyage to a search for a mysterious maiden called Yillah, the narrator is taken by the Mardians to be a demigod and is given the name of Taji. Then in the third and last section the search for Yillah is almost entirely superseded by a satirical travelogue, and Taji virtually disappears. Instead, more and more space is given to the observations and opinions of a "philosopher" named Babbalanja who in effect supplants Taji. The story is arranged to allow him to comment sardonically on universal human problems as well as on the men and manners of various countries that are allegorically represented by islands in the archipelago of Mardi. Babbalanja's consistently negative stance leads King Media to call him a "lunatic" and Babbalanja readily admits that he has been "crazy" from his birth because he is "possessed by a devil." The devil in fact is given a name: Azzageddi.

The character of Babbalanja warrants careful examination particularly because it throws light on Melville's conception of Ahab's madness. Babbalanja is a man of high intelligence who is nevertheless regarded by other characters as well as by himself as a madman or lunatic. His insanity is sometimes attributed to demonic possession. It finds expression in denunciations of injustices such as the abuse of the poor by the rich and powerful. Since Babbalanja reminded a contemporary reader of Teufelsdröckh in Carlyle's *Sartor Resartus*, it is appropriate to recall Teufelsdröckh's query: "what is Philosophy throughout but a continual battle against Custom; an ever-renewed effort to *transcend* the sphere of blind Custom, and so become Transcendental?" Generally speaking, however, in Melville's early books he treats the idea of insanity quite casually. For example, the narrator of *Mardi* refers to a rabidly jingoistic orator in "the grand council of Vivenza" as a "crazy man" and a "lunatic," and his speech is a "delirium." Even when Melville occasionally uses a technical vocabulary to refer to states of mind, he does so without emphasis. Yillah's confused account of her early life makes Taji fear she may be "some beautiful maniac." The term "monomania" occurs at least twice in *Mardi* in situations where insanity is not involved, just as, in Our Old Home, Hawthorne says of Delia Bacon, "Unquestionably, she was a monomaniac."

In Melville's next book, *Redburn* (also published in 1849), the spiritual alienation exemplified by Azzageddi is more fully developed in the character Jackson, whom Alan Lebowitz calls "a direct forerunner of Ahab." Jackson has "Ahab's overawing power and his strange, dictatorial magnetism." The first-person narrator says that Jackson "seemed to be full of hatred and gall against everything and everybody in the world; as if all the world was one person and had done him some dreadful harm, that was rankling and festering in his heart." The young and rather naive narrator adds: "Sometimes I thought he was really crazy." Despite the striking similarities, Ahab is of course much more complex than Jackson. The suggestion of madness, in particular, undergoes elaborate development in the later character. There are indications that in the interval Melville has become aware of the technical definition of monomania, for he makes use of this information in depicting Ahab's madness. The term, and with it the notion of a disease with specific symptoms, had become current only recently. Isaac Ray, the leading American authority on mental diseases in Melville's day, said in 1838 that it had been introduced by the noted French physician J. E. D. Esquirol; and this opinion is confirmed by the British psychiatrist James C. Prichard, who noted in 1835 that the term had appeared in English "within a few years." The *Oxford English Dictionary* places the first use of the word in 1823. It had gained currency quickly in England and America because of a controversy over the validity of the plea of "moral insanity," of which monomania was considered to be one type, as a defense in criminal prosecutions. Chief Justice Lemuel Shaw of the Supreme Judicial Court of Massachusetts (whose daughter would become Herman Melville's wife in 1847) stated in an opinion written in 1844 that in cases of monomania, "The conduct may be in many respects regular, the mind acute, and the conduct apparently governed by rules of propriety, and at the same time there may be insane delusion, by which the mind is perverted." In such cases, "the mind broods over *one idea* and cannot be reasoned out of it." Shaw was evidently trying to recognize a new model of the psyche (he held for the defendant) but he could not free himself from the traditional assumption that all insanity is a disturbance of cognition.[1]

The British common-law test of insanity was set forth in the McNaughton decision in 1843, which used as a criterion the individual's ability to distinguish right from wrong. The notion of "moral insanity" upset this principle by implying that man might be fully aware of the immorality of a possible course of actions, yet be unable to resist his impulse to follow it. Ray, for example, quotes the German psychiatrist Johann C. Hoffbauer to the effect that "The maniac may judge correctly of his actions without being in a condition to repress his passions, and to abstain from the acts of violence to which they impel him." Elsewhere Ray asserts that a sufferer from "partial moral mania," "while he retains the most perfect consciousness of the impropriety and even enormity of his conduct, ... deliberately and perseveringly pursues it." Amariah Brigham, director of the New York State Lunatic Asylum at Utica and editor of the *American Journal of Insanity*, made an astute observation in that journal in October 1844 concerning the attitude of the general public toward the novel idea of moral insanity:

> The disbelief in a kind of insanity that does not disturb the intellect, arises perhaps from the common phraseology, that the affections, passions, and moral qualities, have their seat in the *heart* and not in the *brain*, and therefore are not likely to be disordered by disease of the latter organ. But in fact the orderly manifestations of our moral faculties, our affections, and intellectual powers, are alike dependent on the healthy state of the brain. *The heart has nothing to do with either* [italics in original].

Ishmael (evidently serving as a mouthpiece for Melville) makes the point that Ahab is suffering from a disease of his moral powers, not his reason: "Now, in his heart, Ahab had some glimpse of this, namely: all my means are sane, my motive and my object mad. Yet without power to kill, or change, or shun the fact; he likewise knew that to mankind he did long dissemble; in some sort, did still. But that thing of his dissembling was only subject to his perceptibility, not to his will determinate."

For the plot of *Moby-Dick*, the significant feature of the conception of monomania was that Ahab, as a sufferer from the disease, could pursue an insane course of vengeance against the White Whale, yet present the appearance of sanity to the owners of the *Pequod* and retain his full capacity to command the vessel and dominate the crew. It was also necessary that, despite Ahab's madness, he should be capable of the impressive intellectual feat of determining where the whale would most probably reappear by analyzing ocean currents and records of previous sightings. Ray, summarizing his wide reading in British and Continental authorities, asserts that, in monomania, "the mind is not observed to have lost any of its original vigor, and its soundness on every other topic remains unimpaired"; indeed, "we are occasionally struck with the acuteness of the reasoning power displayed by monomaniacs." Perhaps, too, the doctrine that moral insanity exonerates one of guilt might render Ahab more acceptable as a tragic hero.

Evidently, then, Melville draws upon received scientific opinion in depicting Ahab's madness, and provides a recognized cause of monomania in the mutilation that he suffered in his first encounter with the White Whale: Ray says that mania may be caused by "external injuries" as well as by "moral shocks." Thus the writer establishes the plausibility of a plot that sends a crazy skipper with his crew across the oceans of the world in a hunt for a specific giant killer whale.

Chapter 41, "Moby Dick," where Ishmael makes his most prolonged effort to explain "What the white whale was to Ahab," contains a narrative account of the Captain's first encounter with Moby-Dick. Infuriated by what whalers generally regarded as this animal's "treacherous retreats," his practice of swimming away from his pursuers in apparent alarm, then turning suddenly to attack them, Ahab, "seizing the line-knife from his broken prow, had dashed at the whale, as an Arkansas duelist at his foe, blindly seeking with a six inch blade to reach the fathom-deep life of the whale." In retaliation the whale had "reaped away Ahab's leg." This mutilation, says Ishmael, was followed by "long months of days and weeks" of suffering that changed a mere "sudden, passionate, corporal animosity" into a "final monomania." Thereafter, "Ahab cherished a wild vindictiveness against the whale, all the more fell for that in his frantic morbidness he at last came to identify with him, not only all his bodily woes, but all his intellectual and spiritual exasperations."

We have then two stages in the development of Ahab's madness: a first stage, of indeterminate length, in which his exasperations accumulate and burst forth in the fury of his futile single-handed attack on the whale; and a second stage, following the mutilation, during which Ahab becomes insane. But because his madness is a "cunning and feline" monomania, he is able to conceal "the mad secret of his unabated rage" while he plans the "audacious, immitigable, and supernatural revenge" that is the hidden goal of the voyage of the *Pequod*. Having begun his analytic account of the changes going on inside Ahab's mind, Melville had the impulse to perform his task thoroughly. He does not, however, provide any details about the "intellectual and spiritual exasperations" which had accumulated in Ahab before his first encounter with Moby-Dick. This seems to me a weakness in the story. For if Ahab is to acquire the status and enact the role of tragic protagonist, he must elicit a degree of identification from the reader, and the identification depends heavily on the reader's being able to enter imaginatively into the protagonist's sufferings.

Melville magisterially begs this question. We are given no particulars concerning Ahab's exasperations beyond the following—a celebrated, powerful flight of rhetoric, but one that is singularly abstract:

The White Whale swam before him as the monomaniac incarnation of all those malicious agencies which some deep men feel eating in them, till they are left living on with a half a heart and half a lung. That intangible malignity which has been from the beginning; to whose dominion even the modern Christians ascribe one-half of the worlds; which the ancient Ophites of the east reverenced in their statue devil;—Ahab did not fall down and worship it like them; but deliriously transferring its idea to the abhorred white whale [sic], he pitted himself, all mutilated, against it. All that most maddens and torments; all that stirs up the lees of things; all truth with malice in it; all that cracks the sinews and cakes the brain; all the subtle demonisms of life and thought; all evil, to crazy Ahab, were visibly personified, and made practically assailable in Moby Dick. He piled upon the whale's white hump the sum of all the general rage and hate felt by his whole race from Adam down; and then, as if his chest had been a mortar, he burst his hot heart's shell upon it.

The passionate eloquence of this passage tends to distract the reader's attention from the fact that it is not anchored in time or place, or in any actual experience. The injury inflicted on Ahab by the whale brings into focus a pervasive hostility that was already present in Ahab. Indeed, the latter part of the passage implies that an elite of "deep men," since the time of Adam, has felt a "general rage and hate" directed toward "all the subtle demonisms of life and thought." But the reader is offered almost no novelistic specification concerning the process through which Ahab developed his share of this universal rage and hate. The items are meager: at his birth he was given the name of a wicked Old Testament king by a "crazy" mother who died soon after; and a shadowy Indian sorceress predicted he would justify the name. After he reached manhood he was injured in some fashion off Cape Horn. Finally, he became involved in an altercation "afore the altar in Santa," perhaps by spitting in a ritual vessel. But even if we knew more about these incidents, it is not clear they would throw more light on the origins of Ahab's hostility toward the universe.

I pursue the inquiry into the genesis of Ahab's madness because the question is so intimately and basically related to the larger question of what attitude Melville expects the reader to take toward this astonishing character. When I speak of begging the question, I mean that the author assumes the reader will share Ahab's assumption that malicious forces control the universe. Yet Melville at the same time drops many intimations that this assumption is the basis of Ahab's madness. Even here, however, a further ambiguity appears, for possibly Ahab's madness does not consist in conceiving of the universe as being controlled by forces hostile to man, but simply in imagining that these forces are embodied in, or adequately represented by, a single whale.

So far I have been discussing what might be called the referential or metaphysical aspects of Ahab's madness—its bearing in the outside world. Melville takes an equal or even greater interest in exploring the subjective or psychological aspect of it. In the chapter we have been noticing, Melville makes a strenuous effort to find metaphors adequate to depict the structure of Ahab's psyche. First, he draws an analogy between the Captain's monomania and the Hudson River. As Ahab gradually recovered physically from the loss of his leg, says Ishmael, his "full lunacy subsided not, but deepeningly contracted; like the unabated Hudson, when that noble Northman flows narrowly, but unfathomably through the Highland gorge. But, as in his narrow-flowing monomania, not one jot of Ahab's broad madness had been left behind; so in that broad madness, not one jot of his great natural intellect had perished. That before living agent, now became the living instrument." Realizing that his imagery is growing more and more involved, Melville nevertheless, with an apology, tries yet another analogy: "If such a furious trope may stand, his special lunacy stormed his general sanity, and carried it, and turned all its concentrated cannon upon its own mad mark; so that far from having lost his strength, Ahab, to that one end, did now possess a thousand fold more potency than ever he had sanely brought to bear on any one reasonable object."

It appears that before Ahab's condition stabilized itself as a monomania, he suffered from a "full lunacy" or "broad madness." Furthermore, we are to conceive of a "general sanity" preceding the condition of broad madness; and this broad madness had been (to adopt the technical vocabulary of the day) a moral insanity, involving no impairment of Ahab's "great natural intellect." But whereas originally the intellect had been the dominant "agent" in Ahab's psyche, the intellect became the instrument or tool of the madness, and continued to be merely the instrument or tool of the monomania when Ahab's "special lunacy stormed his general sanity."

This explanation is so complicated as to be all but unintelligible. Even if we recognize that Melville is using "agent" in an etymological sense which has been lost in the twentieth-century usage, to mean the power in command, the executive (whereas we customarily use "agent" as a synonym for Melville's "instrument"), the metaphors become so twisted and involved that they convey little or no meaning. The same can be said of a later passage in which once again Melville tries to present a detailed description of the structure and functioning of Ahab's psyche through the use of an apparatus of hypostatized faculties in the manner of early nineteenth-century academic psychological theory. Because the passage is central to the present inquiry, I shall quote it entire:

> Often, when forced from his hammock by exhausting and intolerably vivid dreams of the night, which, resuming his own intense thoughts through the day, carried them on amid a clashing of phrensies, and whirled them round and round in his blazing brain, till the very throbbing of his life-spot became insufferable anguish; and when, as was sometimes the case, these spiritual throes in him heaved his being up from its base, and a chasm seemed opening in him, from which forked flames and lightnings shot up, and accursed fiends beckoned him to leap down among them; when this hell in himself yawned beneath him, a wild cry would be heard through the ship; and with glaring eyes Ahab would burst from his state room, as though escaping from a bed that was on fire. Yet these, perhaps, instead of being the unsuppressible symptoms of some latent weakness, or fright at his own resolve, were but the plainest tokens of its intensity. For, at such times, crazy Ahab, the scheming, unappeasedly steadfast hunter of the white whale; this Ahab that had gone to his hammock, was not the agent that so caused him to burst from it in horror again. The latter was the eternal, living principle or soul in him; and in sleep, being for the time dissociated from the characterizing mind, which at other times employed it for its outer vehicle or agent, it spontaneously sought escape from the scorching contiguity of the frantic thing, of which, for the time, it was no longer an integral. But as the mind does not exist unless leagued with the soul, therefore it must have been that, in Ahab's case, yielding up all his thoughts and fancies to his one supreme purpose; that purpose, by its own sheer inveteracy of will, forced itself against gods and devils into a kind of self-assumed, independent being of its own. Nay, could grimly live and bum, while the common vitality to which it was conjoined, fled honor-stricken from the unbidden and unfathered birth. Therefore, the tormented spirit that glared out of bodily eyes, when what seemed Ahab rushed from his room, was for the time but a vacated thing, a formless somnambulistic being, a ray of living light, to be sure, but without an object to color, and therefore a blankness in itself. God help thee, old man, thy thoughts have created a creature in thee; and he whose intense thinking thus makes him a Prometheus; a

vulture feeds upon that heart for ever; that vulture the very creature he creates.

This passage, not surprisingly, has given difficulty to commentators.
The most determined efforts to interpret it with which I am familiar are
those of Paul Brodtkorb and Robert Zoellner, neither of whom seems to me
to discover a usable meaning in Melville's tormented prose. Mr. Brodtkorb
observes accurately (*Ishmael's White World: A Phenomenological Reading of
Moby Dick*): "The passage is full of complex abstractions, qualifications,
extensions, synonyms with subtle distinctions implied between them,
and second thoughts.... there are loose ends to the precision of Ishmael's
analysis; he makes too many abstract synonyms." In order to account for
the discrepancies between Ishmael's generalizations about Ahab and the
character's actual behavior, Mr. Zoellner (*The Salt-Sea Mastodon: A Reading
of Moby Dick*) postulates a "psychic paradigm" in which a "preliterary" or
"pretextual Ahab" is modified by the events of the plot. But this seems a
desperate measure somewhat like the "Cycle and epicycle, orb in orb" of
predecessors of Copernicus. I think the upshot of the matter is that Melville
found he could not construct a satisfactory model of Ahab's mind by using
an apparatus of faculties, even with the addition of uncanonical faculties such
as "life-spot" or "living principle" or "common vitality." Paradoxically, this
failure reveals the subtlety of his psychological insight and his responsibility
to observed fact: he is superior to the professionals of his day in recognizing
(even though inarticulately) that the psyche is not a structure of faculties and
cannot be imagined as functioning mechanically, no matter how complex the
mechanism is taken to be.

The other frontal attack on the problem of Ahab's psyche is the "halls
of Thermes" passage in the pivotal Chapter 41. Here Melville undertakes
to describe "Ahab's larger, darker, deeper part" by analogizing it to the
half-buried Roman baths beneath the Hôtel de Cluny in Paris. To descend
into these subterranean chambers is to venture "far beneath the fantastic
towers of man's upper earth," where Ahab's "root of grandeur, his whole
awful essence sits in bearded state; an antique buried beneath antiquities,
and throned on torsoes! So with a broken throne, the great gods mock that
captive king; so like a Caryatid, he patient sits, upholding on his frozen
brow the piled entablatures of ages. Wind ye down there, ye prouder, sadder
souls! question that proud, sad king! A family likeness! aye, he did beget ye,
ye young exiled royalties; and from your grim sire only will the old State-
secret come." Although no reader can fail to be dazzled by the gorgeous
imagery and moved by the powerful emotion in this passage, it resembles the
description of Ahab's nightmares in being almost impervious to the kind of

attention we ordinarily bring to novelistic prose. It is a lyric poem rather than a contribution to characterization. The underground cavity is a metaphor for Ahab's psyche below the level of consciousness, but at the same time the seated statue (a "captive king") is an emblem of Ahab as he appears to others. By implication he has suffered some immense injustice; like Prometheus, he is being punished by the gods, although his acts of rebellion are nameless. Yet this archetypally aggressive son is at the same time a father; he possesses a secret of universal importance that he can conceivably transmit to the royal sons—like him, exiled—whom he has begotten. There is no indication, however, what that secret is. At most, the reader understands that it is not the delusion of a madman, but the wisdom of a sage.

The upshot of my inquiry is that Ahab's madness proves to be beyond the reach both of the conventional terminology of faculties and the audacious metaphor of the. buried statue. But Melville's inventiveness and inexhaustible energy offered him several others lines of approach. One of these was the chasm opening within Ahab "from which forked flames and lightnings shot up, and accursed fiends beckoned him to leap down among them." The flames of hell and the accursed fiends have their source in a tradition of demonology in popular culture reaching back to medieval Christian folklore, as exemplified for example in the paintings of Hieronymous Bosch, and kept alive in Gothic fiction. Closely related to such material, although not explicitly involving demonic possession, are Ahab's ranting speech when the corposants appear at mastheads and yardarms during the storm, and his ceremony of magnetizing a fresh needle when atmospheric electricity reverses the poles of the compass. The twentieth-century reader is likely to assume that at these moments Ahab is play-acting, like Mark Twain's Connecticut Yankee staging "miracles" to impress a naive audience. But this assumption is called in question by Ishmael's—and apparently Melville's— attitude toward Fedallah and the oriental boatmen whom Ahab conceals below decks (presumably to avoid arousing the resistance of the crew to his project of revenge). Ahab reveals the boat-crew only with the first lowering against the White Whale. On this occasion, says Ishmael, "what it was that inscrutable Ahab said to that tiger-yellow crew of his—these were words best omitted here, for you live under the blessed light of the evangelical land. Only the infidel sharks in the audacious seas may give ear to such words, when, with tornado brow, and eyes of red murder, and foam-glued lips, Ahab leaped after his prey." Fedallah is in some sense supernatural, a devil haunting and exercising control over him. Yet one of the most amusing touches of humor in this grim book is Stubb's sardonic joking to his boat crew about the "five more hands come to help us—never mind from where— the more the merrier." Melville seems only half-serious in his use of these

Gothic paraphernalia; and not even his most devoted admirers are inclined to defend it nowadays.

Along with the ancient linkage in popular culture between madness and demonology, Melville was aware of a conception of madness transmitted as a part of high culture that regarded it as supernatural but benign rather than malevolent. The learning and scholarly ingenuity that have been brought to bear on *Moby-Dick* have shown that the most important single component of Ahab's character is the Romantic notion of genius. Throughout history the madman had been classed among the wretched of the earth. When he could not be cared for by his relatives, he had been allowed to wander about begging, or had been locked up in the same prison with paupers and criminals. But even in his rags and his misery, the lunatic had been viewed with a touch of superstitious awe, and this hint of mystery in the unreason of madness was caught up and developed in the Romantic notion of a small company of supremely gifted geniuses whose abilities and accomplishments could not be accounted for within the intellectual horizon of ordinary humanity.

Goethe, recalling Socrates' *daimon*, had explained the superior powers of these extraordinary mortals by saying they possessed a demonic element, capable of evil as well as good because it operated without regard to commonplace criteria of right and wrong, yet responsible for all the supreme achievements of the race. The relation between genius and madness is elaborated further in Carlyle, whose, half-grotesque hero Teufelsdröckh writes:

> Witchcraft, and all manner of Spectre-work, and Demonology, we have now named Madness and Diseases of the Nerves. Seldom reflecting that still the new question comes upon us: What is Madness, what are Nerves? Ever, as before, does Madness remain a mysterious-terrific, altogether *infernal* boiling up of the Nether Chaotic Deep, through this fair-painted Vision of Creation, which swims thereon, which we name the Real. Was Luther's Picture of the Devil less a Reality, whether it were formed within the bodily eye, or without it? In every the wisest Soul lies a whole world of internal Madness, an authentic Demon-Empire; out of which, indeed, his world of Wisdom has been creatively built together, and now rests there, as on its dark foundations does a habitable flowery Earth-rind.

Melville was particularly impressed by the suggestion that true wisdom must be rooted in "a whole world of internal Madness, an authentic Demon-

Empire." In this regard Ahab conforms to a familiar Romantic pattern. Both his insanity and his extraordinary powers on intellect are mentioned by Ishmael even before Ahab appears. Among the "fighting Quakers" of Nantucket, we are told, arise from time to time men who gain "from the audacious, daring, and boundless adventure" of their careers in the whale fishery "a thousand bold dashes of character, not unworthy a Scandinavian sea-king, or a poetical Pagan Roman."

> And when these things unite in a man of greatly superior natural force, with a globular brain and a ponderous heart; who has also by the stillness and seclusion of many long night-watches in the remotest waters, and beneath constellations never seen here at the north, been led to think untraditionally and independently; receiving all nature's sweet or savage impressions fresh from her own virgin, voluntary, and confiding breast, and thereby chiefly, but with some help from accidental advantages, to team a bold and nervous lofty language—that man makes one in a whole nation's census—a mighty pageant creature, formed for noble tragedies.

In mid-nineteenth-century America such a claim of direct access to nature amounted to a virtually carte-blanche endorsement of the character. Equally important, however, is the "half wilful over-ruling morbidness at the bottom of [Ahab's] nature." For, Ishmael adds, "all men tragically great are made so through a certain morbidness. Be sure of this, O young ambition, all mortal greatness is but disease." "Morbid" is Coleridge's term for Hamlet, and Melville's conception of Ahab owes a debt to Shakespeare. It is important to notice that Ahab's madness is not an unfortunate accident that has befallen a potentially great man, but an essential element in his greatness, the element that makes it tragic.

The disease of greatness invariably involves suffering. When Ahab first shows himself on deck, he stands before the crew "with a crucifixion in his face; in all the nameless regal overbearing dignity of some mighty woe." Melville's consistent linkage of Ahab's insanity with suffering is one of the most convincing indications of his superior insight into abnormal states of mind. He may have learned something from the tendency of professional psychological theory in his day to broaden the definition of insanity to include "moral" (that is, emotional) processes as well as cognition. But his conception of the nobility of suffering derives rather from literary tradition, from the conception of tragedy—which (as the reference to the crucifixion reminds us) is inseparable in our culture from Christian theology. Ahab's suffering confers status on him. It earns forgiveness for his otherwise intolerable arrogance.

It has been ably argued that in the two successive chapters, "Moby Dick" and "The Whiteness of the Whale," Ishmael intends to distinguish his own attitude (which is taken to be sane) from Ahab's (which is monomaniacal) on the basis of Ahab's dogmatic certainty that the Whale is indeed the agent of invisible forces embodying all the evil in the universe, whereas Ishmael believes that the reality behind the presented surface of the world is simply a blank, "the colorless, all-color of atheism." Is Ahab's vision of cosmic evil in the whale an insane projection, but Ishmael's agnostic view sane? We must not forget Melville's often-quoted declaration to Hawthorne: "I have written a wicked book, and feel spotless as a lamb." Much of the power of the novel is generated by the fact that Melville was of two minds while he was writing it—that he did, like Ishmael, have a strong impulse to identify himself with Ahab, and only by a relatively narrow margin was able to reestablish his control over his materials and achieve something like a catharsis at the end in the description of Ahab's death. Even so, Ishmael, the force of health and moderation, is a shadowy figure beside Ahab. The first-person narrator disappears for long sequences in the course of the book, and has little tangible experience to offer in support of his essentially ideological declaration in "A Squeeze of the Hand": "For now.... by many prolonged repeated experiences, I have perceived that in all cases man must eventually lower, or at least shift, his conceit of attainable felicity; nor placing it anywhere in the intellect or the fancy; but in the wife, the heart, the bed, the table, the saddle, the fireside, the country." The lower intensity of this insight, in comparison with some of the moments of tragic recognition elsewhere in the book, is well signaled by the charming frivolity of the remainder of the paragraph: "now that I have perceived all this, I am ready to squeeze case eternally. In visions of the night, I saw long rows of angels in paradise, each with his hands in a jar of spermaceti."

Although the plot of *Moby-Dick* establishes a precarious balance between the attitudes of the two protagonists, it is difficult to avoid viewing Ahab as the embodiment of significant unconscious drives (in Henry A. Murray's words, "the culturally repressed dispositions of human nature") and Ishmael as the embodiment of a conscious rationality that is considerably less powerful. The impulses represented in Ahab are accorded much more space and are portrayed much more vividly. We can readily accept Melville's declaration to Hawthorne that the true motto of the book is Ahab's blasphemous, Gothic invocation at the tempering of his specially forged harpoon in the blood of the three harpooners: "Ego non baptizo te in nomine patris, sed in nomine diaboli!" Charles Olson, who discovered these words in Melville's handwriting on a flyleaf of the volume of his set of Shakespeare containing *Lear*, *Othello*, and *Hamlet*, reports (in *Call Me Ishmael*) that the next words in the note are, "madness is undefinable—It & right reason extremes of one—not the (black art) Goetic but Theurgic magic—seeks converse with the Intelligence, Power, the Angel."

Melville's statement to Hawthorne implies a temporary identification with Ahab and a conscious acceptance of Ahab's madness as a kind of demonic possession. But the jotting on the flyleaf reinterprets the diabolic aspect of that madness as somehow related to angelic inspiration. Olson interprets the note as follows: "I take 'it' to refer to the 'madness' of the previous sentence. 'Right reason,' less familiar to the 20th century, meant more to the last, for in the Kant-Coleridge terminology 'right reason' described the highest range of the intelligence and stood in contrast to 'understanding.'" I am dubious about the allusion to Emerson's faculties of Understanding and Reason. Melville was ordinarily impatient with this kind of technical philosophizing; furthermore, "right reason" is, if not foreign to the Romantic vocabulary, at least rare in it: the Emersonian phrase was usually "the higher Reason" or simply "Reason." Yet I think Olson's interpretation points in the right direction. He has to fill in by hypothesis a considerable hiatus in logic but Melville's meaning does indeed come out something like this: Ahab's madness leads him to extremes of language and apparent paradoxes, such as invoking the Devil in a travesty of the baptismal service. Yet this is not so depraved as it might seem; it represents primarily a repudiation of the sterile, routine correctness of established formulas and decorums. Melville's invocation of the Devil is perhaps to be taken in the sense of Emerson's "Self-Reliance":

> On my saying, "What have I to do with the sacredness of traditions, if I live wholly from within?" my friend suggested,—"But these impulses may be from below, not from above." I replied, "They do not seem to me to be such; but if I am the Devil's child, I will live then from the Devil." No law can be sacred to me but that of my nature. Good and bad are but names very readily transferable to that or this; the only right is what is after my constitution; the only wrong what is against it.

In this sense, Ahab's madness can properly be called a mode of transcendence. Henry A. Murray is correct when he asserts that "Melville's target in *Moby-Dick* was the upper-middle-class culture of his time." More fully, Ahab's enemy, and Melville's, was "the dominant ideology, that peculiar compound of puritanism and materialism, of shallow blatant optimism and technology, which proved so crushing to creative evolutions in religion, art, and life."

This flat statement is no doubt an oversimplification, if only because it leaves out of account the extraordinary shifts in narrative perspective that result from Melville's use of two protagonists, and the audacious changes from first-person narration to an overtly dramatic form, or again to an omniscient point of view that allows the narrative voice full entry into the mind of any character. To take Melville's identification with Ahab as an axiom, ignoring the significant limitations imposed on it by the presence of Ishmael, is in effect to rewrite the book. Nevertheless, Murray is in my opinion more nearly right than wrong. Furthermore, the author of *Moby-Dick* exhibits more than a trace of the conception of madness which attained wide currency a few years ago in what we used to call the counterculture: the conception, that is, of the British psychiatrist R. D. Laing, who maintains that the madman (specifically, the schizophrenic) can often be, "even through his profound wretchedness and disintegration, the hierophant of the sacred." More than once Melville's depiction of Ahab's monomania seems to be implying propositions that Laing states as follows: "Madness need not be all breakdown. It may also be breakthrough. It is potentially liberation and renewal as well as enslavement and existential death."

Maintaining, as Ishmael does (with Melville's evident approval), that "man's insanity is heaven's sense," comes close to Laing's contention that

> Our civilization represses not only "the instincts," not only sexuality, but any form of transcendence. Among one-dimensional men, it is not surprising that someone with an insistent experience of other dimensions, that he cannot entirely deny or forget, will run the risk of being destroyed by the others, or of betraying what he knows.
>
> In the context of our present pervasive madness that we call normality, sanity, freedom, all our frames of reference are ambiguous and equivocal.

In this larger frame of reference, the difference between Ishmael's and Ahab's metaphysical positions seems a matter of degree only. The more detached Ishmael believes that in concentrating his hostility upon a single creature, even though that creature be the White Whale, Ahab has narrowed his field of vision unduly, and at the same time has introduced a manichean distortion into the limited part of the cosmic horizon that he does perceive. Ishmael is aware of a majesty and a terrible beauty in Moby-Dick to which Ahab seems wilfully blind. Yet both these protagonists are alter egos of the author, they are both committed to an underlying structure of assumptions and values that Melville shares. It is only a slight oversimplification to say that these shared assumptions and attitudes are given condensed expression in the mysterious "six-inch chapter" (ch. 23, "The Lee Shore") which has rightly been recognized by Brodtkorb as a capsule statement of the theme of the novel. The chapter is devoted to the character Bulkington, who serves briefly as steersman of the *Pequod* when the ship sets sail on Christmas night. Melville evidently feels a strong emotional attachment to an actual person whom he introduces in this puzzling fashion. Bulkington has just returned from a four-year voyage, and for reasons that are never explained has immediately shipped again. His choice is made to seem portentous: Ishmael says that in refusing to stay ashore, but instead setting forth once again to challenge the boundless ocean, Bulkington illustrates "that mortally intolerable truth; that all deep, earnest independence of her sea; while the wildest winds of heaven and earth conspire to cast her on the treacherous, slavish shore." But "in landlessness alone resides the highest truth, shoreless, indefinite as God."

Ahab's madness is his rejection of the slavish shore of order and sanity; it is his mode of transcending the mediocrity of a culture that lacks all distinction, and worse still, is basically hypocritical. But Melville's great book is defective, in my opinion, to the extent that the truth to which Ahab maintains his loyalty is never adequately set forth. In the absence of more specific evidence about the bases for Ahab's attitude of rebellion against the universe at large, his pursuit of the White Whale runs the danger of seeming to be merely an effort at revenge for a specific injury. I put the case bluntly in order to call attention to a difficulty of interpretation that is often overlooked. The difficulty can be stated as a question concerning the nature of Ahab's madness. Is it a textbook case of monomania, brought on by the trauma of physical mutilation? Or an instance of demonic possession? Or a mystical experience in which Ahab gains transcendent wisdom at the cost of suffering and death?

NOTE

1. The last sentence of this paragraph was inadvertently omitted in the *Yale Review*. I found it in an erratum slip tipped into an offprint inscribed by Henry Nash Smith.—Ed.

CAROLYN PORTER

Call Me Ishmael, or
How to Make Double-Talk Speak

1

The voice that begins *Moby-Dick* by announcing "Call me Ishmael" directs our attention immediately to a narrative perspective identified by its cultural dislocation, its displaced stance in a region somewhere beyond the borders of both the normal and the normative. By actively choosing the name of an outcast, Ishmael emphasizes his exiled stance. He proceeds to confirm if not his abnormality, at least his eccentricity, when he explains why he went to sea by adducing a series of reasons that culminate in the claim that going to sea is his way of avoiding suicide, his "substitute for pistol and ball." Yet he ends the opening paragraph by insisting that "if they but knew it, almost all men ... cherish very nearly the same feelings toward the ocean with me" (Chap. 1). If Ishmael is fast an exile whose very name invokes the boundary between outcast and society, by the end of the paragraph he has crossed that boundary to speak in the name of "all men." By shifting from eccentricity to normality, Ishmael establishes in embryo a pattern to be repeated and developed in the chapter as a whole, where boundaries are invoked in order to be crossed and finally blurred. First, and most notable, is the boundary between land and sea.

Ishmael begins by emphasizing the line dividing sea from land, focusing our attention on the "insular city of the Manhattoes ... belted round

From *New Essays on* Moby-Dick, Richard H. Brodhead, ed., pp. 73–108. © 1986 by Cambridge University Press

133

with wharves as Indian isles by coral reefs" and surrounded by "commerce," so that we have before us an image of Manhattan as not only bounded but forcibly "belted" in. To the water's edge have come "crowds of water-gazers" whom Ishmael describes as "leaning against the spiles" and "looking over the bulwarks," as if "striving to get a still better seaward peep." These "landsmen" seem to have poured down the "streets" that "take you waterward" in order to "get just as nigh the water as they possibly can without falling in."

The imagery of magnetism Ishmael uses to portray these water-gazing landsmen suggests that were they not "pent up in lath and plaster—tied to counters, nailed to benches, clinched to desks," the "magnetic" force exerted by the "compasses of all those ships" would compel them to emulate Ishmael in his decision to "sail about a little and see the watery part of the world." As Ishmael proceeds to multiply examples of the universal appeal of water, he not only calls forth the reader's assent to the claim that all men cherish a feeling for the ocean, but more importantly, he makes that feeling seem fundamental to human nature itself. In the interest of explaining his own desire to sail the seas as representative rather than exceptional, he has already begun to substitute sea for land as the locale of man's ontological condition, and thus to move us toward the position finally symbolized by Bulkington.

Appearing for the second and last time in "The Lee Shore," the chapter that marks the moment at which the *Pequod* leaves the shore, the figure of Bulkington not only provides Ishmael with an emblem of man's essential landlessness but also serves as a signal that we have already accompanied Ishmael across the boundary between land and sea. From this vantage point, it is no longer the sea that is dangerous. The land that once seemed our home, the scene of "safety, comfort, hearthstone, supper, warm blankets, friends," is now revealed as both "treacherous" and "slavish" when seen from across the *Pequod*'s prow (Chap. 23). But by now it is clear that to cross the boundary between land and sea amounts to more than a simple shift of perspective. The normal attributes of land and sea have been inverted, so that, once at sea, we are compelled to regard the land as inaccessible and our desire to return within its comforting limits as not only dangerous but suspect. For though "mortally intolerable," the conclusion to which Bulkington testifies is that "in landlessness alone resides the highest truth, shoreless, indefinite as God."

The rhetorical strategy used in Chapter 1 is designed, then, to loosen our attachment to the ground beneath our feet, so as to situate us eventually in Bulkington's position. As we will eventually learn, to embrace landlessness in these terms is to trade certainty for doubt and thus to find ourselves, like Ishmael, compelled not only to wander but to wonder. Crossing the border dividing sea from land ultimately threatens to blur all the categories of difference that order our apprehension of the world, bleaching it to a sinister and maddening whiteness. Ishmael's distinctive pattern of boundary crossing; then, operates to a purpose, a point that grows clearer as we observe his next rhetorical maneuver in Chapter 1.

Having invoked and then blurred the line between land and sea, Ishmael proceeds to subject the class divisions between passenger and mariner, officer and sailor, to similar treatment. Ostensibly, Ishmael wishes to specify the terms on which he sailed, and so to specify further his identity: "I do not mean to have it inferred," he begins, "that I ever go to sea as a passenger." Passengers are first distinguished from sailors by having a "purse," and a "purse is but a rag," Ishmael remarks, "unless you have something in it." In short, Ishmael's purse is empty. Yet this fact in itself eventually reveals a second reason for his shipping as a sailor rather than as a passenger: They pay sailors, "whereas they never pay passengers a single penny." Noting that "there is all the difference in the world between paying and being paid," Ishmael celebrates the joys of being paid in contrast to the pain of paying, "perhaps the most uncomfortable affliction that the two orchard thieves entailed upon us" (Chap. 1).

Since this discussion is divided into two parts and separated by Ishmael's related treatment of officers, the logical necessity at its heart is partially obscured; if someone is paying, someone else is being paid. To pay is to empty one's pockets and become the man in need of pay, whereas to *be* paid is to fill one's pockets and so be ready to pay again. Although there is a "difference ... between paying and being paid," then, the line marking that difference begins to blur when the deed of paying and being paid actually takes place. When the roles of payer and payee are acted out, in other words, the actors can be seen constantly changing places with one another, a point of some consequence when, as here, these roles are designated by the class-defined terms of passenger and common sailor. In crossing the line rhetorically; Ishmael undermines its social force.

Initially embarrassed by poverty, Ishmael disclaims any desire to be a passenger; "passengers get sea-sick—grow quarrelsome—don't sleep of nights," he insists, as if his lack of money were a minor issue in his decision, an issue best treated in the abstract. But the very articulation of the abstract difference between paying and being paid serves rhetorically as the hinge by which Ishmael swings from the position of the man whose pockets have been emptied in the painful act of paying to that of the man happily anticipating being paid. He ends by imagining himself engaged in the "urbane activity" of receiving money, speaking now in the tones of the gentleman passenger when he ironically alludes to his Christian faith by noting how "marvellous" it is that we are so pleased to receive money when "we so earnestly believe money to be the root of all earthly ills."

Sandwiched within this discussion of passengers versus sailors, with its implicit subversion of class differences, is a treatment of sailors versus officers in which that subversion is made explicit. Here again, the pattern is repeated. The line dividing "a Commodore, or a Captain, or a Cook" from a "simple sailor" is drawn and then blurred. Indeed, Ishmael is already blurring it when he includes cooks in the same category with captains and commodores, since the cook we will soon meet on the *Pequod*, like many we might have met in the merchant service of the day, is a black. Abjuring as he does "all honorable respectable toils" carrying "glory and distinction," Ishmael confesses to a slight temptation when it comes to the "considerable glory" of being a cook. Yet it turns out that it is not the cook, but the cooked that attracts Ishmael, and so he displaces the honor due the "respectable toils" of the former onto the tastiness of the latter. "Once broiled, judiciously buttered, and judgmatically salted and peppered," he remarks, "there is no one who will speak more respectfully, not to say reverentially, of a broiled fowl than I will." Unless, he implies, it be the "old Egyptians" whose "idolatrous dotings ... upon broiled ibis" resulted in "their huge bake-houses the pyramids." The reverential language of honor attached to captain and commodore is first undermined by its transference to cooks and then exploded by its application to broiled fowl as the object of idolatry.

It remains for Ishmael to face squarely the socially degraded status of the common sailor. After a bravado gesture worthy of Whitman, presenting himself as the sailor "right before the mast, plumb down into the forecastle, aloft there to the royal masthead," Ishmael admits that no matter how far and wide he may move, he moves at the dictates of others. "They rather order me about some," he acknowledges, but when he adds that they "make me jump from spar to spar, like a grasshopper in a May meadow," his simile evokes an image of springtime freedom already undermining the force of the point it illustrates. Ishmael then marks the line between sailor and officer in terms that give it both personal and social resonance when he notes that such treatment "touches one's sense of honor, particularly if you come of an old established family in the land, the Van Rensselaers, or Randolphs, or Hardicanutes." In itself, the implication that Ishmael comes from such a family begins to destabilize the very social division he is acknowledging, for if a common sailor can be the son of a gentleman, class lines are already blurred. Further, the juxtaposition of the Van Rensselaers and the Randolphs with the Hardicanutes, whose demise has long since been accomplished, obviously serves to relativize and so undercut the force of the "old established family" as a social category.

But finally, in order to blur the line between officer and sailor effectively, Ishmael must address the core issue of authority, of who gives and who takes, orders. Noting that his "transition ... from a schoolmaster to a sailor" has been a "keen one," Ishmael appeals to the authority of the New Testament and the viewpoint of the "archangel Gabriel," in whose eyes all men are spiritual equals. From this perspective, "who aint a slave?" Ishmael asks, and goes on to insist that "however much they may thump and punch" him, the "universal thump is passed round" in a circuit that includes "everybody." As in the case of paying and being paid, the roles of thumping and being thumped are passed around, and so the distinction loses its significance, if not from a "physical" at least from a "metaphysical point of view."

Although the class line between captain and sailor has been seriously questioned and its force partially suspended, it is important to notice that it has by no means disappeared. Such boundary lines, whether between land and sea or between gentleman and sailor, are crucial to Ishmael's discourse. They must be there if they are to be crossed and blurred, whether by appeals to the New Testament's teaching on spiritual equality and the evils of money, or by the burlesque on flatulence with which Ishmael concludes his commentary on the commodore, who "gets his atmosphere at second hand from the sailors on the forecastle."

Ishmael rounds out the chapter by invoking and then blurring the line to which he will return in "The Mat-Maker," that between fate and free will. From the start, Ishmael has accounted for his decision to ship as a common sailor in terms that presuppose that it was a decision. Indeed, the entire chapter up to this point derives much of its ironic force from the disparity between Ishmael's tone of reasoned judgment and the personal exigencies clearly behind his alleged choices. But faced with the need to explain his choice of a whaler as his berth, Ishmael falls back on Fate and the "grand programme of Providence." He now insists that Fate dictated his choice, all the while cajoling him into the delusion that it was a "choice" made by an "unbiased freewill and discriminating judgment." But at the same time, he turns Fate itself into a joke. He takes the "programme of Providence" literally, excerpting it when he lists "whaling voyage by one Ishmael" as an event in small print squeezed in between "Grand Contested Election for the Presidency of the United States" and "Bloody Battle in Afghanistan." He humbly admits his inability to explain why "those stage managers, the Fates," gave him "this shabby part of a whaling voyage," whereas others were accorded roles in "high tragedies" or "genteel comedies" or "farces," leaving to our judgment which genre fits events such as the "grand contested election for the presidency."

In closing the chapter, Ishmael returns to the point where he began, the magnetic attraction of water, now objectifying it in the "overwhelming idea of the great whale himself." Swayed by the attractive force of the "mysterious monster" and the "wild and distant seas where he rolled his island bulk," Ishmael returns across the boundary between normality and eccentricity as he admits that "with other men, perhaps, such things would not have been inducements." But he can now afford to acknowledge that his "itch for things remote" may be idiosyncratic because he has now established a narrative voice that commands some authority over its own territory—a no-man's-land, a marginal space between the known and the unknown. By transgressing boundaries, by subverting the force of fixed oppositions, Ishmael has established a voice that can now move back and forth across them with head-spinning speed: "Not ignoring what is good, I am quick to perceive a horror, and could still be social with it—would they let me." The lines dividing good from evil, familiar from alien, individual freedom from coercive force, are crossed in swift succession, in a passage that itself carries us from the rebellious freedom of sailing "forbidden seas" and landing on "barbarous coasts" to the image of the world as a prison where "it is well to be on friendly terns with all the inmates" (Chap. 1).

2

A narrator who persistently blurs the very distinctions to which he appeals in introducing himself and his story speaks from a peculiar position, one likely to make extraordinary demands upon us as readers, forced as we are into a dizzying effort to keep up with a voice we justifiably suspect is bent upon carrying us away—away from our moorings among familiar assumptions and out to a sea where all assumptions are in doubt. But our troubles are as nothing compared to Melville's. To understand how Ishmael's voice is empowered, his unique perspective authorized, is to appreciate both the problems Melville faced and the skill with which he solved them.

Where, to begin with, do you ground the perspective of a narrator who resembles those "judicious, unincumbered travellers in Europe" who "cross the frontiers into Eternity with nothing but a carpet-bag,—that is to say, the Ego?" So, in a famous letter to Hawthorne, Melville characterized those men who had the courage to say "No! in thunder" to the age's smug beliefs.[1] To praise such a man, however, is one thing; to give him a voice and a place to stand is another.

We have already begun to see how Melville met this problem in *Moby-Dick*. As Ishmael crosses and blurs the boundary dividing sea and land, his voice takes up residence *at* the boundary, occupying the marginal space between the familiar and the unknown that he creates and expands by traversing it, over and over again. In other words, Melville turns the boundary itself into the locus of Ishmael's narrative voice.

Yet such a voice remains necessarily unstable, since it is always undermining the very boundaries from which it speaks. Such instability, indeed, becomes part and parcel of Ishmael's identity as narrator. He is, for example, notorious for reporting soliloquies he cannot pretend to have witnessed, and indeed, for disappearing entirely on occasion. Further, he shows only the most sporadic respect for the ordinary conventions of narrative, such as plot or character development. Yet there is a rhetorical method in his narrative madness, one we can appreciate more fully by broadening our focus from the opening chapter to the opening movement of *Moby-Dick*, Chapters 1 through 23, which take us from Ishmael's self-introduction to the moment marked by "The Lee Shore," the moment when the *Pequod* plunges "like fate into the lone Atlantic" (Chap. 23).

These twenty-three chapters depict Ishmael's own "waterward" course to Nantucket, and his preparations for setting sail—preparations both "physical" and "metaphysical." These chapters also serve to prepare *us* as readers for setting sail by establishing both the commercial (physical) and the religious (metaphysical) implications of the voyage to come. Yet it is Ishmael's meeting with Queequeg and their developing friendship that provides the novel's opening movement with its narrative center. Not only are nine of the twenty-three chapters centrally concerned with Queequeg, but once he appears in Chapter 3, we never lose sight of him completely, even in Father Mapple's chapel.

Queequeg's prominence is the more striking in view of the fact that he will play a far smaller role in the story to come than we are led to expect here. So marked is the disparity between his introduction in the novel's opening section and his diminished role in the rest of the tale that it has served as evidence for the theory of the "two *Moby-Dicks*."[2] Yet whatever its compositional history, the misleading prominence of Queequeg in these chapters as they stand in the finished text can best be accounted for by understanding his role as essentially played out by the time he and Ishmael set sail—the role of initiating Ishmael into the tribe of the whalemen, those "renegades and castaways" of all colors and cultures who make up an "Anacharsis Clootz deputation" representing a global citizenry of marginal men, or what Ishmael calls "Isolatoes" (Chaps. 26–27). Queequeg's presence continues to be felt, to be sure, but largely as a result of the bond formed in these chapters, a bond so deep that Queequeg becomes virtually a double, a shadow self for Ishmael. That bond must be secured at the outset if Ishmael is to assume full membership in the company of whalemen. In short, as he becomes "social" with the particular "horror" that is Queequeg, Ishmael's unstable narrative identity is provided with a social dimension.

In becoming Queequeg's "bosom friend," Ishmael is subjected to a cultural identity crisis from which he emerges with the social identity required to support the narrative perspective we have begun to observe in action. Ishmael's encounter with Queequeg—his initial fear, his weakening defenses, both "melting" into a profound love and admiration for the cannibal—is less an extended episode in a story than a passage through a "liminal" state in which the boundaries between civilized and savage, Christian and cannibal, are simultaneously crossed and blurred.[3] But Ishmael's ritual initiation deviates markedly from the pattern set by earlier accounts of travel among savages, in which the encounter with alien people serves to reconfirm the boundaries of the civilized.

For example, Richard Henry Dana, Jr.'s, *Two Years Before the Mast*, which set many of the conventions for the travel adventure of Melville's day, presents a young voyager who rounds Cape Horn and lands on the coast of California, where he encounters a host of alien creatures, with one of whom he even becomes good friends.[4] Yet throughout his narrative, Dana remains an observer whose ultimate crisis, significantly, centers on getting home. Initiated into the hard life of a sailor and exposed to a host of culturally alien customs and people, Dana undergoes a rite of initiation that leads back to Boston and to his reconfirmed sense of himself as a gentleman. He crosses boundaries, to be sure, but only to return with a renewed sense of his original civilized self.

Nor is the pattern that informs Dana's narrative limited to the literary realm. As T. Walter Herbert has shown, the encounters with the South Sea islanders recorded in the travel accounts of Charles Stewart and David Porter display the same reconfirmation of the civilized self.[5] We will have occasion to return to these models shortly, but for now they can serve to point up the singularity of Ishmael's case. For Ishmael hardly emerges from his encounter with Queequeg as a reconfirmed member of civilized society. On the contrary, he has become the "bosom friend" of a cannibal with whom he has formed a lasting bond of love, ritually celebrated in a pagan rite (Chap. 10). Having crossed the boundary between civilized and savage, he does not return. Yet neither is he transformed into a savage cannibal himself. Rather, he finds himself on the border between the two realms, translated by his bond with Queequeg into a man alienated from civilized society, and yet an alien to the savage world from which Queequeg has come. He thus resembles no one more than Queequeg himself.

It is worth recalling that Queequeg has left a royal family behind on his native island. Like Ishmael, he has responded to an "itch for things remote" by leaving home to sail about the world (Chap. 1). And like Ishmael, he now finds himself suspended between two worlds. In "Biographical," we are told that "Queequeg's wild desire to visit Christendom" proved so strong that he forced a Sag Harbor captain to let him stay aboard his ship, and was forthwith "put down among the sailors and made a whaleman." So, like Ishmael, he has been precipitously demoted from the upper to the lower classes, and, like Ishmael, he has "disdained no seeming ignominy" as a common sailor, despite his noble origins (Chap. 12). Further, Queequeg's biography mirrors Ishmael's, for Queequeg has crossed the boundary between the savage and the civilized from the other side, yet with similarly alienating results.

Queequeg's motives for impressing himself into the ship's company ironically mirror the missionaries' motives for spreading the gospel in the South Seas: "he was actuated by a profound desire to learn among the Christians, the arts whereby to make his people still happier than they were; and more than that, still better than they were." Discovering that Christians are both "miserable and wicked," he has decided to "die a Pagan" but has remained an exile, living "among these Christians" and trying "to talk their gibberish." No only alienated but corrupted, Queequeg believes himself now "unfitted for ascending the pure and undefiled throne of thirty pagan Kings," contaminated as he is by his exposure to "Christianity, or rather Christians" (Chap. 12).

Melville's ironic inversion here of the story Americans were telling themselves about the savages, whose culture they were in fact contaminating and destroying in the name of Christianity, presupposes the rhetorical strategy at work throughout his treatment of Queequeg. He situates Ishmael and Queequeg together by a double process; as the alien grows familiar, the familiar grows alien, so that Queequeg is no longer a startling, multicolored savage but a man with a biography, and one that resembles Ishmael's in key respects.

This process has already begun in Chapter 6, "The Street," where, after spending his first night with Queequeg, Ishmael saunters out "for a stroll" in New Bedford. His initial "astonishment" at seeing "Queequeg circulating among the polite society of a civilized town" fades in the light of day and the now apparent fact that this "civilized" seaport is populated not only by sailors but by "savages outright." To see "actual cannibals stand chatting at street corners" renders the cannibals familiar and the street corners strange. To see among the "Feegeeans" and "Tongatabooans"—the "green Vermonters" makes the latter "more comical" and equally alien. "New Bedford is a queer place" indeed, where the rich live in "patrician-like houses" fenced in by "iron emblematical harpoons." Not only do Queequeg's peculiarities turn out to be normal, but the normal becomes strange, until finally the line between civilized and barbaric is impossible for Ishmael to discern. It is the barbaric whalemen, after all, who are responsible for civilizing New Bedford itself; "Had it not been for us whalemen, that tract of land would this day perhaps have been in as howling condition as the coast of Labrador," Ishmael concludes (Chap. 6).

Melville has foreshortened the matter of the alien encounter, then, and encapsulated it in the novel's opening section. He puts his narrator through an initiation into pagan life from which he emerges not, as convention demands, at the end of a voyage but at the outset of one, and not with a reconfirmed identity but with a radically fluid one. The outcast who introduced himself as Ishmael has, by forming a bond with a cannibal, joined that company of whalemen and other "queerest looking nondescripts" he finds populating an allegedly civilized New Bedford as well as the decks of the *Pequod*.

Yet the social identity thus accorded Ishmael's narrative voice only complicates Melville's task, for an alliance with such sailors and savages hardly renders Ishmael respectable or trustworthy as a narrator. A man who speaks from what Melville's contemporaries regarded as the margins of civilization, from what Americans today still marginalize when they refer to it as the Third World, is ill-placed, to put it mildly, for authorizing his voice. Ordinarily, the travel writers of Melville's day commanded authority by speaking from a position securely fixed within the society for which they wrote. Thus, Dana narrates his adventure from the perspective it served to resecure—that of the young Boston gentleman. The narrative itself steadily maintains its distance upon the alien worlds of both ship and shore that Dana observes. Similarly, in David Porter's account of the Marquesas, the natives are objects—of observation, coercion, and finally slaughter. In Charles Stewart's account, they are objects ripe for conversion.[6] In *Moby-Dick*, savages and sailors retain their otherness, but they are not regarded as objects at a distance. Ishmael, as he tells us, "was one of that crew" (Chap. 41).

In short, insofar as the voice of Ishmael has acquired a habitation and a name, it is neither local nor familiar. Further, what kind of discourse is available to a man who speaks from the boundaries? To occupy Ishmael's position entails what his voice everywhere reveals—a deeply subversive relation to all forms of discourse. The discourse of savages and sailors remains alien and unauthorized, whereas those authorized by his own culture are necessarily subjected to an alienation effect that distances and renders them suspect. In short, Ishmael's voice may have been grounded in a social identity, but the question remains, how is his discourse to find authority?

It is this question of how to authorize the discourse of a socially marginalized and culturally alienated narrator that takes us to the heart of

Ishmael's rhetoric in *Moby-Dick*. But to understand Melville's solution to this problem, at once a literary and a personal one, we need to return to the point at which it first arose for him, at the outset of his career as a writer. When he published *Typee* in February, 1846, Melville was already crossing and blurring a boundary, although he did not yet know it. He was not, however, allowed to remain in ignorance for long.

3

On April 17, 1846, *The Morning Courier & New York Enquirer* reviewed *Typee*, damning it as a "fiction." Conceding that the author may have "spent some time in the Marquesas Islands," the reviewer nonetheless insisted:

> We have not the slightest confidence in any of the details, while many of the incidents narrated are utterly incredible.... This would be a matter to be excused, if the book were not put forth as a simple record of actual experience. It professes to give nothing but what the author actually saw and heard. It must therefore be judged, not as a romance or a poem, but as a book of travels—as a statement of facts;—and in this light it has, in our judgment, no merit whatsoever.[7]

In this reviewer's view, Melville had violated the boundary between fact and fiction. His charge, moreover, was echoed on both sides of the Atlantic. Some skeptics, indeed, questioned whether Melville had even *been* to the Marquesas, and the more sardonic of them went further, asking whether "Herman Melville" was a real person.[8]

In crossing and blurring the line between fact and fiction, the young author committed a sin whose seriousness in Melville's day Michael Bell has recently demonstrated.[9] Modern scholarship, moreover, has found him guilty. As Leon Howard sums up the case, *Typee* "well deserved to come under suspicion."[10] Among other things, Melville altered the time span from the four weeks he had actually spent on the island to the four months recorded in the narrative. He portrayed a lake on an island that has none. He borrowed from previous accounts by Stewart, Porter, Ellis and Langsdorff, although disavowing such debts.[11]

Given such departures from fact, what are we to make of Melville's claims that *Typee* is "based upon facts ... which have come immediately under the writer's cognizance"? (p. xiv) By and large, critics have interpreted Melville's responses to his reviewer's skepticism as covering up the bad faith of an incipient romancer. Thus, after a close scrutiny of the

Preface Melville composed after his English publisher, John Murray, had voiced his skepticism, Leon Howard concludes, "Caught by a publisher's unanticipated demand that his 'yarn' be certified as the 'truth', he could only ask with jesting Pilate 'What is truth?' and evade, as best he could, the answer" (p. 293).

Given the demonstrated fictional elements in *Typee*, and given the subsequent record of Melville's capacity for ironic duplicity toward his readers, it is hardly surprising that we have come to view Melville's first book as the product of an imagination already caught in the act of disguising itself. Since *Typee* is not entirely factual, in our sense of the term, we have come to interpret his responses to the charges at the time that it was a fiction as the evasions of an author caught out in lies he at least half knew he had told. Yet the evidence adduced for Melville's conscious duplicity in the matter is far from compelling, and points just as persuasively, if not more so, to a different claim: Melville kept insisting that he had told the truth because he really believed he had.

For one thing, his letters at the time reveal a man alternately befuddled and outraged by people who insist on not believing him. The more his word is questioned, the more ardently he seeks to defend it. Indeed, when we look at his correspondence, it is hard to believe that this twenty-seven-year-old novice author was yet capable of the duplicities charged against him by modern scholars. Consider, for example, his response to the *New York Enquirer*'s hostile review. Melville composed a piece to be placed anonymously in the same newspaper and sent it to a friend who had agreed to serve as conduit. The piece itself has not survived, but the letter accompanying it reveals a man whose deep discomfort with *this* duplicitous act is readily apparent:

> Herewith you have the article we spoke of. I have endeavoured to make it appear as if written by one who read the book and believed it—& moreover—had been as much pleased with it as most people who read it profess to be. Perhaps, it may not be exactly the right sort of thing. The fact is, it was rather an awkward undertaking any way—for I have not sought to present my own view of the matter (which you may be sure is straightforward enough) but have only presented such considerations as would be apt to suggest themselves to a reader who was acquainted with & felt friendly toward the author.[12]

Aware that his own name cannot be used, since it is after all his own word that is in doubt, Melville has written a friendly review of his own book, and even "modelled" it "upon hints suggested by some reviews" already published.[13] His closing remarks make it clear that he has been driven to this stratagem by his fear that the "obnoxious review," now widely reprinted, will "do mischief unless answered," impairing "the success of the book here as a genuine narrative."[14] As a travel writer, Melville may already have behaved deviantly, but he is not yet comfortable with being devious.

In any case, Melville never deviated from his insistence that *Typee* was essentially accurate, except implicitly when he cut from the revised edition the passage in which he disclaimed any knowledge of Porter's or Stewart's accounts of their Marquesan visits. Whether he had read these accounts when he actually wrote this early passage is unclear. That he *had* read them at least by the time he completed the manuscript has been demonstrated.[15] That he chose to eliminate his claims to the contrary *may* reveal that he had originally lied, but it surely indicates a desire to correct any such misrepresentation.

Nor does Melville's rhetoric in the Preface to *Typee* necessarily support Howard's interpretation of duplicity. The Preface is clearly designed to win the reader's confidence, and was no doubt composed, as Howard notes, after Melville "had been put on the defensive by John Murray's queries and demands." Howard reads the Preface as a series of evasions designed to excuse the author from the duties of a "meticulous historian," and finds even Melville's closing insistence upon his "anxious desire to speak the unvarnished truth" telling for its failure actually to state "that he *had* spoken the unvarnished truth" (p. 293).

Yet when we read the Preface not in order to find traces of guilty evasion, but simply as the testimony of an author whose word has been doubted, what first strikes us is his sustained attention to his readers' expectations as these have been determined by the conventions of the travel narrative as he understands it, and his overriding desire to explain his deviations from such conventions in terms that will inspire the reader's confidence.

For instance, he notes that unlike other "writers of travels among barbarous communities," he "refrains in most cases" from trying to account for the "origins and purposes" of their peculiar "customs," and asks to be excused for this "culpable omission" in the light of the "very peculiar circumstances in which he was placed" (p. xiii). Again, he acknowledges the prominent attention normally accorded "dates" in "many published narratives," but explains that since he "lost all knowledge of the days of the week," he could not follow this convention (p. xiv). And again, he explains his partial orthographic deviation from "several works descriptive of the islands in the Pacific" on the grounds that these works have often failed to convey "many of the most beautiful combinations of vocal sounds ... by an over-attention to the ordinary rules of spelling" (p. xiv).

In each case, Melville explains his deviations from convention on the grounds dictated by his actual experience. Howard treats such rhetoric as a ploy, yet it need not imply the conscious duplicity of motive Howard infers when he says, for example, that when Melville explained the lack of dates, he was trying "to protect himself against the one charge which fortunately was not raised but to which he knew he was most vulnerable—that of falsifying the time period" (p. 293). It is just as likely that Melville's strategy here is more directly concerned with accounting for his break with the convention—one used by Dana, for example—of ordering a travel narrative by reference to dates, than with consciously covering up deliberate falsehood. He was certainly aware, of course, that he had extended the length of his adventure, but he was also very likely telling the truth when he said that he had lost track of time while on the island. The point is that we need not read any conscious duplicity into Melville's defensive strategy here in order to account for a rhetorical maneuver more simply explained by the hypothesis that he was struggling to make his story credible by connecting it to the tradition of travel writing to which he saw himself contributing at this point in his career. By apologizing for his deviations from this tradition, he simultaneously drew himself more visibly into the company of others whose testimony had been credited and authorized with the public.

The Preface does deserve a skeptical reading, but its tensions derive less from a conflict between the truth of Melville's experience and the account he had delivered in the pages to follow than from a conflict between that account and the assumptions informing the genre upon which his readers' expectations were based. For if Melville's aim here is to buttress the authority of his testimony by bringing it more closely into relation with the conventions of travel writing, he is also palpably aware that beneath the conventions he has innocently violated lie a set of values and beliefs he has not so innocently called into question. In other words, the source of the rhetorical strain in the Preface lies in the cross purposes to which Melville is driven when forced to ground his credibility as author in a tradition whose authority he has also questioned in the text to follow.

Accordingly, while paying homage to that tradition by begging forgiveness for his deviation from its conventions, he cannot avoid registering his awareness of what such deviations actually signal—a positive difference from, and in some cases a repudiation of, the accounts whose veracity he himself is questioning. For example, the polite disclaimer of any explanations concerning native customs acquires its irony from the fuller explanation provided in the text proper for this "culpable omission": "There is a vast deal of humbuggery in some of the accounts we have from scientific men concerning the religious institutions of Polynesia." (p. 170) It is after all those who have *not* omitted such explanations who are "culpable." On this reading, the Preface reveals a Melville less concerned to cover his tracks than to authorize his perspective, by trying to ground it in a tradition whose conventions and dominant values he has actually violated.

In effect, Leon Howard is right, but for the wrong reasons. Melville's readers did have good reason to be suspicious, not because of the extent to which he had embellished his tale, but rather because of the threat his narrative posed to their culturally inscribed defenses. Nor was this threat merely a matter of *Typee*'s outspoken attacks on the civilizing missionaries. Rather, it was Melville's marked tendency to "dismantle" the civilized self, as T. Walter Herbert has put it, which provoked such outrage.[16] As narrator, Tommo not only deliberately depicts, but unwittingly reveals, a dismantled self, one whose partial absorption into an alien culture has destabilized his perspective far more seriously than Melville apparently realized at the time of writing. If, as Herbert has argued, Melville adopted in *Typee* the narrative perspective of the "gentleman-beachcomber," he remained largely innocent of the radical instability of such a contradictory synthesis.[17] He spoke as a gentleman, but his views were too often those of the beachcomber, a marginal man, half proletarianized by his shipboard life as a sailor, half estranged by his four years of exposure to foreign peoples with dark skins.

Thus his genuine astonishment when faced with such "numbskulls," as he called them, who "heroically avow their determination not to be 'gulled'."[18] "How indescribably vexatious," he wrote to Murray in response to a request for "documentary evidences," when "one really feels in his very bones that he has been there, to have a parcel of blockheads question it."[19] Melville could not comprehend the charges brought by his skeptical reviewers because they were questioning his authority in terms that served to obscure the root source of their stated doubts. They accused him of lying; he insisted he had told the truth. But the two parties to this quarrel were already speaking different languages.

As Michael Bell has made clear, in mid-nineteenth-century America the distinction between fiction and nonfiction was far more central than that between the novel and the romance. Indeed, according to Bell, Hawthorne's careful effort to carve out the romance as his province, and to define its limits and operative assumptions, was itself a defensive strategy designed to undermine the suspiciousness with which fiction was regarded by those of his contemporaries who regarded it as contaminated by imagination and riddled with deceit. The line between fiction and nonfiction was charged defensively against the multiple dangers seen in the increasingly popular fictional forms invading the literary marketplace.[20]

In a larger sense, the opposition between fact and fiction operated variously to mark off the true from the false, the good from the bad, the healthy from the diseased, the real from the illusory, the honest from the deceitful. In effect, the distinction between fiction and nonfiction became charged by the very threats it had arisen to defuse, and thus was likely to be invoked most forcefully when threatened most directly. This *Typee* accomplished. The popular travel narrative achieved its credibility as factual not, finally, by any scrupulous attention to dates or orthography but by the distance it preserved, and even reinforced, between civilization and savagery, familiar and alien, safe and dangerous. By collapsing that distance, Melville's narrative voice called into question the opposition it ordinarily served to maintain. His narrative therefore became, for many readers, literally incredible. Whatever the embellishments and inventions Melville had used to make his narrative entertaining, these were not the source of the skepticism voiced by his reviewers. These readers, after all, did not have before them the evidence adduced by modern scholarship. Their incredulity arose in response to a narrative voice that was itself destabilized by the experience it sought to report, and that therefore destabilized, their own most basic assumptions about the world.

Thus, because he had blurred the line between the civilized and the savage, Melville was accused of violating that between fiction and fact. Nor could he counter such charges. His only recourse was to underscore his book's generic identity, and his own class identity, by means of the rhetorical alliance he attempted in the Preface to the revised edition of *Typee*. Just as in *Typee* proper, he could only call the line between civilized and savage into question from a supercivilized vantage point that depends for its authority on the very category of the civilized that he was questioning,[21] so in the Preface he can only authorize his word by relating it to that of the very authorities whose word he is questioning. It is this same double bind, however, in which narrative authority must be derived from the discourse of those whose authority he is questioning, that Melville ultimately unravels and exploits in order to authorize Ishmael's voice in *Moby-Dick*.

Before returning to Ishmael's voice, it is worth noting that the distinction between fiction and nonfiction in Melville's early work, an issue to which scholars have devoted considerable attention, needs to be resituated in relation to the struggle for narrative authority that began with *Typee*. Among other things, this approach would allow us to relate Melville's tendency to mix fictional and nonfictional genres to the well-known story of his hostility to his audience.[22] For example, when Melville shifted from the nonfictional travel narrative to the romance in *Mardi*, he cryptically prefaced his book by announcing his decision "to see whether the fiction might not, possibly, be received for a verity; in some degree the reverse of [his] previous experience."[23] The experiment failed, to be sure, but we have not fully appreciated all that was at stake for Melville in it.

We have generally seen *Mardi* as a turning point in Melville's career because it reveals him moving away from fact toward fiction, a view that quite logically leads to the conclusions reached by Nina Baym when she argues that Melville's adoption of fictional genres proved incompatible with his consistent aim of truth telling.[24] Truth, displaced from the factual to the fictional, from the physical to the metaphysical realm, turned out to be impossible to tell, according to Baym, and Melville's career as a fictionist is thus marked by a serial rupture of genre after genre, as each proves resistant to the truth teller's efforts. On this view, Melville's unwavering devotion to the "great Art of Telling the Truth" was only frustrated by his choice of fiction as a medium.[25]

No doubt this is accurate enough, and yet it obscures an issue just as basic to Melville's needs and aims here. If we take seriously the implicit challenge he hurled at his audience in *Mardi*'s Preface—"You want a romance? I'll give you a romance!"—it becomes clear that Melville made the shift to fiction at least in part in an effort to find a discourse in which his voice might be authorized. Encompassing and motivating the search Baym has described Melville pursuing, for a fictional genre in which to tell the truth, is a fundamental and longer-lived need to find an authorized discourse. In a sense, Melville was seeking the authority he felt he had lost at the very moment he had claimed it, the authority of his own word. Underlying the shift from nonfiction to fiction, and woven throughout his quarrel with a hostile and indifferent audience, is a search for some authority to replace that which turned up missing in *Typee*.

If we followed Melville's career to its end from this vantage point, we would see more clearly why he finally abandoned fiction. For eventually, fictional discourse by itself would prove as unreliable a source of authority as nonfictional discourse had, operating as it did in accord with codes of consistency and verisimilitude that became, to Melville, manifestly false. He bid farewell to fiction with *The Confidence-Man*, whose implicit motto could have echoed that with which he turned away from nonfiction in *Mardi*: "You want to be gulled? I'll gull you!" His subsequent career as a poet, a choice itself partly informed by the same need to authorize his voice, only continues a long and tortured story in which Melville found that the truth lacked authority, and that authority—the authorized discourses of his era—lacked truth.

Yet at the center of that career is *Moby-Dick*, a book whose extravagant violations of generic boundaries have always rendered it virtually unclassifiable, whereas the imaginative genius of its language continues to outstrip our expectations at each reading. For once, Melville found a narrative voice fully adequate to the demands he placed on it. This is not to say that only with *Moby-Dick* did he succeed as an artist—far from it. Nor is it to suggest that *Moby-Dick* was met with widespread praise. It was not. Nor is this lack of responsiveness surprising, for in Ishmael, Melville created a narrator who speaks with the full authority of the culture whose authority he is out to subvert.

4

Ishmael, as we have seen, blurs boundaries for a purpose. He aims to undermine our most basic and fixed assumptions and beliefs, to destabilize our culturally inscribed patterns of perception, to decenter our rooted perspective as landsmen. He ought to be a threat. Yet he has usually been regarded by modern readers as genial, tolerant, open-minded—in short, as a comic and sane counterweight to the mad Ahab. Although Ishmael's narrative relationship to Ahab, as we shall see, contributes to this effect, the major source of Ishmael's miraculous talent for radically destabilizing our perspective without provoking our hostility lies elsewhere—in his double-voiced discourse.[26] It is such discourse, in fact, that enables him to cross and blur boundaries with impunity, for it allows him to voice the other, the alien, while ostensibly speaking the language of the culturally legitimate.

We can see such double-voiced discourse at work most clearly in those chapters like "The Affidavit," where Ishmael speaks a readily identifiable language. Here it is the lawyer who undertakes, with characteristic circumlocution, to "take away any incredulity which a profound ignorance of the entire subject may induce in some minds, as to the natural verity of the main points of this affair." Disavowing any hope of proceeding "methodically," Ishmael nonetheless tries to provide a legal brief, consisting in "separate citations of items" from which "the conclusion aimed at will naturally follow of itself." The first group of such items is divided into two categories, personal and general knowledge, and the "conclusion aimed at" is that specific, identifiable whales can be and have been encountered twice by the same whalemen, thus making plausible Ahab's calculated pursuit of the particular whale that dismasted him. The second group demonstrates that the "Sperm Whale is in some cases sufficiently powerful, knowing, and judiciously malicious, as with direct aforethought to stave in, utterly destroy, and sink a large ship." The chapter is punctuated with firstly's and secondly's, and replete with lengthy quotations from texts whose "testimony," Ishmael assures us, is "entirely independent of my own" (Chap. 45).

Yet Ishmael's legalistic format breaks down almost immediately, as if the eager witness had become befuddled by the need to organize his "items" in so artificial a form. He claims to have "personally known three instances" in which a whale has been harpooned, escaped, and "been again struck by the same hand." But instead of enumerating each instance in orderly fashion, he confuses them to the point of absurdity. He seems particularly obsessed, for example, with the "three year instance," in part no doubt because it echoes, and seems to underscore, his opening claim that he knows of three instances of a harpooned whale being reharpooned by the same man. The number three is repeated nine times in the course of one paragraph: five times in reference to the number of years between first and last encounters, three times in reference to his instances, and once as a guess regarding how many times the whale in the three year instance "circumnavigated the globe." Meanwhile, no doubt in an effort to stretch the interval between first and second sightings, he twice qualifies the three year instance, which "may have been something more than that," at least he is "pretty sure it was more than that." This, despite the story he tells about the man who reencountered the whale in the three year instance, a man who happened "in the interval" to join a trading ship to Africa, go ashore, and travel inland with a "discovery party ... for a period of nearly two years" (Chap. 45). It is not that one couldn't resolve these apparent contradictions by reconstructing Ishmael's argument. The man in question could have spent two years in Africa, returned to sea, and some time later, at least a year and probably "something more than that," met up with his whale. The point is that as Ishmael recounts such "instances," they are garbled by the very numbers designed to organize and verify them.

Nor is the purpose of verification served by the little flight of fancy used to depict the three year instance man's African adventure, in which he was "endangered by serpents, savages, tigers, poisonous miasmas, with all the other common perils incident to wandering in the heart of unknown regions." Ishmael clearly wants to emphasize the improbability of the man's second encounter with his whale; he moves deep into Africa while the whale is "brushing with its flanks all the coasts of Africa," and yet both are unwittingly set on a course that will lead them back to each other. But the more Ishmael tries to make his primary point—that such encounters are not as unlikely as they may seem—the more confused his argument becomes. Digression gives way to the simple and repeated insistence, "I say, I, myself, have known three instances ..." The reductio ad absurdem arrives with his claim that in the three year instance he was "on the boat, both times," and recognized the whale by the "huge mole" under its eye (Chap. 45).

Since the three year instance is taken from an actual account, which Melville could have simply quoted, as he in fact does with other accounts later in the same chapter, Ishmael's peculiar handling of his evidence obviously results from a deliberate strategy.[27] He is, of course, parodying the legal discourse he struggles so arduously to deploy, but the effect of this form of parody is complex. As it keeps collapsing, Ishmael's visible effort to marshall his argument behind "separate citations of items" ends by discrediting not his own word but the legal discourse in which he tries to speak. In other words, if the passage were fully ironic, the parody would undermine Ishmael's credibility altogether, sweeping his claims into the heap of refuse that is piled up by his "instances" and "items." Yet because his struggle with the language of the "affidavit" is so palpable, it is the language, and not his testimony itself, that is discredited. At the same time that it is being parodied and discredited, however, this legal language is already beginning to authorize the very voice that fails to speak it successfully. Ishmael's veracity is actually being supported by his audible inability to fit what he knows to be true into the conventions inscribed in the testimonial discourse. Rather than regarding his evidence as doubtful, we begin to feel that the truth does not sound like evidence.

There are, in effect, two voices speaking here. One speaks in the cadences of legal testimony, and the other can be heard struggling against its limits. But the second voice can be heard only because it clashes so discordantly with the first. Indeed, that is why the legal discourse is voiced in the first place: to make audible the voice that cannot speak it fluently. The purpose, then, is not only to parody legal discourse but to circumscribe and reify it, so that its boundaries come into view, set in relief as an artificial limit against the expanse of alien knowledge Ishmael has no direct means of communicating. Consequently, Ishmael's voice is authorized ironically, by its capacity to expose the limits of the authorized discourse in *which* he is compelled to speak. In the act of parodying legal discourse, he usurps its authority.

Here Ishmael's authentic voice sounds, against the legal discourse because he so audibly fails to mater its conventions, but this is only one means by which double-voiced discourse is set into operation in *Moby-Dick*. Ishmael is by no means always so incompetent. On the contrary, he often reveals so profound a mastery of the discourse he is voicing that he can apply it readily to novel areas of knowledge or experience. But the effect is similar; the limits of the parodied discourse are exposed at the same time that its authority is appropriated. For example, in the next section of "The Affidavit," Ishmael adopts the pose of a learned authority on the "Sperm Whale Fishery."

"It is well known in the Sperm Whale Fishery," he begins, "however ignorant the world ashore may be of it," that "a particular whale" becomes "popularly cognisable," a fact to which "several memorable historical instances" attest. Here, the Sperm Whale Fishery designates the whaler's ocean world as if it were a specific delineated realm, a nation to itself with its own history, which Ishmael is engaged in describing to us from behind a lectern. Translated into this historian's pedagogical discourse, tall tales become cultural history in which particular whales acquire their fame from a "terrible prestige of perilousness" to which "the fatal experiences of the fishery" give rise (Chap. 45).

The information Ishmael proceeds to deliver about "famous whales" actually comes from whaler's lore, the kinds of stories that other writers kept at arm's length in their accounts. Thomas Beale, for example—a major source for Melville throughout *Moby-Dick* and a specific source for this passage—regards such "strange" stories as that of "Timor Jack" as "probably much exaggerated."[28] Ishmael himself has already acknowledged the "fabulous rumors" abounding in the Sperm Whale Fishery. In Chapter 41, "Moby Dick," he has made it clear that he knows a tall tale when he hears one, but this does not prevent such tales from circulating at sea to profound effect, as when "some whalemen" are found to believe that Moby Dick is "ubiquitous" and "immortal" (Chap. 41). Thus, "Timor Jack" becomes "Timor Tom" in his account, in which the very fact that the whale has a name serves to corroborate his claim that "famous whales enjoy great individual celebrity" in the Sperm Whale Fishery (Chap. 45). Speaking as one of the "students of Cetacean History," to whom such names are "as well known as Marius or Sylla to the classic scholar," Ishmael becomes the historian of an alien world, but one after all no more alien than the Roman. Indeed, he has himself been so deeply absorbed by the culture of the Sperm Whale Fishery that he speaks finally as its epic poet in a series of apostrophes: "Was it not so, O Timor Tom ... O New England Jack! ... O Morquan! ... O Don Miguel!" This momentary seizure is itself foregrounded as epic discourse when Ishmael abruptly concludes it by returning to "plain prose." In such a passage, Ishmael immerses us in the alien culture of the Sperm Whale Fishery by means of a learned discourse appropriated from the shore world. As the discourse itself is parodied, it serves to authorize not only a knowledge to which it is alien, but the very voice that is engaged in the parody.

In "The Affidavit," the ironically self-authorizing effects of Ishmael's double-voiced discourse are unusually clear. As the parody grows more extravagant, Ishmael himself grows more persuasive. He ends the chapter by extending the scope of his "historical instances" back to the sixth century and Procopius's account of a sea monster, which Ishmael construes, by means of a manifestly preposterous reasoning process, to "have been a sperm whale." The alien worlds of the Sperm Whale Fishery and the Romans are forced to coalesce here, in a parody of the speculative historian intent upon bending his evidence to suit his argument. "A fact ... set down in substantial history," Ishmael insists, "cannot easily be gainsaid"; never mind that he has admitted the "substantial history" in question to be faulty "in some one or two particulars" and the "fact" in question to be far too vaguely reported to count. The "precise species" of Procopius's sea monster is not mentioned, but Ishmael clears up this detail by resorting to a marvel of circular reasoning. He has been arguing for several pages that the sperm whale is capable of destroying ships. Now he decides that the sea monster must have been a whale, "as he destroyed ships" (Chap. 45).

In this extravaganza, Ishmael repeatedly makes explicit reference to "the best authorities" whose discourse he is simultaneously parodying. Where before he spoke as the fully initiated epic poet of the Sperm Whale Fishery, here, he seems to embrace just as thoroughly the landsman's logic (a tactic he will employ to similar effect in "Jonah Historically Regarded"). Yet as before, the parodied discourse serves primarily as a sounding board for Ishmael's authentic voice, as if he were a ventriloquist smiling at the nonsense his own dummy is made to speak. By voicing the discourses he is constrained to speak through, Ishmael submits them to an alienation effect, while all the time appropriating their authority. As a result, this chapter can actually serve the purpose for which it is named. As an affidavit, it can disarm skepticism. At least it did for one reviewer at the time. After reading Chapter 45, he said, "all improbability of incongruity disappears, and Moby Dick becomes a living fact, simply doubtful at first, because he was so new an idea."[29] Although hardly representative, this reviewer's response testifies to the potential power of Ishmael's double-voiced discourse as a strategy for usurping authority.

The same double effect can be seen in Ishmael's parodic voicing of scientific and philosophical discourses, where the authority inscribed in the landsman's culturally bound and legitimized discourses is both undermined and exploited, enabling Ishmael to cross and blur boundaries in the name of the boundary keepers themselves.

In Chapter 32, "Cetology," for example, he opens with his characteristic humility, avowing his inability to perform the task before him—"the classification of the constituents of chaos." Yet in this case, such helplessness immediately allies him with "the best and latest authorities" who, like Beale, themselves attest to the "utter confusion" that "exists among the historians of this animal." "Cetology" is a chapter famous for its parody of erudite naturalists, and nowhere is Ishmael more explicit in his appeal to existing authorities, actually listing their names, from "the Authors of the Bible" on through Coffin, Olmstead, and Cheever. The cetological information Ishmael provides here is largely plundered from such sources, as is the metaphor of sovereignty, taken from Beale, which Ishmael weaves through his discussion, though to an effect far beyond any predictable from Beale.[30] Thus, "the Greenland whale is an usurper upon the throne of the seas" whom Ishmael proclaims "deposed" by the "great Sperm Whale" who "now reigneth." Again, despite Linnaeus's declaration, "I hereby separate the whales from the fish," Ishmael insists that "down to the year 1850, sharks and shad, alewives and herring, against Linnaeus's express edict," swam "the same seas with the Leviathan." (Insofar as Linnaeus unwittingly echoes God in Genesis, Ishmael parodies the same source.) But if whales and fish refuse to abide by the edict of "A.D. 1776" and separate themselves, Ishmael himself usurps Linnaeus's authority when he denies pig-fish and saw-fish "their credentials as whales" and dismisses them from "the Kingdom of Cetology." In short, Ishmael mixes the discourse of the naturalist with that of political sovereignty, just as he organizes his cetological information by reference to the sizes of books, in accord with the fact that "though of real knowledge there be little, yet of books there are plenty" (Chap. 32).

Here, then, Ishmael in effect uses one discourse to satirize another, so that the authorities whose voices he is parodying undermine each other. Meanwhile, Ishmael's voice absorbs the authority it is all the while draining from these discourses, which are left beached, as it were, like those "uncertain whales" whose names are "mere sounds, full of Leviathanism, but signifying nothing" (Chap. 32).

As this allusion to *Macbeth* indicates, Ishmael's voice is by now a virtual sponge, capable of soaking up an infinite number of voices and squeezing out their discourse into a pool as large as the ocean he sails. The scholarship devoted to tracing Melville's borrowings and allusions in *Moby-Dick* is itself comparably infinite.[31] Nor have critics failed to note that, as Joseph Flibbert puts it, Melville "parodies his source at the same time that he plunders it for information."[32] What I wish to add is that he plunders his sources for their authority as well, a rhetorical feat that relies upon Ishmael's double-voiced discourse.

Understood as the locus of such discourse, Ishmael represents a solution to the problem of self-authorization that Melville had first confronted when met with the skeptical responses to *Typee*. For if Ishmael's voice operates, as I have argued it does, to absorb the authority of the very discourses he parodies, then he serves as a rhetorical device skillfully designed to exploit the double bind by which Melville was trapped in the Preface to *Typee*. But Ishmael is more than a rhetorical solution to Melville's long-standing problem. He is also the narrator of *Moby-Dick*, and his role in the novel requires further scrutiny.

5

Ishmael's double-voiced discourse, although not limited to his digressive chapters, explains one of their major purposes, for in these long-winded digressions, Ishmael's voice not only absorbs authority but disperses it. As a narrator who has begun by assuming a stance on the boundaries, allied there with socially marginal outcasts, Ishmael ends by speaking in the name of a global community of men, "an Anacharsis Clootz deputation" representing the human race at large (Chap. 27). The digressions on whaling, from "Cetology" to "The Whiteness of the Whale," from "The Advocate" to "The Affidavit" and beyond, are crucial to this process.

Having undergone his ritual initiation at Queequeg's hands into the world of the Sperm Whale Fishery, Ishmael, as we have seen, acquires the social identity of the whaleman. He immediately begins establishing his professional credentials in "The Advocate," a chapter that parodies oratorical debate in its defense of the honor and dignity of "the business of whaling." By means of the same double-voiced discourse we have seen him deploy in "The Affidavit" and "Cetology," Ishmael appropriates for the whale ship the honor accorded "Martial Commanders" and the "heroes of Exploring Expeditions," whose exploits have opened access to distant lands and thus enlarged the scope of "the enlightened world" (Chap. 24). As usual, Ishmael is undermining the values inscribed in the discourse he uses, exposing its contradictions right and left. "If American and European men-of-war now peacefully ride in once savage harbors," he declares, it was the "whale-ship which originally showed the way," as if war ships brought peace, as if the proud Americans were not literally "men-of-war," as if "savage harbors" had not been peaceful themselves prior to such civilizing invasions. Yet at the same time that he exposes the rhetoric of imperialism, Ishmael is himself expanding the provenance of his voice, enlarging its scope by according the Sperm Whale Fishery the status it deserves. What begins as self-parody, when Ishmael remarks how "ridiculous" it would be for a harpooner to add the initials "S.W.F." to his "visiting card," ends with the avowal that "a whale-ship was my Yale College and my Harvard" (Chap. 24). As he mimics the rhetoric of honor and respectability, Ishmael empowers his voice as that of a cosmopolitan and professional.

By the same token, as he voices the discourses of philosophers, scientists, and politicians, Ishmael absorbs their authority, displacing it to the society of whalemen, whose esoteric knowledge and marginal status thereby become normal, even normative. In short, such digressions provide Ishmael with the sea room he needs to move from social outcast to social spokesman. As a member of the Anacharsis Clootz convention that the *Pequod's* crew symbolizes, Ishmael gives voice to an alien sea world. But he does so by speaking through and against the familiar discourse of the shore, and in the process he displaces and disperses the latter's authority, delivering it over to the democracy of the "meanest mariners, and renegades and castaways" he represents (Chap. 26).

Yet as embodied in the *Pequod's* crew, Ishmael's discursive democracy reveals remarkably little capacity to resist virtually total submission to Ahab's authority. It is not only his institutionalized authority as captain, but a primitive tribal authority to which the crew subject themselves in the pagan ritual described in Chapter 36, "The Quarter-Deck." When we recall that Ishmael was "one of that crew" and filled with a "wild, mystical, sympathetical feeling," welding his "oath" to "theirs," his rhetorical behavior as narrator is cast in a different light (Chap. 41). If, by subverting and appropriating the authority inscribed in the discourses he voices, Ishmael is enabled to blur the boundaries between the familiar and the alien with impunity, his narrative position on the boundaries also serves to construct—for both himself and his reader—a defense against the threat represented by Ahab.

Ahab's authority is beyond the reach of Ishmael's parodic voice. A mark of Ahab's discursive impunity is his tendency to speak in monologues. Ahab talks primarily to himself, addressing others only in the line of duty to his overarching obsession, as in "The Quarter-Deck," where he ignites the crew with the fire of his maniacal zeal. Although he must use language to achieve his ends, Ahab's authority over the crew finally depends less on his verbal discourse than on the discourse of ritual, dramatic action he manipulates so skillfully. Accordingly, Ahab comes to us as a man incapable of dialogue, for conversation as a social medium requires at least the equality of a shared discourse, even if not of a shared social status, and Ahab shares neither. Even when he appears to converse, Ahab places his interlocutor at such a distance that, like the carpenter, he is justified in asking, "What's he speaking about, and who's he speaking to?" (Chap. 108). Only with Fedallah does Ahab seem to enjoy the communion of genuine dialogue, but finally as the quest for Moby Dick reaches its climax, the two "never ... speak," so "yoked together" are they by "the unseen tyrant driving them" (Chap. 130).

Except with the Parsee, then, when Ahab speaks he is performing either before his company, as on the Quarter-Deck, or for himself, as in the following chapter, "Sunset." Yet his performance is by no means fraudulent. When he conducts the ritual designed to merge the brew's will with his own, he himself participates fully, with no ironic distance. And when he talks to himself, he is similarly fully present in his own speech. Yet it is not his speech, but that of Lear and Hamlet, among others, that flows from his mouth. Because Ahab hears no speech but his own, he cannot recognize that it is not his own that he speaks. He is a man possessed, wholly in the grip of the inspired language he speaks, just as he is totally consumed by the demon within that drives him along "iron rails" to his "fixed purpose" (Chap. 37). Just as Ahab acknowledges no boundaries to his will, he exhibits no sense of discursive boundaries. Whether he is talking with others or speaking from Shakespeare's stage, Ahab is always addressing the blank, mute universe he so woefully inhabits, trying to get a voice out of silence but doomed to hear nothing but his own voice, since he is deaf to the voices of others.

Yet this very discursive isolation both reflects and fosters Ahab's autonomous authority. Acknowledging no other authority than himself, Ahab seizes all authority for himself. In relation to his crew, he does so by an appeal to atavistic instincts; in relation to the reader, he does so by a discourse purified by amnesia of any "mortal inter-indebtedness" to others (Chap. 108). In this sense, Ahab represents a wish fulfillment on Melville's part, for his discursive amnesia enables Melville to pose the ultimate questions in a voice charged with epic energy but owning allegiance to no authority save its own.

Ahab's authority, then, lies beyond the range of Ishmael's double-voiced discourse for the same reason it exerts such a powerful attraction, for Ahab's authority seems to be self-generated. Like the godlike Prometheus, "who made men, they say," Ahab taunts Starbuck with the question, "Who's over me?" (Chaps. 108, 36). Yet although he claims that he would "strike the sun if it insulted" him, Ahab is revealed as in thrall himself to the sun's element (Chap. 36). If "right worship is defiance," what Ahab worships "defyingly" as the "clear spirit of clear fire" is the devil, in whose name he baptizes his harpoon, just as Melville was to baptize his book (Chap. 119).[33] Owning his allegiance to the "speechless, placeless power" of fire, Ahab allies himself with the fires of hell; "for what's made in fire must properly belong to fire," he says, "so hell's probable" (Chaps. 119, 108). An authority wholly generated out of the self, in short, is an authority doomed to serve the forces of evil.

Ahab's power, then, is irresistible because demonic, sealed by a pact with the devil—Fedallah, Ahab's dark shadow self—and manifested in his capacity to subordinate the crew's will by "magnetically" charging them with "the same fiery emotion accumulated within the Leyden jar of his own magnetic life" (Chap. 36). Even Starbuck cannot finally resist the primitive power upon which Ahab depends to divert the *Pequod* from its appointed economic ends. Given that Ishmael has testified to the sea's magnetic attraction for him, and that he has already undergone a ritual transformation in becoming Queequeg's friend, it is hardly surprising that his "shouts had gone up with the rest" (Chap. 41). As "one of that crew," Ishmael is irresistibly drawn by the force of Ahab's will, by the self-generated authority he exercises over the ship and aims to impose on nature itself.

Yet in telling his tale, Ishmael develops a rhetorical defense against the threat that Ahab's fatal quest unveils. If his narrative stance on the boundaries enables Ishmael to undermine the landsman's authority, it also enables him to resist the threat of absolute boundary violation that is at the heart of Ahab's madness.

Ahab's obsessive revenge is, after all, itself a response to the violation of his boundaries—as free man, as autonomous human, as whole body. Ahab's boundaries, both physical and metaphysical, have been violated so decisively that he has been driven mad. As his empathy with Pip's madness reveals, Ahab has survived an experience in which the lines dividing man and nature, self and world, have dissolved. His monomaniacal quest, then, is fueled by the need to resecure the boundaries that Moby Dick has violated. As Michael Rogin has argued, Ahab's obsession is itself a defense "against chaos, against the panic of rage without a target."[34] Ahab's madness derives from the dissolution of the most personal as well as the most universal of boundaries, for not only has the integrity of his body been violated, but the integrity of his mind and his soul as well. The white scar that some believe runs from Ahab's "crown to sole" brands him as a man riven in two, clinging fast to a monomaniacal purpose that alone holds him together. His vengeful pursuit of the White Whale is fueled by a need as desperate as it is doomed, the need to reinstate the boundaries that the whale's dismembering attack has dissolved. But as the case of Pip serves to indicate, once such boundaries have been dissolved, they cannot be reconstituted. For the vision of chaos and the experience of absolute vulnerability to which such a crisis leads render all boundaries suspect, artificial, and finally sinister. All "visible objects" become for Ahab "pasteboard masks," and for Ishmael, "though ... this visible world seems formed in love, the invisible spheres were formed in fright" (Chaps. 36, 42).

Wonder ye then, as Ishmael might say, at the value of clinging to the boundaries? To cross and blur boundaries is one thing; to violate them absolutely, another. Just as Ishmael requires the discourses of others to make his own voice heard, he depends upon the authority invested in those discourses as a virtually infinite resource on which to draw, not only for his own authority as narrator, but also as a defense against the threat inscribed in Ahab's autonomous authority—the threat of total annihilation. As Robert Zaller has argued, rebellion is for the Melvillean hero a dialogue with power

in which assassination must be avoided because it would break the circuit.[35]
By the same token, Ishmael never kills the authority vested in the discourses
he parodies; rather, it is as if he borrows the authority of one, then another
source. His stance on the boundary, then, not only enables him to blur it but
to defend it against the total dissolution that would render him, like Pip, a
mad mimic rather than a sane one.

This built-in resistance to the magnetic attraction of Ahab's demonic
authority underlies Ishmael's ability to destabilize without threatening us as
readers, to make us "social" with the "horror" to which he opens our eyes.
Ishmael both subverts authority and clings to it, just as he advises us to cling
to the Mast-Head. For to blur all boundaries is to lose one's footing, as has
Ahab, who would "like to feel something in this slippery world that can hold"
(Chap. 108).

In his desire for a self-generated authority, Ahab served Melville as an
expressed wish fulfillment, but his mad captain also testifies to Melville's fear
of boundary dissolution, the same fear that provided *Typee* with its dramatic
suspense: Will I be eaten by these friendly natives? In Ishmael, however, he
constructed a narrative perspective that could express both wish and fear
with impunity. By speaking from the boundaries in a voice authorized by the
very discourses it subverts, Ishmael is empowered to defend against the very
threat of boundary dissolution to which this stance makes him vulnerable. In
the Epilogue, as in the story it concludes, Ishmael floats "on the margin," and
though "drawn towards the closing vortex," he is miraculously saved. Just as
Queequeg's friendship accorded him a socially designated place to stand on
the boundary between civilized and savage, Queequeg's coffin provides him
with a "life-buoy" on which he floats along "a soft and dirge-like main,"
unharmed by "sharks" and "sea-hawks," until the *Rachel* appears to find
"another orphan." As reported, Ishmael's survival is almost as implausible as
his narrative behavior is outrageous, but both reflect the "cunning spring"
and "buoyancy" of his double-voiced discourse (Epilogue).

NOTES

1. "To Nathaniel Hawthorne," April 16, 1851, *Moby-Dick*, ed. Harrison Hayford and
Hershel Parker (New York: Norton, 1967), p. 555.

2. George R. Stewart, "The Two *Moby-Dicks*," *American Literature* 25 (January 1954):
417–48.

3. On liminality, see Victor W. Turner, *The Ritual Process: Structure and Anti-Structure*
(Chicago: Aldine, 1969).

4. Richard Henry Dana, Jr., *Two Years Before the Mast* (New York: Penguin, 1981), pp.
207ff.

5. T. Walter Herbert, *Marquesan Encounters* (Cambridge, Mass: Harvard University
Press, 1980).

6. For a brief but useful discussion of Dana's narrative perspective, see Thomas Philbrick's Introduction to *Two Years Before the Mast*, op. cit., pp. 7–29. For an extended analysis of Porter and Stewart, see Herbert, *Marquesan Encounters*, pp. 51–148.

7. Jay Leyda, *The Melville Log*, 2 vols. (New York: Harcourt, Brace, 1951), vol. I, pp. 211–12.

8. "A doubt has existed on the part of some reviewers, whether it is the genuine production of the reputed author." Ibid., vol. 1, p. 228. For an overview of the skeptical reception accorded *Typee* and then *Omoo*, which was contaminated by association, see ibid., vol. I, pp. 204–49. An example of the sardonic reviewers: "The train of suspicion once lighted, the flame runs rapidly along.... And Herman Melville sounds to us vastly like the harmonious and carefully selected appellation of an imaginary hero of romance.... Of the existence of Uncle Gansevoort, of Gansevoort, Saratoga County, we are wholly incredulous." Ibid., vol. I, p. 249.

9. Michael Davitt Bell, *The Development of American Romance* (Chicago: University of Chicago Press, 1980).

10. "Historical Note" in Herman Melville, *Typee: A Peep at Polynesian Life*, ed. Harrison Hayford, Hershel Parker, and G. Thomas Tanselle (Evanston, Ill: Northwestern/ Newberry, 1968), p. 291.

11. See Charles R. Anderson, *Melville in the South Seas* (New York: Columbia University Press, 1939).

12. Leyda, *Log*, vol. I, p. 214.

13. Ibid.

14. Ibid., pp. 214, 215.

15. Anderson, *Melville*, pp. 117–78.

16. Herbert, *Marquesan Encounters*, p. 178.

17. Ibid., p. 153.

18. Leyda, *Log*, vol. I, p. 214.

19. Ibid., p. 236.

20. Bell, *American Romance*, pp. 25–36.

21. Herbert, *Marquesan Encounters*, pp. 152–5.

22. For the best introduction to Melville's relationship to his audience, see Ann Douglas, *The Feminization of American Culture* (New York: Alfred A. Knopf, 1977), pp. 349–95.

23. Herman Melville, *Mardi, and A Voyage Thither*, ed. Harrison Hayford, Hershel Parker, and G. Thomas Tanselle (Evanston, Ill: Northwestern/Newberry, 1970), p. xvii.

24. Nina Baym, "Melville's Quarrel with Fiction," *PMLA* 94 (October 1979): 909–23.

25. "Hawthorne and His Mosses," in Hayford and Parker, ed., *Moby-Dick*, p. 542.

26. The term "double-voiced discourse" is taken from Mikhail Bakhtin, on whose theory of language and the novel the following discussion draws heavily. See "Discourse in the Novel" in Bakhtin, *The Dialogic Imagination*, trans. Caryl Emerson and Michael Holquist (Austin: University of Texas Press, 1981), pp. 259–422.

27. The account is Henry T. Cheever's, and the relevant passage is provided in "Explanatory Notes," *Moby-Dick*, ed. Luther S. Mansfield and Howard P. Vincent (New York: Hendricks House, 1952), p. 720.

28. Ibid., p. 720.

29. William T. Porter, "Spirit of the Times," in *The Recognition of Herman Melville*, ed. Hershel Parker (Ann Arbor: University of Michigan Press, 1967), p. 47.

30. Thomas Beale's use of the metaphor of sovereignty is apparent in the passage cited in "Explanatory Notes," Mansfield and Vincent, ed., *Moby-Dick*, p. 674.

31. A start on this infinitude may be made with F. O. Matthiessen, *American Renaissance* (New York: Oxford University Press, 1941), and the "Explanatory Notes" in Mansfield and Vincent, ed., op. cit.

32. *Melville and the Art of Burlesque*, in Robert Brainard Pearsall, ed., *Melville Studies in American Culture*, Vol. 3 (Amsterdam: Rodopi N.V., 1974), p. 65.

33. "To Nathaniel Hawthorne," June 29, 1851, in Hayford and Parker, ed., *Moby-Dick*, p. 562.

34. *Subversive Genealogy: The Politics and Art of Herman Melville* (New York: Alfred A. Knopf, 1983), p. 115.

35. "Melville and the Myth of Revolution," *Studies in Romanticism* 15 (Fall 1976): 607–22.

CHARLES OLSON

A Moby-Dick *Manuscript*

It is beautifully right to find what I take to be rough notes for *Moby-Dick* in the Shakespeare set itself. They are written in Melville's hand, in pencil, upon the last fly-leaf of the last volume, the one containing *Lear*, *Othello* and *Hamlet*. I transcribe them as they stand:

> Ego non baptizo te in nomine Patris et
> Filii et Spiritus Sancti—sed in nomine
> Diaboli.—madness is undefinable—
> It & right reason extremes of one,
> —not the (black art) Goetic but Theurgic magic—
> seeks converse with the Intelligence, Power, the Angel.

The Latin is a longer form of what Melville told Hawthorne to be the secret motto of *Moby-Dick*. In the novel Ahab howls it as an inverted benediction upon the harpoon he has tempered in savage blood:

> Ego non baptizo te in nomine patris, sed in nomine diaboli.
> I do not baptize thee in the name of the father, but in the name
> of the devil.

From *Call Me Ishmael: A Study of Melville*, pp. 51–62. © 1947 by Charles Olson.

The change in the wording from the notes to the novel is of extreme significance. It is not for economy of phrase. The removal of Christ and the Holy Ghost—Filii et Spiritus Sancti—is a mechanical act mirroring the imaginative. Of necessity, from Ahab's world, both Christ and the Holy Ghost are absent. Ahab moves and has his being in a world to which They and what They import are inimical: remember, Ahab fought a deadly scrimmage with a Spaniard before the altar at Santa, and spat into the silver calabash. The conflict in Ahab's world is abrupt, more that between Satan and Jehovah, of the old dispensation than the new. It is the outward symbol of the inner truth that the name of Christ is uttered but once in the book and then it is torn from Starbuck, the only possible man to use it, at a moment of anguish, the night before the fatal third day of the chase.

Ahab is Conjur Man. He invokes his own evil world. He himself uses black magic to achieve his vengeful ends. With the very words "in nomine diaboli" he believes he utters a Spell and performs a Rite of such magic.

The Ahab-world is closer to *Macbeth* than to *Lear*. In it the supernatural is accepted. Fedallah appears as freely as the Weird Sisters. Before Ahab's first entrance he has reached that identification with evil to which Macbeth out of fear evolves within the play itself. The agents of evil give both Ahab and Macbeth a false security through the same device, the unfulfillable prophecy. Ahab's tense and nervous speech is like Macbeth's, rather than Lear's. Both Macbeth and Ahab share a common hell of wicked, sleep-bursting dreams. They both endure the torture of isolation from humanity. The correspondence of these two evil worlds is precise. In either the divine has little place. Melville intended certain exclusions, and Christ and the Holy Ghost were two of them. Ahab, alas, could not even baptize in the name of the Father. He could only do it in the name of the Devil.

That is the Ahab-world, and it is wicked. Melville meant exactly what he wrote to Hawthorne when the book was consummated:

I have written a wicked book, and feel as spotless as the lamb.

Melville's "wicked book" is the drama of Ahab, his hot hate for the White Whale, and his vengeful pursuit of it from the moment the ship plunges like fate into the Atlantic. It is that action, not the complete novel *Moby-Dick*. The *Moby-Dick* universe contains more, something different. Perhaps the difference is the reason why Melville felt "spotless as the lamb." The rough notes in the Shakespeare embrace it.

"Madness is undefinable." Two plays from which the thought could have sprung are in the volume in which it is written down: *Lear* and *Hamlet*. Of the modes of madness in *Lear*—the King's, the Fool's—which is definable? But we need not rest on supposition as to what Melville drew of madness from *Hamlet*, or from *Lear*: *Moby-Dick* includes both Ahab and Pip. Melville forces his analysis of Ahab's mania to incredible distances, only himself to admit that "Ahab's larger, darker, deeper part remains unhinted." Pip's is a more fathomable idiocy: "his shipmates called him mad." Melville challenges the description, refuses to leave Pip's madness dark and unhinted, declares: "So man's insanity is heaven's sense."

The emphasis in this declaration is the key to resolve apparent difficulties in the last sentence of the notes in the Shakespeare volume:

> It & right reason extremes of one,—not the (black art) Goetic but Theurgic magic—seeks converse with the Intelligence, Power, the Angel.

I take "it" to refer to the "madness" of the previous sentence. "Right reason," less familiar to the 20th century, meant more to the last, for in the Kant-Coleridge terminology "right reason" described the highest range of the intelligence and stood in contrast to "understanding." Melville had used the phrase in *Mardi*. What he did with it there discloses what meaning it had for him when he used it in these cryptic notes for the composition of *Moby-Dick*. *Mardi*:

> Right reason, and Alma (Christ), are the same; else Alma, not reason, would we reject. The Master's great command is Love; and here do all things wise, and all things good, unite. Love is all in all. The more we love, the more we know; and so reversed.

Now, returning to the notes, if the phrase "not the (black art) Goetic but Theurgic magic" is recognized as parenthetical, the sentence has some clarity: "madness" and its apparent opposite "right reason" are the two extremes of one way or attempt or urge to reach "the Intelligence, Power, the Angel" or, quite simply, God.

The adjectives of the parenthesis bear this reading out. "Goetic" might seem to derive from Goethe and thus Faust, but its source is the Greek "goetos," meaning variously trickster, juggler and, as here, magician. (Plato called literature "Goeteia") Wherever Melville picked up the word he means it, as he says, for the "black art." "Theurgic," in sharp contrast, is an accurate term for a kind of occult art of the Neoplatonists in which, through self-purification and sacred rites, the aid of the divine was evoked. In thus opposing "Goetic" and "Theurgic" Melville is using a distinction as old as Chaldea between black and white magic, the one of demons, the other of saints and angels, one evil, the other benevolent. For white or "Theurgic" magic, like "madness" and "right reason," seeks God, while the "black art Goetic" invokes only the devil.

Now go to *Moby-Dick*. In the Ahab-world there is no place for "converse with the Intelligence, Power, the Angel." Ahab cannot seek it, for understood between him and Fedallah is a compact as binding as Faust's with Mephistopheles. Melville's assumption is that though both Ahab and Faust may be seekers after truth, a league with evil closes the door to truth. Ahab's art, so long as his hate survives, is black. He does not seek true converse.

"Madness," on the contrary, does, and Pip is mad, possessed of an insanity which is "heaven's sense." When the little Negro almost drowned, his soul went down to wondrous depths and there he "saw God's foot upon the treadle of the loom, and spoke it." Through that accident Pip, of all the crew, becomes "prelusive of the eternal time" and thus achieves the converse Ahab has denied himself by his blasphemy. The chapter on THE DOUBLOON dramatizes the attempts on the part of the chief active characters to reach truth. In that place Starbuck, in his "mere unaided virtue," is revealed to have no abiding faith: he retreats before "Truth," fearing to lose his "righteousness." ... Stubb's jollity and Flask's clod-like stupidity blunt the spiritual.... The Manxman has mere superstition, Queequeg mere curiosity.... Fedallah worships the doubloon evilly.... Ahab sees the gold coin solipsistically: "three peaks as proud as Lucifer" and all named "Ahab!" Pip alone, of all, has true prescience: he names the doubloon the "navel" of the ship—"Truth" its life.

"Right reason" is the other way to God. It is the way of man's sanity, the pure forging of his intelligence in the smithy of life. To understand what use Melville made of it in *Moby-Dick* two characters, both inactive to the plot, have to be brought forth.

Bulkington is the man who corresponds to "right reason." Melville describes him once early in the book when he enters the Spouter Inn. "Six feet in height, with noble shoulders, and a chest like a coffer-dam." In the deep shadows of his eyes "floated some reminiscences that did not seem to give him much joy." In the LEE SHORE chapter Bulkington is explicitly excluded from the action of the book, but not before Melville has, in ambiguities, divulged his significance as symbol. Bulkington is Man who, by "deep, earnest thinking" puts out to sea, scorning the land, convinced that "in landlessness alone resides the highest truth, shoreless, indefinite as God."

The rest of the *Pequod*'s voyage Bulkington remains a "sleeping-partner" to the action. He is the secret member of the crew, below deck always, like the music under the earth in *Antony and Cleopatra*, strange. He is the crew's heart, the sign of their paternity, the human thing. And by that human thing alone can they reach their apotheosis.

There remains Ishmael. Melville framed Ahab's action, and the parts Pip, Bulkington and the rest of the crew, played in the action, within a narrative told by Ishmael. Too long in criticism of the novel Ishmael has been confused with Herman Melville himself. Ishmael is fictive, imagined, as are Ahab, Pip and Bulkington, not so completely perhaps, for the very reason that he is so like his creator. But he is not his creator only: he is a chorus through whom Ahab's tragedy is seen, by whom what is black and what is white magic is made clear. Like the Catskill eagle Ishmael is able to dive down into the blackest gorges and soar out to the light again.

He is passive and detached, the observer, and thus his separate and dramatic existence is not so easily felt. But unless his choric function is recognized some of the vision of the book is lost. When he alone survived the wreck of the *Pequod*, he remained, after the shroud of the sea rolled on, to tell more than Ahab's wicked story. Ahab's self-created world, in essence privative, a thing of blasphemies and black magic, has its offset. Ahab has to dominate over a world where the humanities may also flower and man (the crew) by Pip's or Bulkington's way reach God. By this use of Ishmael Melville achieved a struggle and a catharsis which he intended, to feel "spotless as the lamb."

Ishmael has that cleansing ubiquity of the chorus in all drama, back to the Greeks. It is interesting that, in the same place where the notes for *Moby-Dick* are written in his Shakespeare, Melville jots down: "Eschylus Tragedies." Ishmael alone hears Father Mapple's sermon out. He alone saw Bulkington, and understood him. It was Ishmael who learned the secrets of Ahab's blasphemies from the prophet of the fog, Elijah. He recognized Pip's God-sight, and moaned for him. He cries forth the glory of the crew's humanity. Ishmael tells their story and their tragedy as well as Ahab's, and thus creates the *Moby-Dick* universe in which the Ahab-world is, by the necessity of life—or the Declaration of Independence—included.

CAPTAIN AHAB AND HIS FOOL

Life has its way, even with Ahab. Melville had drawn upon another myth besides Shakespeare's to create his dark Ahab, that of both Marlowe and Goethe: the Faust legend. But he alters it. After the revolutions of the 18th–19th century the archetype Faust has never been the same. In Melville's alteration the workings of *Lear* and the Fool can also be discerned.

The change comes in the relation of Ahab to Pip. Ahab does not die in the tempestuous agony of Faustus pointing to Christ's blood and crying for His mercy. He dies with an acceptance of his damnation. Before his final battle with the White Whale Ahab has resigned himself to his fate.

His solipsism is most violent and his hate most engendered the night of THE CANDLES when he raises the burning harpoon over his crew. It is a night of storm. The setting is *Lear*-like. Ahab, unlike Lear, does not in this night of storm discover his love for his fellow wretches. On the contrary, this night Ahab uncovers his whole hate. He commits the greater blasphemy than defiance of sun and lightning. He turns the harpoon, forged and baptized for the inhuman Whale alone, upon his own human companions, the crew, and brandishes his hate over them. The morning after the storm Ahab is most subtly dedicated to his malignant purpose when he gives the lightning-twisted binnacle a new needle. Melville marks this pitch of his ego:

> In his fiery eyes of scorn and triumph, you then saw Ahab in all
> his fatal pride.

In a very few hours the change in Ahab sets in and Pip—the shadow of Pip—is the agent of the change. Like a reminder of Ahab's soul he calls to Ahab and Ahab, advancing to help, cries to the sailor who has seized Pip: "Hands off that holiness!" It is a crucial act: for the first time Ahab has offered to help another human being. And at that very moment Ahab speaks Lear's phrases:

> Thou touchest my inmost centre, boy; thou art tied to me by
> cords woven of my heart-strings. Come, let's down.

Though Ahab continues to curse the gods for their "inhumanities," his tone, from this moment, is richer, quieter, less angry and strident. He even questions his former blasphemies, for a bottomed sadness grows in him as Pip lives in the cabin with him. There occurs a return of something Peleg had insisted that Ahab possessed on the day Ishmael signed for the fatal voyage. Peleg then refuted Ishmael's fears of his captain's wicked name—that dogs had licked his blood. He revealed that Ahab had a wife and child, and concluded:

> hold ye then there can be any utter, hopeless harm in Ahab? No,
> no, my lad; stricken, blasted, if he be, Ahab has his humanities!

These humanities had been set aside in Ahab's hate for the White Whale. One incident: Ahab never thought, as he paced the deck at night in fever of anger, how his whalebone stump rapping the boards waked his crew and officers. The aroused Stubb confronts Ahab. Ahab orders him like a dog to kennel. For Stubb cannot, like Pip, affect Ahab. When it is over Stubb's only impulse is to go down on his knees and pray for the hot old man who he feels has so horribly amputated himself from human feelings.

Pip continues to be, mysteriously, the agent of this bloom once it has started. Says Ahab: "I do suck most wondrous philosophies from thee!" He even goes so far as to ask God to bless Pip and save him. BUT before he asks that, he threatens to murder Pip, Pip so weakens his revengeful purpose.

Though Pip recedes in the last chapters, the suppleness he has brought out of old Ahab continues to grow. Pip is left in the hold as though Ahab would down his soul once more, but above decks Ahab is no longer the proud Lucifer. He asks God to bless the captain of the *Rachel*, the last ship they meet before closing with Moby-Dick, the vessel which later picks Ishmael up after the tragedy. The difference in his speech is commented on: "a voice that prolongingly moulded every word." And it is noticed that when, toward the last days, Ahab prepares a basket lookout for himself to be hoisted up the mast to sight Moby-Dick, he trusts his "life-line" to Starbuck's hands. This running sap of his humanities gives out its last shoots in THE SYMPHONY chapter: observe that Ahab asks God to destroy what has been from the first his boast—"God! God! God! stave my brain!" He has turned to Starbuck and talked about his wife and child! And though this apple, his last, and cindered, drops to the soil, his revenge is now less pursued than resigned to. His thoughts are beyond the whale, upon easeful death.

In the three days' chase he is a tense, mastered, almost grim man. He sets himself outside humanity still, but he is no longer arrogant, only lonely: "Cold, cold ..." After the close of the second day, when Fedallah cannot be found, he withers. His last vindictive shout is to rally his angers which have been hurled and lost like Fedallah and the harpoon of lightning and blood. He turns to Fate, the handspike in his windlass: "The whole act's immutably decreed." That night he does not face the whale as was his custom. He turns his "heliotrope glance" back to the east, waiting the sun of the fatal third day like death. It is Macbeth in his soliloquy of tomorrow, before Macduff will meet and match him. On the third day the unbodied winds engage his attention for the first time in the voyage. Even after the White Whale is sighted Ahab lingers, looks over the sea, considers his ship, says goodbye to his masthead. He admits to Starbuck he foreknows his death: the prophecies are fulfilled. In his last speech he moans only that his ship perishes without him:

Oh, lonely death on lonely life! Oh, now I feel my topmost greatness lies in my topmost grief.

He rushes to the White Whale with his old curse dead on his lips.

The last words spoken to him from the ship had been Pip's: "O master,
my master, come back!"

What Pip wrought in Ahab throws over the end of *Moby-Dick* a veil of
grief, relaxes the tensions of its hate, and permits a sympathy for the stricken
man that Ahab's insistent diabolism up to the storm would not have evoked.
The end of this fire-forked tragedy is enriched by a pity in the very jaws of
terror.

The lovely association of Ahab and Pip is like the relations of Lear to
both the Fool and Edgar. What the King learns of their suffering through
companionship with them in storm helps him to shed his pride. His hedging
and self-deluding authority gone, Lear sees wisdom in their profound
unreason. He becomes capable of learning from his Fool just as Captain
Ahab does from his cabin-boy.

In *Lear* Shakespeare has taken the conventional "crazy-witty" and
brought him to an integral place in much more than the plot. He is at center
to the poetic and dramatic conception of the play. Melville grasped the
development.

Someone may object that Pip is mad, not foolish. In Shakespeare the
gradations subtly work into one another. In *Moby-Dick* Pip is both the jester
and the idiot. Before he is frightened out of his wits he and his tambourine
are cap and bells to the crew. His soliloquy upon their midnight revelry
has the sharp, bitter wisdom of the Elizabethan fool. And his talk after his
"drowning" is parallel not only to the Fool and Edgar but to Lear himself.

A remark in *Moby-Dick* throws a sharp light over what has just been said
and over what remains to be said. Melville comments on Pip:

> all thy strange mummeries not unmeaningly blended with the
> black tragedy of the melancholy ship, and mocked it.

For Pip by his madness had seen God.

CHRISTOPHER STEN

Sounding the Whale: Moby-Dick *as Epic Novel*

At the end of his now famous review, written in the late summer of 1850 while composing Moby-Dick, Melville predicted that Hawthorne *Mosses from an Old Manse* would one day be regarded as his masterpiece. "For," he explained, "there is a sure, though a secret sign in some works which prove the culmination of the powers (only the developable ones, however) that produced them." Whether Melville had read any of Hawthorne's other works at this time is unclear. Still unacquainted with the man himself, or so he professed, he apparently did not know that Hawthorne had published *The Scarlet Letter* earlier that same year.[1] Even so, Melville had the good sense to hedge his bets by adding that he hoped the older writer would yet prove his prediction wrong, "Especially," he explained, "as I somehow cling to the strange fancy, that, in all men, hiddenly reside certain wondrous, occult properties—as in some plants and minerals—which by some happy but very rare accident (as bronze was discovered by the melting of the iron and brass in the burning of Corinth) may chance to be called forth here on earth; not entirely waiting for their better discovery in the more congenial, blessed atmosphere of heaven."[2]

What is remarkable about this rather droll version of Emersonian philosophy is that it captures the same conviction regarding the potency of transcendent powers, the same conception of life, even the same theory of

From *Sounding the Whale:* Moby-Dick *as Epic Novel*, pp. 1–26. © 1996 by Kent State University Press.

art that Melville was then trying to infuse into his own masterwork. The calling forth of wondrous, occult properties, that rare but happy accident in the life of humankind, is the central subject of Melville's great story. In its most heightened form, it is also the subject of the world's great modern epics, particularly spiritual epics, such as the *Divine Comedy* and *Paradise Lost*, that tell the story of a hero who makes a life-transforming journey into the deepest realms of the self and back out again.

Since 1950, when Newton Arvin and Henry F. Pommer first examined the matter in some detail, many critics have gone on record as calling *Moby-Dick* an epic or acknowledging it has significant ties with the epic tradition.[3] But there have also been many who have questioned such a designation and argued instead for the influence of some other genre, particularly tragedy, romance, or anatomy, or some heterogeneous combination of genres. Even some who advocate reading the book as an epic, such as Arvin or, more recently, John P. McWilliams, have expressed reservations about the term or claimed the book finally eludes generic classification. Clearly, Melville's critics are far from agreement on the matter, despite the fact that it is one of the most analyzed texts in all of American literature. Even among critics who are predisposed to see the book as an epic, there is some disagreement about the qualities that make it so.

While there are several reasons for such disagreement, much of it, I would say, stems from the fact that even as an epic *Moby-Dick* is an unusually ambitious work that brings together two epic traditions rather than one: the ancient or primitive national epic of combat or conflict, as in the *Iliad* or *Beowulf*, and the modern universal epic of spiritual quest, of the search for a transcendent order or significance to human life, as in the *Divine Comedy* or *Paradise Lost*. Though in Melville's treatment the two are in fact woven together to form a single story, with each of the two major characters crossing the line into the other's epic territory, the first can be said to focus generally on Ahab and the second on Ishmael.

While much of my discussion centers on Ahab and the ancient epic of combat, my principal point of focus throughout is on *Moby-Dick* as a spiritual epic. The later tradition envelopes the earlier one, as Ishmael's story envelopes Ahab's. As more and more critics in the twentieth century have testified, this is Ishmael's story even more than it is Ahab's, important as Ahab's is, and so the parallels with the spiritual epic are more pervasive, and more profound, than the parallels with the primitive epic of physical courage. Moreover, given Melville's symbolic technique, which in an epic work is designed to infuse the quotidian world with significance and elevate mundane matters to the supernatural plane, the theme of the quest for the soul takes on an overriding importance. The ancient epics, too, of course had a spiritual dimension in that they were intended to explain the intrusions of the gods into the affairs of humankind; they were, as Arthur Hutson and Patricia McCoy, among others, have said, concerned in a fundamental way with mythology.[4] But, beginning with Dante, the epic became essentially inward, and not simply psychological but spiritual, centering on the search for the soul or the soul's salvation. As an epic of the universal story of mankind, therefore, *Moby-Dick* is more than a local instance of myth-making or nation-building, comparable for its time and place to the *Odyssey* of ancient Greece or the *Aeneid* of early Rome. It is also Melville's attempt to show that the powers behind the great spiritual epics of the world are the same powers that propelled its major religious mythologies—Judeo-Christian, Hindu, Egyptian, among others Melville knew quite thoroughly[5]—and that they were alive in his own day as they had been in those earlier times.[6]

My understanding of Melville's conception of epic writing has been much informed by several searching studies of the epic poem, especially work by Lascelles Abercrombie, Albert Cook, and John Kevin Newman.[7] However, my understanding of Melville's conception of the epic journey or quest in particular is even more deeply indebted to the work of several modern students of psychology, religion, and myth, especially C. G. Jung, Mircea Eliade, and Joseph Campbell, who define life, and the quest, in terms of individuation or spiritual awakening and otherwise explore, from a modern, broadly psychological point of view, the gap between the seen and the unseen, the known and the unknown worlds. Campbell offers the classic formulation, in *The Hero with a Thousand Faces*, though he in no way restricts his discussion to the epic per se, when he says that the hero's journey is structured like the "monomyth" found in rites of passage, with their three-part structure of separation, initiation or trial, and return. As Campbell says, "A hero ventures forth from the world of common day into a region of supernatural wonder: fabulous forces are there encountered and a decisive victory is won: the hero comes back from this mysterious adventure with the power to bestow boons on his fellow man."[8] The Greek legends of Prometheus and Jason, the biblical narratives of Moses and Christ, the legend of the Buddha, and the epic stories of Odysseus and Aeneas all follow this basic pattern, typically represented in terms of the hero's being swallowed by a monster and then being reborn.

When seen in relation to *Moby-Dick*, such a scheme, with its emphasis on transformation and the turning toward spiritual self-knowledge, naturally points to Ishmael as the true hero of the book; he alone completes an initiatory test and returns to tell about it, though the nature of his "boon" may at first seem problematic. By contrast, Ahab resists the test, even as he resists all reminders of his mortality. In Eliade's terms, he clings to his existence as a "natural" man and is never "born to the spirit."[9] As is often the case, however, there are larger social and political consequences to such resistance. Entrusted with the power to rule others, Ahab is an instance of the public man turned private person. Like the king who becomes a tyrant, a dangerous figure known in myth and folklore as "Holdfast," he sacrifices the public good for his own benefit.[10] Unredeemed and unreborn, Ahab is incapable of recognizing anything beyond his own egoistic needs, and as a consequence he brings not health nor treasure nor sacred knowledge but ruin and death to his people and to himself.

In the following discussion, I have taken a cue from Ishmael, a model anatomist, and dissected *Moby-Dick* into pieces, in this case five sections of nearly equal length. I have done so for practical reasons and as a convenience to the reader, who would no doubt otherwise find this an impossibly long discussion. But I have done so also to call attention to a five-part structure that I believe is inherent to the narrative itself. This structure takes its definition from the stages in the whale hunt that forms the basic story line of the book: (1) preparations for the hunt (chapters 1–23); (2) presentation of the lore of the whaling industry (chapters 24–47); (3) the pursuit of the whale (chapters 48–76); (4) capturing the whale (chapters 77–105); and (5) the trial in the whale's "belly" (chapters 106–35). For each of these parts, I have appropriated a corresponding section title from T. S. Eliot *The Waste Land* to indicate in a shorthand form how Melville unfolds the central themes of the hunt for the great White Whale. Both works, in fact, the one for the nineteenth century and the other for the twentieth, make extensive use of many of the same central images, of death and burial, of games and the hunt, of fire and water, of lightning, thunder, and rain. More importantly, both are epic works that tell much the same story of a devastated land, a wounded fisher king, and the search for a holy elixir or precious fluid, whether of whale oil or water.[11]

The first clues that *Moby-Dick* belongs with the world's great epics are to be found in the etymology and extracts sections of the book's frontmatter. Here, Melville creates the impression that his subject is universal and that, like the old oral epics, his story is a work of bricolage. To appropriate a distinction first made by Lascelles Abercrombie, one of the pioneering students of the form, the extracts are the epic material— "fragmentary, scattered, loosely related, sometimes contradictory"—out of which Melville's epic poetry was made.[12] Even before the current storyteller, in this case Ishmael, had come along to put together the pieces, there had been earlier bards, in sundry cultures and languages, who sang of his subject. By implication, the whale is everywhere and immortal. The etymologies and extracts help to establish the epic stature, formidableness, and inexhaustibility of Ishmael's subject, and they serve to place the reader in an appropriate mood of awe or wonder.

Yet they also help to establish the character of Melville's storyteller, even before he introduces himself. They suggest the compiler himself to be a broken, searching, strangely modern figure, sometimes a lexicographer, sometimes a sub-sub-librarian, and at other times an author or a whaler, whose world is fragmented almost beyond repair—a man so preoccupied with the beast of destruction as to be at once possessed and at the same time paralyzed. Like Tiresias, the narrator of Eliot's poem, he is all but overwhelmed by the oppressiveness of death and destruction, trapped in a past without change, and can therefore do little more than murmur, "These fragments I have shored against my ruins."[13] Together, the extracts reveal the compiler's fixation on Leviathan, the ancient initiator of the Last Things, at the same time they reveal his numbness, or shock, and his inability to make sense of what he has lived through.

But the opening extracts have a redemptive function as well.[14] Like the scattered pieces of a fertility god, they await the water that will restore life to the dead land, and its people, in some distant spring. In effect, they are like seeds of the hero's renewal, as the writings of the past often are. But their mystery first must be unlocked; a worthy hero who can show the way must make himself known. Even before the story begins, then, Melville hints at important parallels between his story of the wounded Ahab, named for a despised *Old Testament king*, and the ancient myth of the impotent Fisher King, whose land has been devastated by his own selfishness and who now awaits a cure.

One final word of introduction: As almost anyone who has ever looked closely into Melville's novel knows, *Moby-Dick* is an incredibly rich and complex work with as intricate a set of symbols, image patterns, and motifs as is to be found in a work of literature anywhere in the world. One of the things I hope to show in the succeeding pages is that there is a logic to Melville's patterning, a logic driven by his understanding of and excitement for the epic genre but given form by a language of nature that is universal—of decay and rebirth, of seasonal cycles, of water, fire, thunder, lightning. I cannot, of course, say whether Melville himself was fully conscious of the intricate web of relations I trace in this chapter. But I believe that, as he himself said in his review of Hawthorne Mosses, there is something "wondrous" or "occult" about certain instances of the creative process that make them transcend what can normally be expected in such matters. Certainly to those of us who have never written an epic, particularly one of such depth and grandeur and richness as *Moby-Dick*, there is something preternatural about the form itself.

Perhaps it is true, too, that there is something preternatural also about the effort required to produce one.

I. The Burial of the Dead

Like the *Divine Comedy*, *The Waste Land*, and other spiritual epics, *Moby-Dick* opens with its hero in a fallen state of emotional torpor and confusion. Starting his story before his transforming experience on the *Pequod*, Ishmael says he is like a spiritually dead man in a spiritually dead land, seeking the relief of the condemned everywhere. He has grown weary of existence, as one does when his youth is spent and he finds himself, as Dante said at the start of his story, "In the middle of the journey of our life." He experiences depression, morbidness, even thoughts of suicide, and he hungers for change or escape.

Like Ahab, Ishmael suffers from a malaise or schism in the soul, an aggression so intense as to prove deadly to himself and others. As Ishmael confesses, it is only by holding to "a strong moral principle" that he can keep himself from "deliberately stepping into the street, and methodically knocking people's hats off." Whenever he finds himself overtaken by such an urge, he knows it is "high time to get to sea as soon as I can." However, whether this is to be viewed as a still surer means of realizing a deep-seated death wish or as an alternative to it, a means of regaining his health, Ishmael himself seems a little unsure. Going to sea, he says equivocally, "is my substitute for pistol and ball."[15] Even if he himself is unsure, his unconscious knows there must be a dying to the world before there can be a rebirth. That is the only way one can ever hope to overcome the death of the spirit. Ahab's example attests to that by his failure, as Ishmael's example does by his success. For the hero to come back as one reborn, filled with creative energy, as Ishmael does when he returns to tell his tale at the end, he must first give up the world and everything in it.

It is significant, but not widely recognized, that Ishmael is not alone in his suffering, that he is a representative figure or exemplary hero. "If they but knew it," he writes, "almost all men in their degree, some time or other, cherish very nearly the same feelings towards the ocean with me," and as proof he has to look no further than his own fellow "Manhattoes." Everywhere he looks, on a dreamy Sunday afternoon, he sees "crowds of water-gazers," thirsting for the adventure that will free them from the land and the deadly routine of their lives. All of them, "thousands upon thousands of mortal men fixed in ocean reveries," hunger for that deeper, vivifying knowledge of the spirit that going to sea makes possible. "Meditation and water," Ishmael explains, "are wedded forever" because, as the Greeks were the first to learn, introspection is the way to self-understanding (3–4). However, as the example of Narcissus warns, such inwardness can be a dangerous business; it must not lead simply to a love for the self or a fascinated preoccupation. It has to be conducted as an active search for and testing of the self; it has to involve a trial. Few people get beyond the stage of being weekend water-gazers because they are afraid of the challenge of the new, afraid of what the unfamiliar might hold. They thus remain among the dead, "victims" whom one day a more adventurous soul, like Ishmael, will come back to try to rescue, and so on, in an endless cycle.

What distinguishes Ishmael from these more timid Manhattanites is simply that he accepts the call to the sea. He does so, to be sure, without full understanding of what he is doing or why, but he is the sort of man who lives intuitively and knows to trust his inner promptings wherever they might lead him. Because the episodes in his journey represent trials of the spirit, psychological trials, his passage is inward as much as it is across land or water—"into depths where obscure resistances are overcome," as Campbell explains, "and long lost, forgotten powers are revivified, to be made available for the transfiguration of the world."[16]

In *Moby-Dick* this inner realm is of course represented by the sea, a universal image of the unconscious, where all the monsters and helping figures of childhood are to be found, along with the many talents and other powers that lie dormant within every adult. Chief among these, in Ishmael's case, is the complicated image of the Whale itself, which is all these things and more and also serves as the "herald" that calls him to his adventure. At the end of chapter 1, "Loomings," with its promise of some distant, portentous engagement, Ishmael reveals that his chief motive for wanting to go whaling "was the overwhelming idea of the great whale himself." But that he is responding as much to a lure from within the self as from without is suggested in the final lines of this opening chapter, when he asserts that, having examined his motives and finding the idea of going whaling to his liking, "the great flood-gates of the wonder-world swung open, and in the wild conceits that swayed me to my purpose, two and two there floated in my inmost soul, endless processions of the whale, and, midmost of them all, one grand hooded phantom, like a snow hill in the air" (7). For Melville's hero, this phantom whale that is later incarnated as the great White Whale is the beginning and the end, and it represents all the instinctual vitality locked deep within the self. It is in this sense that the Whale is synonymous with "the ungraspable phantom of life" that is "the key to it all" (5).

Because the way of the hero is through a strange realm filled with danger and hardship, he requires the help of a guide or wisdom figure, some master of the world beyond who can provide the kind of assistance that, to the neophyte, seems magical. As in any initiatory experience, the novice has to be instructed in the rules of the game and have the way pointed out to him. Also, usually the guide supplies a charm or fetish that will serve to ward off danger or insulate the hero from the dark forces unleashed during this process. While the guide is sometimes a woman, like Beatrice in Dante's vision, more typically it is a man, as in the *Divine Comedy* again, where Virgil assumes the role in the early stages. So in *Moby-Dick* Ishmael is guided through the early episodes of his journey by the masterful harpooner and mystagogue, Queequeg, a deeply if comically religious man whose home is a mythical island called Kokovoko. In keeping with such mysterious figures generally, Queequeg is both protective and forbidding, nurturing and threatening, like the complex powers of the unconscious that he symbolizes.[17]

When Ishmael meets Queequeg, on his first night at the Spouter-Inn, while en route to his initial whaling adventure, the unlettered cannibal seems a most unlikely candidate for a mentor in any regard, except possibly the art of embalming. Queequeg, who has been out late peddling shrunken heads in the streets of New Bedford, looks like something out of a nightmare (Ishmael, it will be noted, had been struggling to fall asleep when the savage makes his entrance into his room), with strange tattoos all over his body, a hideous scalp-knot on his head, and a frightful tomahawk at his side. Ishmael, who admits to being "as much afraid of him as if it was the devil himself" when he first glimpses him, is initially horror-struck that he might lose his own head to this "abominable savage" (22). As it turns out, of course, Queequeg is not a cannibal; but, in the logic of the book, his reputation as a man-eater does make him an appropriate guide for a novice like Ishmael, whose initiation will require that he be swallowed by a Whale. Though Ishmael "ain't insured!" as he exclaims in desperation to the landlord, he could hardly do better than to trust himself to this implausible guide who will one day save him from the wrath of the great White Whale. Even on this first night, after all the proper introductions have been made, he comes somehow to sense that this peculiar figure is a kind of blessing in disguise, so much so that, after dismissing Peter Coffin, he turned in, as he says, "and never slept better in my life" (24). Having once before that evening gone to bed commending himself "to the care of heaven" (20), he can do so now with a true sense of security. To the hero who can bring himself to believe in the ultimate benevolence of the creation, all the security of an assisting providence will be given.

Still, if Ishmael knew how to read the signs, he would know his destiny had brought him to the one man who can lead him through the maze of his future trials and on to the final, life-changing encounter with the beast of destruction. The next morning, waking to find Queequeg's arm thrown over him in a loving, protective embrace, he sees only that "this arm of his [was] tattooed all over with an interminable Cretan labyrinth of a figure" (25). Ishmael is too green at this point to recognize that this figure represents a map of the path in and out of the maze of the Minotaur, the beast he must slay to gain whatever treasure awaits him. He can hardly be expected to know, at this early stage of the hunt, that he himself will become an American version of Theseus. However, much later in the narrative, in "A Bower in the Arsacides" (chapter 102), he will turn up with a tattoo on his own right arm bearing the dimensions of a gigantic whale, whose labyrinthine skeleton he has wandered into and out of again. An experienced whaler himself by this time, Ishmael is then ready to lead his readers into the belly of the whale and out again. In the end, he becomes their guide and protector, the hero who shows the way.

The next morning, though, when Ishmael ventures into the streets of New Bedford, he is startled to find himself in the midst of an entire society completely devoted to the business of whaling. Virtually all the males of the town are living at a stage much in advance of the Manhattanites who manage to get only as far as the water's edge in their longing to go to sea. As Ishmael goes out to survey the local scene, he is astonished to discover the streets are full of seasoned whalers just like Queequeg, not simply "the queerest looking nondescripts from foreign parts," but "savages outright"—Feegeeans, Tongatabooans, Erromanggoans—as well as "scores of green Vermonters and New Hampshire men, all athirst for gain and glory in the fishery" (31). The whole town, the entire industry, it seems, is set up to initiate young men into the ways of the hunt.

But such appearances are deceptive. The rites of passage of New England farmboys are only incidental to the basic mission of America's foremost whaling town, namely, the accumulation of huge fortunes. "Nowhere in all America," Ishmael writes, "will you find more patrician-like houses; parks and gardens more opulent, than in New Bedford." A virtual "land of oil," the "town itself is perhaps the dearest place to live in, in all New England; its wealth all "harpooned and dragged up hither from the bottom of the sea" (32). The whole town, in other words, is dedicated to acquiring only the lowest form of treasure that whaling can bring. Fortunately, Ishmael, who only the night before had escaped the ashy, Gomorrah-like inn called "The Trap," somehow knows not to undertake the hunt for material gain only. Intuitively, he recognizes he must push on to Nantucket, the one place in the world where the simple values of the original whale hunters are still practiced, and embark from there.

Melville spells out the dangers of the hero's quest, particularly the dangers of his seeking only earthly profits, in "The Chapel." Here Ishmael, still a relatively conventional hero seeking a conventional form of strength in a conventional place, becomes one of "a small scattered congregation of sailors, and sailors' wives and widows" who sit in silence contemplating the burial of the dead at sea. On his way to the chapel, he had experienced a sudden change in the weather, from "sunny cold" to "driving sleet and mist," a change that emblematizes the changeability of the earthly realm that is the theme of this chapter (34). Once inside, Ishmael sits with the others staring at a series of marble tablets, which flank the pulpit, bearing the names and other details of the lives of sailors lost at sea—stark reminders of the mutability of human existence and human fortune. Although later, when he signs on the *Pequod*, Ishmael shows a healthy regard for the advantages of earning a good wage, in this scene he comes to recognize that to be paid can never he the chief object of the hunt. For he discovers his own mortality and witnesses the folly of a life dedicated to heaping up material riches. In the chapel, he sees that one must choose between death as an ultimate end and faith in some afterlife or spiritual principle. But he also sees that, for a thinking man like himself, the choice is always tenuous and that true faith is never free of entanglements with the world. As he says, in an odd, haunting image,"Faith, like a jackal, feeds among the tombs, and even from these dead doubts she gathers her most vital hope" (37). Still, the need to conquer death, or look beyond it, to seek the soul and live out of it, is at last clear. This is the true reason for undertaking the hunt for the whale, and in the chapel scene this becomes Ishmael's overriding motive.

Although initially sobered by the many memento mori in the chapel, Ishmael somehow manages to grow "merry" again and jokes that he can even consider a stove boat as a "fine chance for promotion" to a higher realm. "Methinks we have hugely mistaken this matter of Life and Death," he exclaims. "Methinks that what they call my shadow here on earth is my true substance.... Methinks my body is but the lees of my better being. In fact," he says, unconsciously contrasting himself with his future captain, Ahab, who regards every limb as sacred, "take my body who will, take it I say, it is not me. And therefore three cheers for Nantucket; and come a stove boat and stove body when they will, for stave my soul, Jove himself cannot" (37). Despite the obvious bravado of this outburst, Ishmael here makes it clear that he has survived his first test and will emerge from this curious Chapel Perilous a profoundly changed man.

Before looking at the sermon that serves as a gloss on this all-important first step in Ishmael's transformation, it is necessary to look briefly at Father Mapple, the complex, sometimes baffling chaplain who delivers it. A man of God, and agent of the Father (as his Catholic-sounding nickname rather obviously implies), he too had gone to sea in his youth and served as a harpooner in the whaling industry. Old in years and experience, then, yet forever young in appearance, he is thus a fit guide for young petitioners. But unlike Queequeg, Mapple counsels caution and obedience. He is in fact an example of a special kind of guide, called in Jung's term a "threshold guardian," who stands at the gateway to the realm of supernatural power and warns the tender or fainthearted to stay away. Conservative and cautious by nature, like the parents of young children, such a figure purposely tries to delimit the hero's world on every side, in accordance with the abilities of the aspirant. When Mapple speaks, therefore, he is like the ancient oracles who guarded the path of the supplicant; he warns the would-be adventurer to stay within the confines of the known world and to flee all fearful encounters with the great powers beyond. To be sure, as a threshold guardian, it is not Mapple's job to frighten away *all* comers; on the contrary, his function is to make sure that the few who finally do come forward are truly ready to take the plunge, that they have the courage and skill to survive the challenges of the next stage of the journey.

After Father Mapple climbs up to his pulpit, he stands to deliver his sermon from behind a copy of the Bible. Immediately sizing him up, Ishmael senses that what he is about to speak is the truth, not because it conforms to the standard Judaeo-Christian view, but because what the chaplain brings to his congregation is the water of renewal. Mapple himself speaks from the very midst of it. "Replenished with the meat and wine of the word," Ishmael explains, "to the faithful man of God, this pulpit, I see, is a self-containing stronghold—a lofty Ehrenbreitstein, with a perennial well of water within the walls" (39). Mapple's sermon, however, is deceptive, as dual-edged as the man himself. What he preaches is indeed a "two-stranded lesson" (42). While on the one hand he speaks to the many whose hearts are not yet ready, preaching against sin and disobedience, and counseling repentance and submission to the will of God; on the other, he also speaks to the few, like Ishmael, who may at that very moment be on the threshold of the potentially deadly yet also potentially glorious adventure of the hero.

Properly understood, the story of Jonah, though couched in the familiar biblical language of sin and trial and deliverance, is a universal tale of one who actively refuses the call to the soul's awakening. It thus serves as a warning, and an invitation, to those who might be resisting or wavering on the brink. What Mapple says is paradoxical: the call is irresistible; the call must be freely accepted. Clearly there is no escaping the experience of being trapped in the belly of the whale, if that is one's destiny. Whether one refuses, like Jonah, or accepts the call, as Ishmael does, there is no avoiding the experience of death and burial, of suffering and dismemberment, when it finally comes.[18] There is only the hope of surviving it in some new form, the hope of some ultimate redemption or miraculous return from the dead, as Jonah returns in the end.

In Melville's conception, the call to adventure, the call to spiritual awakening, was equivalent to the Puritan experience of grace; and, to the rational mind, it entailed the same contradictory dynamic of fate and free will. Like his Calvinist forebears, Melville understood the call as an invitation to experience the woe and delight of the loss of ego that leads to the discovery of the self or the soul, one's core identity. Though one of the smallest books in the Scriptures, Mapple exclaims of Jonah's story, while underscoring the sermon's true theme, "what depths of the soul does Jonah's deep sea-line sound!" (42). The chaplain's rendering of Jonah's tale constitutes a paradigm of the central situation of Melville's epic as a whole, of the trials of the self and its transformation, its breakup and recovery in the belly of the beast. As such, it deserves careful scrutiny.

In Mapple's rendering, the story of Jonah is the story of a man bent on escaping his identity, the identity of his destiny. Jonah's every move, every encounter, reveals this to be so. As he steps onto the ship bound for Tarshish, all the sailors stop to stare at him and wonder *who he is*. And almost immediately, as if in answer to their question, someone calls him a "parricide," a seemingly offhand remark that, ironically, provides an important clue to his identity (43). For in refusing the call to do his Father's bidding, Jonah in effect "kills the father" in himself, the source of spiritual life, of empowering identity, at his center. He refuses to grow up. When the Captain, hearing Jonah coming toward his cabin, calls out "Who's there?" the innocent request to identify himself "mangles" Jonah, an early sign that, for Melville, Jonah's story is linked with Ahab's, as well as Ishmael's, and that the process of dismemberment is symbolic of the pain of personal transformation (44).

It is only when the "hard hand of God" presses on Jonah, forcing him to answer the crew's demands to reveal who he is, that the object of his trial is defined as nothing more or less than the acceptance of his identity. It is only when he begins to confess who he is—first tentatively, "I am a Hebrew," he cries at the height of the storm, thus identifying himself as one of the chosen; then more emphatically, "I fear the Lord the God of Heaven"—that the process of recovering his true self can begin in earnest. For it is then that his shipmates throw him into the sea, where he is carried down "into the yawning jaws awaiting him" (46). There, having owned up to his earthly identity as "one who fears the Lord," he finally accepts God's call, repents his waywardness, and discovers his spiritual identity as one who is delivered by the Lord. In Hebrew Jonah means "dove." And as we know from the story of Noah and elsewhere, the dove carries the sign of peace; it brings news of deliverance from death.

Mapple's sermon does more than warn against refusing the call, however. It also defines the marks of those who do and those who do not refuse it, and as such it provides a means for judging Ishmael's motives, his readiness to undertake the journey, and for determining why Ahab's quest is destined to fail. First of all, until the adventurer owns who he is and recognizes the need to make the journey he is called to, he lives as a man who is already dead, as Jonah does when he "sleeps" with a "dead ear" in his tomblike berth below the ship's waterline (45). That is to say, he feels trapped in his own ego. Secondly, he must "pay" for his own passage. As Mapple says, in this world it is "sin that pays its way" (44). Like Ahab, who in the end pays for his passage on the *Pequod* with the gold doubloon, the "God-fugitive" Jonah is willing to pay much more than the standard fare if that will permit him to escape his destiny (46). But of course those who refuse the call cannot escape having to pay spiritually, too, for their waywardness. That is why they die. Without an infinite source of vitality to sustain them, without a soul, their lives eventually run out.

As it is for Jonah, so it is for these others; the guilty conscience of the resisting hero "is a wound, and there's naught to staunch it" (45). His spiritual lifeblood would all eventually leak away, leaving him dead. Only if it were replenished endlessly, as it would be if he possessed the oil of the whale, would the lamp of his soul burn eternally.[19] In sum, the marks of those who refuse the call, who remain imprisoned by their earthly identity, are these: a feeling of spiritual deadness and entrapment; a sense of life's meagerness, and apprehension at its eventually running out; a desperate desire to hold on, to pay any price but the one required of them; a great fear of God and of not being chosen; and the profound dread that there will be no boon or prize at the end of the game.[20]

In the end, after being reborn "out of the belly of hell," when Jonah is commanded a second time, he answers the call to do "the Almighty's bidding." He agrees to do his duty by preaching "the Truth to the Face of Falsehood"; he goes to Nineveh and brings the prophecy of the deliverance from death of the people there (47–48). Following his own deliverance, Jonah thus becomes an instance of the returning hero, an image of the many figures in *Moby-Dick* who speak as prophets to the dead—of Father Mapple, Elijah, Pip, and finally Ishmael. Melville, however, shows us little of the returning Jonah. Instead, it is Father Mapple who fills out the image of the returning hero in his role as boon-carrier.[21] Significantly, he is a man of the word, an artist, a truth-teller, like Melville himself. When he speaks, the signs are on him that God speaks through him; the "light" that leaps from his eye, the "thunders" that roll away from his brow, these make his listeners look on him with the sense they are looking on the Godhead itself, "with a quick fear that was strange to them" (47).

Yet even Mapple is a reluctant hero; what he shows by his example is how difficult it is to return to the human fold after the intense inwardness and sublimity of the hunt. As he explains to his congregation, "[while] God has laid but one hand upon you; both his hands press upon me." The boon becomes a terrible burden; to be a "speaker of true things," to sound "unwelcome truths in the ears of a wicked Nineveh," to speak to the dead of their deadness and suffer the enmity of the damned is a hard thing.

Fortunately, there is a power to sustain the returning quester—the power of God, of the deepest self. In an image that defines the central meaning of Melville's great symbol of the Whale, there is the power of Leviathan itself, its breeching a trope for the birth of the soul out of the depths of its imprisonment, as it is in Mapple's sermon. Instantaneously, when Jonah finally speaks his own name, when he cries out his identity for the first time, "Then God spake unto the fish [that confined him]; and from the shuddering cold and blackness of the sea, the whale came breeching up towards the warm and pleasant sun, and all the delights of air and earth" (47–48). As this image powerfully suggests, the birth of the self is an occurrence of incredible force, and of transcendent beauty and joy. Though there is a burden to the hero's return, a "woe," it is more than compensated by the "delight" he experiences in performing his true calling. At the culminating moment, when Mapple begins his peroration on the theme of "delight," the chaplain speaks the overriding thesis of his sermon, and of the whole first section of *Moby-Dick*, when he exclaims, "Delight is to him,—a far, far upward, and inward delight—who against the proud gods and commodores of this earth, ever stands forth his own inexorable self" (48).

Chapter 10, "A Bosom Friend," the first of several in the portrait of Queequeg, presents another imposing, yet this time also comic, example of a character who knows how to stand forth "his own inexorable self." Like the New Bedford chaplain, Queequeg is at one with his god and seems to command all the powers of the earth. Where Mapple moves easily through the driving rain (the water that restores or destroys) on his way to the Whalemen's Chapel, Queequeg sits comfortably before the hearth fire (the fire that revives or kills) in the Spouter-Inn. Where Mapple refashions the word of God to suit his ministerial purpose, Queequeg reworks the countenance of his little surrogate god, Yojo, to suit his inner vision. Neither man's action is sacrilegious because both work out of the inner necessity of the returning hero. Both have seen the face of the Father, and now, each in

ıdependent way, they have come back to the fold to relate what they
vitnessed, and to do the work they are bidden to do.

Yet as the title of this chapter suggests, Queequeg is more than the
guide who will show Ishmael the way to the hidden god. He *is* the god, an
image of that "inexorable self" at the center of every successful hero. A pagan,
savage and illiterate, he had a "hideously marred" face with "something in
it," Ishmael says vaguely, "which was by no means disagreeable." Yet what
that something is he then proceeds to identify, with deadpan irony, when he
exclaims, "You cannot hide the soul" (49). Though on the way to Nantucket
a greenhorn mistakes Queequeg for "the devil," Ishmael has already gone far
enough in his initiation to be able to see in the Polynesian's deep, dark eyes
"tokens of a spirit that would dare a thousand devils" (60, 50). If he "looked
like a man who had never cringed and never had had a creditor," as Ishmael
observes of him, no doubt it is because he never had a cause to fear anything
and never had a need to borrow. Wholly centered in himself, he has "no
desire to enlarge his circle of acquaintances"; but when his friends come to
him, as Ishmael does, he is happy to reciprocate, and more (50). Possessing
more of the world's wealth than he himself will ever need, he gives half
his thirty pieces of silver, and more, to his new friend, Ishmael. In his own
example, he thus makes clear that the world will always provide the initiate
whatever he needs to make his journey. To the poor hero like Ishmael, who
has the courage to make the first step, life becomes a veritable cornucopia,
supplying both bed and counterpane, an evening of good talk, a long smoke,
and a friend who "would gladly die for me, if need should be" (51). If he also
has to be forced to take an embalmed head into the bargain, that is because,
unlike Queequeg, he still has no more desire to be reminded of his mortality
than any other poor mortal.

Still, more important than these outward signs of the warming of
the world, in the midst of New Bedford's arctic winter, are the signs of
warming taking place within Ishmael himself, now that he has made friends
with Queequeg. Sitting in their room, the "fire burning low," watching the
cannibal count the pages of a "marvelous book" (presumably the Bible),
he suddenly became "sensible of strange feelings. I felt a melting in me.
No more my splintered heart and maddened hand were turned against the
wolfish world. This soothing savage had redeemed it" (50–51).

Later, after the two have formally declared their friendship, Ishmael
shows the powerful effect of his transformation when, unlike Jonah before
him, he jumps at the chance to do the Lord's bidding. In a comic scene,
Ishmael shows he is, if anything, a little too quick to preach his own religion,
his "particular Presbyterian form of worship," to a real pagan. For, the way
he sees it, he has to "turn idolator" and become a pagan himself first if he is

to have any influence with Queequeg (52). Still, as the result of his efforts, Ishmael goes to bed not alone, as Jonah did, but with a friend; not with a conscience wracked by guilt, as Jonah had, but with one "at peace"; not to sleep like a dead man but to lie abed "chatting and napping" at intervals and then to awake refreshed long before daybreak (53). There, in the cold and the dark, after the fire has gone out, Ishmael speaks for the first time not simply of feeling his "identity" but of feeling it "aright," as if "darkness were indeed the proper element of our essences," he theorizes, "though light be more congenial to our clayey part" (54). Now, warmed by an interior fire, Ishmael has no need for any other kind of flame.

The next day, as the two of them glide down the Acushnet River on the way out of town toward Nantucket, they see ice-crusted New Bedford off to one side, "huge hills and mountains of casks on casks piled upon her wharves" (60). These casks are of course intended to hold the precious whale oil that is the town's principal source of wealth. However, they are really more like stacks of coffins, or caskets, that lie there mutely waiting to serve the burial of the dead instead. To the mind prepared to look for the "meaning" of things, as Ishmael does with comic self-consciousness in the New Bedford chapters, and acknowledge the pervasiveness of death in this wintry landscape, they serve as reminders that America's most affluent town is, after all, a land of the dead and must be abandoned.

By contrast, Nantucket seems impoverished and unpromising. To the worldly eye, it is a wasteland, a desert of sand—"all beach, without a background." But despite the barrenness of the landscape, the people of Nantucket enjoy a wealth and power that those of New Bedford and other whaling centers can hardly appreciate. For like "sea hermits, issuing from their ant-hill in the sea," these "naked Nantucketers" have "overrun and conquered the watery world like so many Alexanders; parcelling out among them the Atlantic, Pacific, and Indian oceans, as the three pirate powers did Poland." As is soon evident in Ishmael's dealings with the Quaker Bildad, the Nantucketers can be shrewd, grasping materialists, but they possess a wealth beyond material riches, too. So at home is the Nantucket whaler while at sea, so attuned to its powerful rhythms, that at night, like the landless gull, he "furls his sails, and lays him to his rest, while under his very pillow rush herds of walruses and whales" (63–64). A nation of adventuring heroes, the people of Nantucket command the wealth of all the seas, the wealth of dreams and the unconscious, as this oceanic image of natural power makes clear.

Like most chapter titles in *Moby-Dick*, "Chowder," the title of the next chapter, is a metaphor or conceit. Besides suggesting something of the mixed character of Ishmael's initial experience of Nantucket, it offers a preview, in miniature, of the mixed nature of the whaling life generally. Arriving at the Try-Pots Inn, Ishmael is immediately reminded by the gallows on the sign outside that there is death and damnation in the whaleman's calling. If one is not killed or maimed in the hunt, the despair at failure can be just as devastating and lead to the same result. Mistress Hussey lectures Queequeg about a recent suicide in her apartments, a young man named Stiggs, who, "coming from that unfort'nt v'y'ge of his," as she says, "when he was gone four years and a half, with ony three barrels of *ile*, was found dead in my first floor back, with his harpoon in his side," a would-be Christ but one forsaken by the Father (67).

However, just as there is both clam and cod on the bill of fare at the Try-Pots Inn, so is there both death and life in the business of whaling. The cook in the kitchen will sometimes mix up the order and serve "clam" (symbol of the recalcitrance of life, of the withholding side of the dual-edged female principle): "that's a rather cold and clammy reception in the winter time, ain't it, Mrs. Hussey?" complains Ishmael facetiously, when his dinner order arrives. But the boldest adventurer will generally get "cod" (symbol of the potency of life, of the providential side of the dual-edged male principle), as Ishmael discovers when he steps to the kitchen window and barks out his order to be sure there will be no mistake about it. "Ask," saith the Lord, according to the well-known proverb, "and ye shall be given." In this world, even the adventuring hero sometimes has to take potluck; but if he is truly fearless about tapping its wealth, he will be rewarded beyond even his wildest dreams. When asked, at the end of this chapter, whether he and Queequeg will take clam or cod the next morning for breakfast, Ishmael responds with the boldness of one who has learned to stand forth his own inexorable self, "Both; and let's have a couple of smoked herring by way of variety," he adds cheekily (67).

"God helps those who help themselves"—that is the unwritten motto of the successful adventurer, and that is the surprising lesson of the following chapter, "The Ship." Though the hero can hardly know such a thing in the beginning, the person who serves as a guide is simply a symbol of the assisting power that dwells within everyone. He is, as in the case of Queequeg, an image of the soul of the adventurer, his task being to instill in his new friend an abiding confidence in his own powers. Thus Ishmael, despite the newfound brazenness displayed at the end of the previous chapter, expresses "surprise and no small concern" when Queequeg informs him that the little god Yojo wants Ishmael himself to be the one to select their ship. Speaking like the novice he is, Ishmael nervously admits that "I did not like that plan at all. I had not a little relied upon Queequeg's sagacity to point out the whaler best fitted to carry us and our fortunes securely." Yet the next morning, his courage screwed up to a pitch, he accomplishes his task quickly and with little worry or internal debate. Ostensibly entrusting everything to the little god Yojo, the comic fetish or charm that seems to protect Ishmael in Queequeg's absence, he in fact falls back on his own intuition in choosing the *Pequod* over the several other ships then in port (67–68). Though in the course of his adventures he sometimes claims to be a victim of the mysterious Fates, it should be recognized that, for the most part, in important ways Ishmael really is the master of his own destiny.

The first part of his day's work successfully completed, Ishmael is nonetheless little wiser than when he began. Boarding the *Pequod* to propose himself as a "candidate" for the voyage, his first response is to look around the quarterdeck "for some one having authority" (70). Clearly, he has not yet figured out that all authority comes from within. Several pages later, though he has by then met with both Captains Peleg and Bildad and taken care of all necessary details, he ends the scene still hungering to see the man who is really in charge. Having only heard about Captain Ahab at this point, Ishmael feels the mystery of his authority deepen. For at this point he learns only that there is much more to know about him. Not until much later are we shown that, behind Ahab, there is a higher authority still, and that Ahab, the son of a "crazy, widowed mother," also seeks the Father (79). Here, however, everything that transpires demonstrates, in an understated way, what Ishmael is not yet prepared to know—namely, that in all essential matters the final authority must reside within the adventurer's own soul.

The encounter with Peleg and Bildad is structured as a second major threshold scene, where Ishmael's resolve and worthiness are tested and he is revealed to be one of the chosen few. Almost literally, in stepping onto the *Pequod*, Ishmael steps into the mouth of the whale, the entrance to the place of trial. For the ship has been rebuilt out of various parts of the whalemen's catch over a long span of years, and the curious wigwam in which he is subjected to Peleg's rigorous questioning is actually supported by the jawbones of a right whale.

Like Father Mapple, Peleg has the job of separating false aspirants from true ones. Those who are not yet ready to follow the path, he tries to dissuade, or intimidate, while those of pure heart and steady purpose he tries to encourage or help smooth their way. Like a holy man conducting an inquest of a heretic, Peleg questions Ishmael about his previous experience at sea. And like a true master, he begins by asking the key question concerning the ultimate test of the whale-hunting hero: "ever been in a stove boat?" Immediately sensing in the politeness of Ishmael's reply ("No, Sir, I never have") that he is a perfect neophyte, Peleg goes back to the beginning and inquires, with the disgust of one who is prepared to hear the worst, "Dost know nothing at all about whaling, I dare say—eh?" When Ishmael confesses his complete ignorance, but then proceeds to mention his previous experience in the merchant service, Peleg cuts him off in disgust and then offers a hint as to the peculiar nature of the whaling enterprise that might help to set him back on track: "Marchant service be damned," he exclaims. "Talk not that lingo to me. Dost see that leg?—I'll take that leg away from thy stern, if ever thou talkest of the marchant service to me again. Marchant service indeed!"(71).

What Peleg hints at here is that those who stray from the true spirit of whaling, who engage in the hunt for worldly, selfish purposes, will suffer the loss of their "standpoint" or leg, symbolic of the phallus or life force, as the captain of the *Pequod* does. It seems hardly a coincidence that, when Peleg hears of such heresy, he suspects Ishmael of being a kind of parricide, accusing him of thinking about "murdering the officers" when he gets to sea. To be sure, Peleg is stringing him along, playing him for the greenhorn he is, as Ishmael eventually comes to realize. But when he returns to the questioning in earnest, asking about Ishmael's motives in wanting to go "a-whaling," Peleg begins to see a little into his heart, and what he finds wins him over to the novice's side: "Well, sir, I want to see what whaling is," Ishmael replies. "I want to see the world" (71). Demonstrating the simple curiosity and innocent wonder of the true aspirant, Ishmael here reveals none of the covetousness or sensualism typical of the men in the merchant service, and none of the egotism that will later emerge in Ahab. After more of Peleg's tough questioning, which Ishmael gets through with relative ease, he is invited "below deck into the cabin," there to sign the ship's papers, and to meet Bildad, in the last test of this early series (73).

Bildad is made of sterner stuff than Peleg, however, and poses a stiffer challenge. Originally "educated according to the strictest sect of Nantucket Quakerism," he is a man who in his later years has resisted all the world's temptations, even "the sight of many unclad, lovely island creatures, round the Horn," as Ulysses resisted the sirens. Known chiefly for his "immutableness," he is one who has himself passed the true whaleman's test, and as such he is thus best suited to administer it to others (74). Like an old sachem or rabbi confronting a young initiate, he asks Ishmael just a single question, composed of two well-chosen words. So masterful is this high priest of whaling—who throughout the interview sits holding the Scriptures in his hands—that he formulates his query using the words of his friend, simply redirecting them to this supplicant. When Peleg informs him that Ishmael says "he's our man, ... he wants to ship," Bildad masterfully turns to the would-be hero and asks him to testify on his own behalf, "Dost thee?" He thus puts to him the one essential question: he asks Ishmael to search his heart and speak his fitness for signing on. That Ishmael speaks truly when he replies "I *dost*" is attested to by the fact that in doing so he slips into the idiom of the old Quaker whaleman, exemplar of Nantucket's great adventurers, and that he does so "unconsciously." For as is repeatedly revealed in *Moby-Dick*, to speak unconsciously is to speak out of the authority of the divine self. In saying "I *dost*," Ishmael does more than assert his readiness, however. He also proclaims his own mortality and thus confesses his dependence on the divine energy to sustain him: "I am dust," he seems to say. At the end of their brief interview, then, Ishmael receives Bildad's laconic blessing or approval. When Peleg asks his friend what he thinks of their young prospect, Bildad responds only with a slightly exasperated but neatly ambiguous, "He'll do" (75).

That Bildad also proves to be exceedingly tight-fisted when it comes to assigning Ishmael his share of the ship's profits may not be so much a sign of hypocrisy in the end, as is generally thought, as it is a sign of consistency. Bildad does have a weaker side, but a case can also be made that he drives a hard bargain because he knows that any worldiness, any sign of hunger for "a princely fortune" (76), may so contaminate the initiate's efforts as to lead him to ruin. Bildad knows that the initiate must put all ideas of making an earthly fortune out of his mind if he is to have any hope of gaining the ultimate reward. As he says, "where your treasure is, there will your heart be also" (77). Indeed, one's heart, or soul, as Melville explains throughout *Moby-Dick*, is one's treasure.

Having affirmed his readiness for the voyage of the *Pequod*, Ishmael is now prepared to speak the name of the "I" who uttered "I *dost*." Returning to his room in the Try-Pots Inn, where Queequeg has been observing his "Ramadan," practicing the sort of asceticism or indifference to the world that Bildad had been trying to instill in Ishmael, Ishmael tries to rouse the Polynesian by speaking softly through the keyhole. In doing so, he announces his identity for the first time in the chronology of the book's events. "Queequeg," he whispers, as though still seeking some external confirmation of himself. "I say, Queequeg! why don't you speak? It's I—Ishmael" (82). Ironically, at the very moment he wants Queequeg to confirm his presence, Ishmael is giving voice to his own deepest self. Here, for the first time, we can begin to appreciate the significance of Ishmael's name, which in Hebrew means "God shall hear," for the biblical Ishmael was more than an outcast or rejected son; he was also one whose name contained the promise of divine redemption. To identify oneself as "Ishmael" is to speak one's faith that the self contains within it all the strength of God the Father. Of course, Queequeg, who is both a simple savage from Kokovoko and an image of the eternal soul within each person, does not stir until he is ready. The soul will not respond simply because it is summoned. At times we may assume that it will succumb to our "polite arts and blandishments," as Ishmael wrongly assumes Queequeg will do in this same scene (84). But generally it comes alive in its own good time, according to a rhythm of its own, as Queequeg finally does the next morning, long after Ishmael has given up trying to rouse him, and the sun first enters their room.

Brief as this scene is, Ishmael nonetheless shows that he has learned to respect the independence of the soul that bides its time. Confident, finally, that Queequeg will eventually follow him to bed, Ishmael takes his own bearskin jacket and, in his last act before retiring, throws it over his new friend, "as it promised to be a very cold night" (84). It is not a gesture that shows much respect for the savage's own wishes, to be sure. But it is an act of real tenderness just the same, one that shows Ishmael to have made a big advance over the smug tolerance he had claimed at the start of this chapter.

As if to confirm that at least a small opening has been made in Ishmael's religious temper, the chapter ends with a reversal of the beginning. Instead of congratulating himself for his noblesse oblige, as he did when he first met Queequeg and learned of his bizarre religious practices, he ends with the sudden recognition that an illiterate savage like Queequeg was capable of feeling much the same way toward himself, thinking that "he knew a good deal more about the true religion than I did" and felt "a sort of condescending concern and compassion" for Ishmael because of his great ignorance (86). Thus, while Ishmael opens the chapter with only a tiny "key-hole prospect" onto Queequeg's Ramadan (and a "crooked and sinister one" at that, as he says), he ends it with the light of day finally dawning on him, literally and figuratively (82). Still a good Presbyterian, garrulously proselytizing to Queequeg even in the last paragraphs of this chapter, Ishmael at least shows signs of becoming more understanding of the religious beliefs and practices of his companion and of learning to appreciate the universal conditions underlying the world's many religions.

Having grown more tolerant himself, now, the naturally loquacious Ishmael finds it but a small step to preaching toleration to others. Chapter 18, "His Mark," ostensibly concerns Queequeg's demonstration of prowess with a harpoon (hitting "his mark") and signing the ship's papers (making "his mark"). But, less obviously, it also concerns Ishmael's growing ecumenicalism, even to the point of showing him in the outrageously funny, unexpected role of Queequeg's evangelist—not his Matthew, Luke, or John, but "His Mark." From the time he enters the story, Queequeg has been something of a Christ-figure to Ishmael, prompting his spiritual awakening, guiding the recovery of his soul, pointing the way to renewed health and happiness. Of course there is a good deal of leg-pulling in Ishmael's exorbitant claim to the Quaker captains that "Queequeg here is a born member of the First Congregational Church. He is a deacon himself, Queequeg is" (88). But beneath the humor of his prevarication and wordplay, the gospel truth of Ishmael's universalism shines through.

Contrary to those, such as H. Bruce Franklin, who argue that *Moby-Dick* shows Melville's preoccupation with one or another religious mythology, I would emphasize the importance of Ishmael's growing ecumenicalism, an ecumenicalism that reaches its high point in this scene. Pressed hard by Bildad to explain himself, Ishmael responds facetiously, "I mean, sir, the same ancient Catholic Church to which you and I, and Captain Peleg there, and Queequeg here, and all of us, and every mother's son and soul of us belong; the great and everlasting First Congregation of this whole worshipping world; we all belong to that ... in *that* we all join hands." "Splice, thou mean'st *splice* hands," Peleg corrects him, thus emphasizing his own recognition, under the sway of Ishmael's rhetoric, of the powerful human bonds, the equality and goodwill, that everyone celebrates in the simple gesture of joining hands (later celebrated in "A Squeeze of the Hand"). Ironically, it is Peleg, then, and not Queequeg, who comes to be converted in this chapter. His heart is changed by the upstart evangelist Ishmael, as he himself humorously confesses. "Young man," Peleg exclaims, at the same time telling them to forget about the cannibal's so-called "conversion" papers and inviting the two of them on board, "you'd better ship for a missionary, instead of a fore-mast hand; I never heard a better sermon" (88).

Bildad is not so easily won over, however. "Eyeing" Queequeg during the signing of the *Pequod*'s papers, afterward he stands and places a tract entitled "The Latter Day Coming; or No Time to Lose," in the cannibal's hands. Only then does he join hands with him, grasping both the little book and Queequeg's hands in his own. Looking "earnestly into his eyes," he warns him to "mind thine eye" and "turn from the wrath to come." But clearly these are wasted words, like the words in the tract that the illiterate Queequeg will never read (nor needs to). As the incarnation of the soul, Queequeg has no ego involvement in the life he leads; unlike Ahab, he does not have to mind his "I." Neither does he have to concern himself with the Last Things, for he has nothing to lose in the end. Instead, as demonstrated earlier, Queequeg keeps his eye on the eye of the whale, the incarnation of the self. For the whale is an image of all Nature, what Emerson called the "Other Me." Like a Buddhist archer, who trains himself to think of nothing but his target, Queequeg is a perfect master, one who can hit the "spot" at will, because he and the whale's eye are one (88–89).

Elijah, the "Prophet" of the next chapter, mysteriously materializes to provide Ishmael his final test before he ships out, asking him whether he has any fear for his soul and darkly hinting that he has committed himself to a fatal undertaking. As the last guardian of the threshold to the magic realm, the prophet tries to shake the initiate's resolve by casting doubt on the ship's whole enterprise; by claiming to know all about its strange past and the captain he enigmatically refers to as "Old Thunder"; and by pretending to have knowledge of the *Pequod*'s future (92). After determining that Ishmael and his friend have just signed the ship's articles, the old sailor inquires ominously, "Anything down there about your souls?" Ironically, Ishmael seems not to comprehend: "About what?" he replies (91). In this case, he is fortunate not to understand Elijah, for we see here by how thin a thread the fate of the would-be adventurer hangs; if Ishmael had comprehended the old prophet, he might have been scared away, or so we are led to assume. However, Ishmael does continue to resist Elijah's sly insinuations, and in the end the old man intimates that Ishmael is made of the true stuff: "I like to hear a chap talk up that way," he says, pretending to call an end to their talk; "you are just the man for him [i.e., Ahab]—the likes of ye. Morning to ye, shipmates, morning!" (93). Despite some lingering doubts after he learns the name of this stranger, Ishmael dismisses them almost entirely by the end of the scene, just a trace of uncertainty remaining to show his mortality.

In the concluding three chapters of this long opening section of *Moby-Dick*, Melville brings to a close the themes of the preparation for the hunt that are his chief concern. "All Astir," which focuses on the preparation of the ship—the purchasing and collecting and the fetching, hauling, and stowing down of its stores—conveys the idea of the world's richness or fecundity, its boundless capacity to provide for the hero's material needs so he can get on with the important business of the quest. Like Mother Nature, the figure called Aunt Charity, who is the *Pequod*'s chief provisioner, is "a lean old lady of a most determined and indefatigable spirit, but withal very kindhearted." She is an image of the eternal woman, always up and doing, forever eager to lend her "hand and heart to anything that promised to yield safety, comfort, and consolation" to the ship's officers and crew. But, even so, there are some needs that even the eternal female cannot supply, some accidents or losses she cannot anticipate or protect against. While the whale ship has been provisioned with "spare boats, spare spars, and spare lines and harpoons, and spare everythings, almost," there can be no supplying, as Ishmael says with both humor and seriousness, of a "spare Captain and duplicate ship" (96). For some things, the men must supply their own insurance; they must be their own protection. How they might accomplish that all-important task is the subject of the next chapter, "Going Aboard," the title of which reiterates a timeless call to adventure.

The next day, when Ishmael and Queequeg make their way past crazy Elijah one last time and step aboard the *Pequod*, it is still early morning, and all is quiet, "not a soul moving." The only person they encounter is a sleeper, a man down in the forecastle spread" at whole length upon two chests" [a fore-image of Ishmael on the coffin/life-buoy at the end], "his face downwards and inclosed in his folded arms," a pose symbolizing self-protection. An old rigger, "wrapped in a tattered pea-jacket," a variation of the earlier image of Queequeg at his Ramadan with Ishmael's coat thrown over him, this curious figure is another likeness of the soul, but the soul in a state of sleep (99). Taking seats at each end of the man, Ishmael and Queequeg pass the time talking and sharing a smoke from the latter's odd tomahawk-pipe. Unaccountably, whenever Queequeg took his turn with the instrument, "he flourished the hatchet-side of it over the sleeper's head," and when Ishmael asks what he is up to, he says only, "Perry easy, kill-e; oh! perry easy!" Still, the action and the explanation together make it clear that Queequeg is acting out a version of the story of Damocles, and that in his version the sword of Fate hangs over the soul that sleeps. The soul must never let down its guard. Like the sleeper who finally wakes to the smoke of his own damnation, the soul must be "all alive now"; it must "turn to." It, too, must be forever up and about its business (100).

What that business consists of Ishmael unwittingly explains when he says that Queequeg's tomahawk-pipe "both brained his foes and soothed his soul" (100). Quite simply, it is the soul's job to slay its enemies; only then can it feel "soothed."[22] In fact, such a notion of the soul's duty provides the rationale for the rest of Melville's epic story. It explains why Ishmael, having found his deepest self, must still go to sea—not to slay the White Whale (which is, after all, Melville's great image of the soul) but to destroy its enemies. Despite this long foreground, then, the journey of Ishmael is only now ready to begin.

At various times in the land-based chapters of *Moby-Dick*, Ishmael shows that he is a fearful man, as well as a man of courage. Whether making his way through the pitch-black streets of New Bedford or facing the prospect of sleeping with a savage; whether contemplating the cenotaphs in the Whaleman's Chapel or standing helplessly outside Queequeg's locked room, Ishmael evidences a nervous, morbid imagination. He is a man who fears death and destruction, and premature burial most of all. In the chapters at the end of this section, his fearfulness even intensifies, as he comes closer and closer to the time when he must cross the threshold of the ship for the last time and move irreversibly into Captain Ahab's domain. The first meeting with Elijah stirs up in Ishmael "all kinds of vague wonderments and half-apprehensions" concerning the *Pequod*, its mysterious captain, and the leg he has lost; and when he sees a group of dim, shadowy figures boarding the ship before dawn the next morning, he has to "beat ... down" his fear when he learns they are nowhere to be found. Significantly, it "seemed,"

Ishmael says, that "Queequeg had not at all noticed" these strange figures (93, 99). Undoubtedly Queequeg did notice them, and everything else besides. The reason he seems not to observe such things is simply that he has no fears, and so he registers no reactions. Unlike the young Ishmael, he is always the master of himself. In the chapter titled "Merry Christmas," when the *Pequod* is making its way out to sea, Ishmael is given a lesson to this effect, a Christmas present in the form of a swift kick in the pants from Captain Peleg, who commands the ship while it is headed out to sea. Ironically, then, even at the start of his quest, Ishmael is offered a "boon," one of the most valuable to be gleaned from his whole journey. Having stopped in the midst of his sailor duties to worry about the perils of starting the voyage with "such a devil for a pilot" as Peleg, who had taken to shouting out his orders in great oaths, Ishmael feels a "sudden sharp poke in my rear"—a timely warning that he needs to pay attention to his duty and not to his fears (103). Clearly, this is a lesson Ishmael takes to heart, for he is never kicked a second time, not even, in the end, by Moby Dick.

"The Lee Shore" is the capstone (a substitute, Ishmael intimates, for a tombstone) of the long opening section of *Moby-Dick* that is so thoroughly permeated by themes of death and burial. A memorial to the questing spirit incarnated in Bulkington, the mariner who hardly lands from one voyage before embarking on another, this chapter offers the promise that the adventuring hero never really dies and is never really buried. "Wonderfullest things are ever the unmentionable," Ishmael exclaims concerning the apparent immortality of this eternally restless figure; "deep memories yield no epitaphs; this six-inch chapter is the stoneless grave of Bulkington" (106). It is important that Ishmael mentions Bulkington as a future "sleeping-partner" of his (16), for like the old rigger whom Ishmael and Queequeg found sleeping in the forecastle on the morning of their departure, Bulkington is next seen "all alive" and tending to business up on the deck, indeed "standing at her helm." What makes Bulkington such a remarkable instance of the adventuring hero is not simply that he can put his fears behind him, as Peleg would have Ishmael do, but that he can put all of his needs for every kind of human comfort behind him as well. As his example suggests, the quest is the most strenuous undertaking imaginable, requiring the most heroic discipline and great personal sacrifice. Like the "storm-tossed ship, that miserably drives along the leeward land," all the power of nature seems to force the quester such as Bulkington toward the shore, the land of his mortal being, inviting him to find rest in comforts that are falsely soothing, or in a peace known only to the dead. "The port would fain give succor; the port is pitiful; in the port is safety, comfort, hearthstone, supper, warm blankets, friends, all that's kind to our mortalities," Ishmael explains. But in that gale, until the agitated adventurer finds true peace, until he slays his enemies, "the port, the land, is that ship's direst jeopardy." Just "one touch of land" would mean instant destruction (106).

Thus all adventuring, Ishmael argues, "all deep, earnest thinking is but the intrepid effort of *the soul* to keep the open independence of her sea; while the wildest winds of heaven and earth conspire to cast her on the treacherous, slavish shore" (emphasis added). Though the quester cannot know while in the midst of his adventure whether he will ever reach his goal, ever slay his enemies or come face to face with the Father, "better is it to perish in that howling infinite [of landlessness], than be ingloriously dashed upon the lee, even if that were safety!" Even so, Ishmael insists, speaking now as one who has already lived through the adventure and, like Queequeg, knows the result to be a truly divine translation, the "agony" of the journey, and the "terrors" of the trial, are not "vain." "Take heart, take heart, O Bulkington! Bear thee grimly, demigod! Up from the spray of thy ocean-perishing—straight up, leaps thy apotheosis!" (107). As in other spiritual epics, Ishmael suggests, the hero will eventually come to appreciate the apparent paradox that in his death is his life. Only by dying to the world, only by being tried in the belly of the whale endlessly, can he hope to experience the continuous rebirth of the soul that keeps it vital.

NOTES

1. While I feel obliged to follow Melville's public testimony here, I suspect Harrison Hayford's theory is right: "Melville wrote the essay not before but after he met Hawthorne." See Hayford's dissertation, "Melville and Hawthorne: A Biographical and Critical Study" 69.

2. Melville, "Hawthorne and His Mosses" 253.

3. Still, the number who have featured the subject of the epic are surprisingly small. In addition to Arvin "The Whale" (in *Herman Melville*) and Pommer's "Poetic and Epic Influences of Paradise Lost" (in *Milton and Melville*), these include just two essays, both from the previous decade: Lord "The Ivory *Pequod* and the Epic of Illusion" and McWilliams "Till a Better Epic Comes Along." Two essays from the 1970s that would seem especially pertinent, Slotkin's "Moby-Dick: The American National Epic" (in *Regeneration through Violence*) and Rosenberry's "Epic Romance: *Moby-Dick*" (in *Melville*), in fact offer little discussion of Melville's novel as an epic per se.

4. See Hutson and McCoy 9ff.

5. See Franklin, *The Wake of the Gods*.

6. As seen in his letter of June 1[?], 1851, to Hawthorne, written while finishing *Moby-Dick*, Melville doubted that his effort would be appreciated, but his mistrust masks his intention: "What's the use of elaborating what, in its very essence, is so short-lived as a modern book? Tho I wrote the Gospels in this century, I should die in the gutter." See Leyda 1:411. In a recent study that indirectly supports my own view, Lawrence Buell has argued that Melville's novel can be read as an instance of scripture; see his "*Moby-Dick* as Sacred Text."

7. See Abercrombie; Cook; and Newman.

8. Campbell, *The Hero with a Thousand Faces* 30.

9. Eliade, "Initiation and the Modern World" esp. 115. Eliade here distinguishes among three types of initiation: puberty rites, initiation into secret societies, and shamanic initiations. These last two both involve the "deepening of the religious experience and knowledge," even to the point of a "death" and "resurrection" wherein the initiate emerges in a new form, namely, as a spiritual being. Shamanic initiations are reserved for teachers or medicine men and "consist in ecstatic experiences (e.g., dreams, visions, trances) and in an instruction imparted by the spirits or the old master shamans (e.g., shamanic techniques, names and functions of the spirits, mythology and genealogy of the clan, secret language)." I see Ishmael's initiation as combining these last two types—initiation into the whaling fraternity and into the ways and knowledge of the shaman or "consecrated individual" (114–16).

10. See Campbell, *Hero with a Thousand Faces* 15.

11. Merchant, in his survey of the form, argues that, while *The Waste Land* lacks the "discursive variety of epic," it has "many features in common" with it and with modern poetic versions of the genre such as Ezra Pound's *Cantos* (92). Because it lacks the amplitude of the true epic, however, Eliot's poem qualifies technically only as a "mini-epic."

12. Abercrombie 16.

13. Eliot, *The Waste Land* 67, l. 431.

14. For an illuminating study of Ishmael as a survivor of an apocalyptic catastrophe, like the survivors of the Holocaust, see the work of my former student, Janet Reno.

15. *Moby-Dick* 3. Subsequent references to *Moby-Dick* are to the Hayford, Parker, and Tanselle edition.

16. Campbell, *Hero with a Thousand Faces* 29.

17. Ibid. 69–73.

18. Note that Mapple's description of Jonah's escape route calls attention to the fact that the Mediterranean is shaped like a whale, thus symbolically conveying the idea that Jonah can be said to be already in the "belly of the whale" even at the moment when he is trying to flee God (43).

19. Cf. "The Lamp," chapter 97, one of many instances of this image that appear throughout *Moby-Dick*.

20. Cf. Melville's remark in his June 1[?], 1851, letter to Hawthorne, written while completing *Moby-Dick*: "The reason the mass of men fear God, and at bottom dislike Him, is because they rather distrust His heart, and fancy Him all brain like a watch." See Davis and Gilman, eds., 128–29.

21. This is an early example of the displacement of roles and multiplication of characters typically found in epics, where themes are built up through variation and duplication to create the effects of richness and resonance, of plenitude and depth, and where indirection is necessarily the overriding method. Virtually everything in *Moby-Dick* is presented indirectly, rather than directly, as if seen in a mirror: Jonah's story is seen through Mapple's eyes; Mapple's story through Ishmael's; even Ishmael's story is presented not as it happens but after the fact, namely, "now that I recall all the circumstances," as he says (7), or after he has had time to reflect on it. It is, of course, in the nature of all literature to work by indirection. But in an epic it is among the chief techniques the poet has at his disposal for generating the sense of heft or weight so characteristic of the genre. In effect, it creates a "double" sense of the subject and thus gives it "double" weight. Thus, the hundreds of instances of "doubling" in the opening chapters of *Moby-Dick* that Harrison Hayford has brought together in his illuminating essay, "Unnecessary Duplicates: A Key to the

Writing of *Moby-Dick*," are not evidences of Melville's failure to edit out the early version of his book from the final one, as Hayford argues. Instead, I believe they are evidences of Melville's epic intentions, some of them, such as the famous tiller that turns into a wheel, presumably playful or ironic in intent.

22. Cf. "The Pipe," chapter 30, where Ahab, finding that his pipe "no longer soothes," tosses it into the sea (129).

JOHN BRYANT

Moby-Dick *as Revolution*

1. TWO *MOBY-DICKS*: LEGEND AND FORM

Legend has it that there are two *Moby-Dicks*. The story varies, depending upon who tells it, but the facts behind this theory of composition are constant. Returning home in February 1850 from London, where he had peddled *White-Jacket*, Melville contemplated basing his sixth book on the neglected Revolutionary War hero Israel Potter. He had retrieved Potter's autobiography from a London bookstall and thought a narrative of the luckless patriot (like that of alienated White-Jacket) would allow him to question democratic hero worship and revolution itself. But the heated events of 1848 might have persuaded him to avoid politics for a while. He put Potter and the seeds of his revolutionary critique aside and turned to what he told his British publisher, Richard Bentley, would be nothing more than "a romance of adventure founded upon certain wild legends in the Southern Sperm Whale Fisheries."[1]

Melville began this new book by writing out of himself. Still, he was quick to invent. Although he could describe the ports of Manhattan and New Bedford from personal experience, he had never been to Nantucket, so he made his own Nantucket. And even though he would be on more familiar "ground" when his narrative took to sea, he knew enough about whaling to know that he did not know it all: not its history, science, practices, or

From *The Cambridge Companion to Herman Melville*, Robert S. Levine, ed., pp. 65–90. ©1998 by Cambridge University Press.

lore. Inevitably, he needed facts. He got himself a library card, checked out William Scoresby's tome on whaling, and began mixing fact and fancy.[2] Or, as he put it on May Day 1850 to Richard Henry Dana, Jr., this "strange sort of book" would pull "poetry" out of "blubber." Given "the nature of the thing," it must itself be as "ungainly as the gambols of the whales themselves" (*Correspondence*, 162). Moreover, "the thing" was already halfway done, so that when he wrote Bentley on June 27, he said it would be ready for publication by late autumn. The "thing" was *Moby-Dick*.

But something happened. First, Melville moved his family from New York City to Arrowhead, a farm in the Berkshires. Second, he met Nathaniel Hawthorne; and that, or so the legend goes, delayed and changed the course of Melville's progress.

Before moving in early August 1850, Melville proposed a week-long party at his uncle's nearby homestead. He invited good friends, neighbors, and literary figures including his editor Evert Duyckinck, the audacious scribbler Cornelius Mathews, the humorist-sage down the road Oliver Wendell Holmes, Holmes's editor James T. Fields, and another of Fields's clients, Nathaniel Hawthorne. On the party agenda was a Monument Mountain picnic during which Hawthorne and Melville finally met, snapping together like magnets. Herman had prepared for the encounter by reading Hawthorne's *Mosses from an Old Manse* and ended up blasting out a praiseful essay, "Hawthorne and His Mosses." Duyckinck read the manuscript and, upon returning to New York, quickly published it in *Literary World*. At this time, Melville also informed Duyckinck that his Whale Fishery romance was "mostly done." Melville, then, seemed on schedule.

However, it would take another year before *Moby-Dick* was ready to print. Surely, the autumn move and subsequent spring planting in 1851 inhibited his writing. And Melville continued to research more whaling books. But, according to legend, the real delay was Hawthorne. Melville discovered in his neighbor those "elective affinities" for aesthetics, metaphysics, and politics that make deep friends. After years of writing tales for the monthlies, Hawthorne, in his mid-forties, had just made his national reputation with *The Scarlet Letter*, and while residing in nearby Lenox, he was working on *The House of the Seven Gables*, which would seal that reputation. Melville, just thirty-one, was also making his bid for national acceptance. In Hawthorne, he had finally found someone with whom he could talk about God, Being, and Fiction. Hawthorne was to him an American Shakespeare, or better: for while Elizabethan politics had kept Shakespeare from speaking the truth, Hawthorne, and Melville too, could speak more frankly in their age of democracy: "the Declaration of Independence makes a difference," Melville had told Duyckinck the year before (*Correspondence*, 122). But though the Revolution may have erased courtly repression, it also placed the "great Art of Telling the Truth" in the hands of the masses,[3] and as Melville complained to Hawthorne, "try to get a living by the Truth—and go to the Soup Societies.... Truth is ridiculous to men" (*Correspondence*, 191). Creating a book true to oneself and one's nation required forging a new relationship with readers or even creating readers anew: it required a revolution.

Scholars have long speculated that Melville's friendship with Hawthorne, as well as his absorption of Shakespeare, triggered a significant reorientation of *Moby-Dick*. The view is that Melville began to write a narrative of whaling fact (like his naval documentary *White-Jacket*) to be completed by fall 1850. This would involve Ishmael, Queequeg, and such strange characters as Peleg, Bildad, and Bulkington, but not Ahab. However, sometime after the August encounter with Hawthorne, Melville recast the book entirely to include the Shakespeareanized story of Ahab. By the spring and summer of 1851, it is surmised, Melville polished the two stories, adding certain interpolated chapters—"shanties of chapters and essays" he called them (*Correspondence*, 195)—in order to enhance the splicing of the two narrative strands into a seamless whole. Try as he might, the seams still showed, but with a deadline to meet and family to feed, Melville surrendered the novel to his printer, telling Hawthorne that all his works were "botches," *Moby-Dick* included.

I call this theory of the two *Moby-Dicks* a "legend" to emphasize that it is, in fact, only a theory, for beyond the few letters revealing Melville's time frame for a "whaling book," a few chapters whose internal references allow us to date them during the period of composition, and several other Ahabian chapters written in a Shakespearean mode, there is little concrete evidence, and nothing at all conclusive, to show that Melville radically altered the structure or conception of his book.[4] Quite possibly Melville had the heavily Shakespeareanized Ahab story in mind from the beginning; after all, his first serious acquaintance with Shakespeare had occurred in 1849 just before his London trip, well before he met Hawthorne. Melville might have gotten his idea of Ahab from Mary Shelley's *Frankenstein*, which he read aloud with his family as he was planning his novel. Or he may have developed Ahab out of his own earlier creation, the angry but sympathetic Jackson in *Redburn*; and there is ample precedence in *Mardi* for the novel's "ontological heroics" without Melville's having to find their inspiration in Hawthorne.[5]

Even so, one cannot read *Moby-Dick* without recognizing that the book is structurally problematic. We begin with a comedy: anxious Ishmael and serene Queequeg bed down, get "married," and take off on a whaling adventure come-what-may. Then, Enter Ahab (Chapter 29): the captain stumps about, throws his pipe overboard, "kicks" Stubb below decks; and suddenly the novel is a play with dialogue, speeches, asides, soliloquies, stage direction, and no Ishmael. But in Chapter 41, Ishmael returns transformed; no longer a central character, he becomes the novel's central consciousness and narrative voice, able to report an interior life in Ahab that he cannot possibly witness. Nevertheless, as his role as a character erodes, his life as a lyrical, poetic meditator upon whales and whaling transforms the novel once again, converting Ahab's drama into a vast essay on things cetological. Along about Chapter 96, "The Try-Works," Ishmael realizes that he cannot follow Ahab's fiery ways, that he will instead seek "attainable felicities" and fly like a Catskill eagle low and high, balancing darkness and light. But Chapter 99, "The Doubloon," returns us to the drama "Ahab," as crew members pull meaning out of the gold coin the captain has offered as a reward to the one who sights Moby Dick. Quickly now the novel gears up its dramatic machinery. Ahab soliloquizes once more in Chapter 114, "The Gilder," about the unendurable cyclicity of human feeling. Conflicts with God and the crew, melodramatic confrontations with his quadrant and the pale fire of "The Candles," the hope of a reversal through the agency of Starbuck and, most significantly, the black cabin boy Pip—all of these theatricalities intensify our anticipation of the coming catastrophe, as if we were caught up in *Lear* or *Macbeth*. Then with three chapters called "The Chase" and their seemingly voiceless, almost cinematic description, and with the brief but symphonic return of Ishmael in the "Epilogue," *Moby-Dick* is done.

There is no wonder that a person reading this book would conclude, as Evert Duyckinck did: "There are two if not three books in Moby-Dick rolled into one."[6] And it is also no wonder that, given its flip-flopping from Ishmael to Ahab—from comedy to tragedy and from lyric meditation to drama—scholars might locate the cause of the novel's structural oddities in its actual composition and assign differently structured sections to different phases of composition. Hence, the theory that Melville wrote two *Moby-Dicks*. And it is perhaps only human for readers trying to make sense of this book to take Melville's dedication of *Moby-Dick* to Hawthorne as a sign of one author's debt to another. Out of such desire, theories become legends.

In fact, the structural peculiarity of *Moby-Dick* is not so peculiar if you consider Melville's formal habits. There is a persistent lub-dub heartbeat built into his works, a large-scale transcendental two-ness of form that derives not from external contingencies of composition but from a deeper personal necessity, a need to discover within our actual world a primal other world of ideality. As Melville put it in his poem "Art," creation pulls meaning out of the sullen matter of existence; it is a wrestling with "Jacob's mystic heart" requiring "Audacity [and] reverence"; it is the fusing of self and other, whether that other be man or God.[7] This essentially Platonic view of creativity relishes the material dust and blubber of our subjectivity (lub) in order to seize a life that transcends all that (dub). In turn, Melville's oscillating literary structure is a mapping of the artist's ontological condition, his physical struggle to experience Being.

Beethoven achieved a similar moment of transcendental form. Deafness let him hear in new ways, and he composed his last piano sonata (Opus 111) in two movements, not the conventional three. Anton Schindler thought the work was a botch. But in fact, the two-part structure embodies a revolution in form and idea, a pairing of two worlds of emotion, linked in contrast and yet combined. The first movement has been called "Sansara": forceful, conflictual, and sullen. The second is "Nirvana," a transcendent heaven of mounting trill upon trill from which there is no return. Melville's structure also confronts us with two phases of our being; he does in literary form what Beethoven does musically.

Melville was not a card-carrying transcendentalist. In a famous letter, he reassured Duyckinck, who had little affinity for Idealism, German or American, that he did not "oscillate in Emerson's rainbow" (*Correspondence*, 121); but he admired the philosopher for his ability to dive and compared him to Shakespeare. Indeed, *Moby-Dick* depicts the struggle to understand the relation between the promise of transcendental thought and its abnegating opposite, the fear of nothingness, which like a jackal gnaws at Idealism: it is the relation of Nirvana to Sansara. And the novel's problematic two-part structure embodies this struggle in its seemingly adventitious but inescapably logical pairing of the bloody world of whaling and the higher world of whale as symbol of being.

This two-part invention was not new for Melville. In earlier works, we often find a "Narrative A" giving way to a "Narrative B," and usually the A-Tale figures an anxious world of work and economy, whereas the B-Tale grasps at ideality. Such structuring is found in *Typee*, *Mardi*, *Pierre*, and *The Confidence-Man*. And though in all cases the transcendental view of Tale B is not so much promoted as darkly critiqued, we can see the inherent desire in Melville's fictional structuring to confront, if not resolve, the problems of ideality as lub gives way to dub. If there seem to be two *Moby-Dicks*, an Ishmaelean and an Ahabian Tale, it is because Melville's literary form recapitulates the revolutions of a mind forced into elemental confrontation with the nature of its being.

My complaint with the two *Moby-Dicks* theory is its presumption that Melville needed Hawthorne or Shakespeare to move from the Ishmaelean Tale A to Ahab's very Shakespearean Tale B. Charles Olson was the first to give gnomic utterance to the idea: "Above all, in the ferment, Shakespeare, the cause."[8] The poet's professor, F. O. Matthiessen, considered the influence to be "almost an unconscious reflex," believing that Shakespeare's phrasings had "hypnotized" Melville and that Melville was "subconsciously impelled to emulation."[9] Leon Howard attempts a more complex chemical argument in saying that Hawthorne "served as a catalytic agent for the precipitation in words of a new attitude toward human nature which his mind had held in increasingly strong solution for some years," and this catalysis allowed Melville his "Shakespearean heights of expression" (Howard, 169). What ties these three positions together is the belief that Shakespeare swept Melville away. The submerged bardolatry in this compositional view has subverted the deeper intertextual enterprise of exploring how Melville used Shakespeare ironically and critically rather than as merely unconscious "emulation."[10]

To be sure, Melville's Shakespearizing shapes some of the deepest moments in *Moby-Dick*. Nevertheless, Melville places the mantel of Shakespeare on Ahab who lives and breathes but also dies by Shakespeare; he takes Shakespeare down with him. If *Moby-Dick* might be reduced to a duel between two idioms—Ahab's relentless Shakespearizing and Ishmael's lyrical poeticizing—it is Ishmael's voice—Homeric yet homely, more biblical than Shakespearean—that survives. Thus, while Melville exploits, even tries to outdo, Shakespeare, he also works the narrative to get him off his back. It is all part of the book's larger cultural declaration. As a purgation of Shakespeare, *Moby-Dick* figures forth a revolution of politics, sexuality, and mind—not only for Melville but also for the reader.

II. Transcendental Doubt: Transcendental Form

At first glance, *Moby-Dick* seems a revolution almost exclusively in its aesthetic modernity. The long, rhythmic lines, the prose poetry, the mixture of genres and multiplicity of voices, the experiments in point of view, symbolism, and psychology, the dramatization of interior life in Ishmael and Ahab, even the novel's tragicomicality—all prefigure the literary sensibilities of James, Joyce, and Faulkner. But the novel's radical politics seem strangely submerged. Surely, we can extract from the novel's veil of allegory a prophetic warning that the American ship of state is heading toward the disaster of Civil War.[11] We can even trick out certain political readings: Ahab as hunter is the capitalist whose rapacity commodifies nature and destroys the communal values; or Ahab as individualist is the demagogue who coopts the culture's expansionist idiom to manipulate the masses and undermine the democracy's fragile community of factions; or Ahab the abolitionist is the extremist eradicating racism in his pursuit of the white whale (its whiteness a symbol of supremacy) despite Pip's healing hand.[12] But these modern political extractions were largely unrecognizable to Melville's contemporaries. And yet, while *Moby-Dick* lacks the overt political agenda of

Harriet Beecher Stowe's more popular *Uncle Tom's Cabin*, its covert message of resistance lies in the rhetorical strategies of its transcendental structure. Finally, *Moby-Dick* is most political in that it makes readers read in ways that politicize and radicalize.

The novel's two-tale narrative is a part of this radicalization. A book is most like revolution when it places the reader in the condition of one caught between deeply felt but conflicting ideologies. Boston-born Ben Franklin arrogantly thanks God for his vanity, claiming it promotes success, but then reverently thanks Providence for giving him success. A utilitarian who cannot get free of puritan rhetoric, he voices the ambivalence of being situated in a moment in history in which new thoughts vie with old and old vocabularies are bent to express new ideologies. No revolt is complete: the tissues of the past obtain. Such nostalgia is a necessity of mind, for desire cannot expel memory. Thus, the revolutionary's necessarily uncertain articulations bespeak an unavoidable condition of conflict and doubt.

In *Moby-Dick*, not only do characters demonstrate these instabilities, but the narrative itself destabilizes readers; it puts us in a revolutionary condition of doubt. As revolution, it makes us inhabit the passions of conflicting ideologies. And this explains the strategy behind the novel's double form. The reader is always caught between Ahab and Ishmael: between the sullen tragedy of vengeance, pride, and authority and the desperate comedy of being; between autocratic sea and domestic shore; between the "other" and the masses, demagogue and cosmopolite.

In Melville's doubled transcendental structure, one cannot programmatically assign Ishmael to material and Ahab to ideal realms, for both inhabit both, each seeking a separate resolution to the same metaphysical and political problems of being and nothingness. The two operate in different modes—one lyrical and comic, the other dramatic and tragic. But, finally, the narrative promotes the more resolvent mode, for just as Beethoven leaves us suspended in his oscillating transcendent trills, Melville ends with Ishmael. And more, Ishmael's comedy frames Ahab's tragedy, so that in fact Ahab's tragic drama is a projection out of Ishmael's comic sensibility. In short, Ahab grows out of Ishmael; his tale is the dramatization of a burning doubt that Ishmael needs to get into and out of, if only to control something deeply self-destructive within him. He is casting out a demon. But the demon Ahab is compellingly sympathetic. Thus, even though we return confidently enough to Ishmael and survive the Ahab tale, we are unnerved by the struggle. Through reading, we become pragmatic idealists left revolving on the edges of Ishmael's maelstrom, staring into the vacant suction of Ahab's political and philosophical idealism.

But rather than allegorizing these experiential modes, our reading places us in the essentially revolutionary condition of "The Transcendentalist," who, as Emerson tells us, must struggle with self-doubt. The problem is not in achieving a mystic transcendence—that momentary sense of oneness like Ishmael's mast-head reveries—but in living on after the experience, returning from ideality to actuality and the "old tricks ... of a selfish society." Adopting the anxious voice of doubt, Emerson concludes, "My life is superficial, takes no root in the deep world; I ask, When shall I die, and be relieved of the responsibility of seeing a Universe which I. do not use? I wish to exchange this flash-of-lightning faith for continuous daylight, this fever-glow for a benign climate."[13]

Ahab voices the same feeling in "The Gilder" (Ch. 114) when he laments the continual flipping between mindless faith and cerebral doubt. If only one could harbor in a final port of balanced repose (aware but calm), but life is a retrogression, and we relive the stages of ideological growth—faith, doubt, repose—repeatedly. Ahab would rather progress linearly in "unretracing gradations," but he spins day for night perpetually, and the revolutions drive him mad.

Emerson's advice to the transcendentalist who cannot and never will experience "continuous day" or Ahab's longed-for "repose of If" is to find a Quakerly contentment in waiting for the light, or as Thoreau would put it, to "anticipate" the day. And this requires a perpetual balance between self-reliance and communality: "the great man is he who in the midst of the crowd keeps with perfect sweetness the independence of solitude" (Emerson, "Self Reliance," 135). Or as Ishmael puts it in a chapter on blubber: "Do thou, too, live in this world without being of it" (307). Ahab, all "fever-glow" and "flash of lightning," cannot, for all his political machinations to gain metaphysical ascendancy, find faith or balance. But Ishmael can.

Ishmael knows the transcendental problem. He begins in crisis, seeing death and the blackness of darkness everywhere. Faith, like a jackal, gnaws at hope. But his deepest fear is not death; he fears that there is nothing beyond our shell of existence; there is no ideal reality beyond the material; there is nothing. This ultimate doubt pushes Ishmael to ask questions not even God can answer: Where does being come from? How does consciousness happen?

Ishmael takes to sea democratically to confront his fear of nothingness, just as Ahab takes to sea autocratically to kill that fear in the form of the white whale. The two approach the matter differently. Ishmael's ideology grows and embraces growth. It begins with a hopeful proposition: "Nothing exists in itself" (53). The postmodern assertion is the seed of his salvation, for if it is true, then all actual things connect, and ideality exists in the connectiveness of actuality. And not only does everything take its being and meaning from everything else, but each thing—you, me, a whale—also connects to a higher reality—the idea of Us. This is the happy, social, Platonic view that denies any threat of nothingness. Ishmael knows he has an inner warmth because his outer nose is cold. He knows he exists because he feels Queequeg's hug; Ishmael defines himself in terms of Queequeg, and vice versa, and the two affirm each other's consciousness. Significantly, Ishmael's democratic politics grow out of his therapeutic exorcism of his fear of alienation.

But Ishmael's punning text belies his confident metaphysics, for his "Nothing exists in itself" contains a deconstruction which may be read thusly: "'Nothing' exists in itself." That is, the "Idea of Nothingness" exists in and of itself: Nothingness is a universal constant with no higher reality. Of course, this inversion prompts another revolution in meaning. The very idea that "Nothingness exists" is a paradox. If Nothingness exists, then Nothingness is a something, beyond which a higher reality may in fact be operating.

Such ironic revolvings and doubts upon doubts drive Ahab to distraction. But they are Ishmael's blood. In "The Mast-Head" (Ch. 35), he finds himself in a transcendental reverie in which all reality becomes one flowing rhythm of life, and yet the moment he yields to this rhythm, he becomes a nonidentity, a nothing. This very awareness triggers a counterimpulse to retain his personal being, his little self in the midst of the larger universal self; and at that moment, he imagines himself falling to his death, his identity returning to him but "in horror," at the very moment (ironically) he has envisioned his nonexistence. In "The Whiteness of the Whale" (Ch. 42), Ishmael contemplates why the color white strikes terror, and the same cycle of identity and negation spins him toward atheism, nihilism, alienation, and even the impossibility of gaining solace from symbolism. But in a later, resolvent mode, Ishmael stares into the fire of "The Try-Works" (Ch. 96) and recognizes that his obsession with Ahab's dilemma of being and nothingness is self-destructive and politically dehumanizing. Instead, as he asserts in "The Squeeze of a Hand" (Ch. 95), whose masturbatory images hearken back to the image in "Loomings" (Ch. 1) of a phantom holding Ishmael's hand and giving solace, he will Seek out the attainable felicities of "the wife, the heart, the bed" (416). Ishmael cannot explain this connective, sexual/metaphysical hand that holds him, but it is enough to pull him back from the fire. It does not remove nothingness, but it gives him something to hold (amusingly enough) while continuing to contemplate. It is Melville's version of maintaining a perfect Emersonian "sweetness" of solitude.

Ahab's approach to the problem of nothingness is denial. In "The Quarter-Deck" (Ch. 36), he rallies the crew by playing fast and loose with transcendental ideas, making the whale out to be a "pasteboard mask" or symbol of an evil and yet reasoning force. Ahab's rhetoric is bad transcendental thinking on two counts. In "The Poet," Emerson argues that we come closest to transcendence when we do what nature does. Since nature is our most immediate example of the creative force of Ideality, doing what nature does means creating, and what nature creates are palpable symbols of universal concepts. Thus, to approach transcendence we must create symbols. Ahab's double heresy, however, is that he attempts to transcend by breaking through and reducing symbols (the whale's pasteboard mask), and does so assuming that destruction, not creativity, is the universal ideal.

Ahab can appear to be performing an authentic act of self-discovery by cutting through nature's surfaces in order to apprehend its ideal reality, but his method is destructive rather than re-creative. Even more problematic is Ahab's pathological denial of the possibility of nothingness. "Sometimes I think there is naught beyond," he admits, "But 'tis enough." This dramatic aside reveals more than Ahab would allow. Ahab is an atheist in denial. His core awareness is that behind the paste-board mask of Moby Dick, there is no god, evil or otherwise; and this primal doubt he cannot bear: "'Tis enough." To deny this fearful nothingness, he erects as a psychological crutch an inverted and shallow form of transcendentalism in which symbol is mere matter (not thought playing upon matter, or fancy upon fact, or poetry upon blubber) and the ideality behind matter is a force of malice, not the Good, or the True, or (as Emerson would have it) Beauty.

Soliloquizing after his speech to the crew, Ahab brashly proclaims, amid images of his iron-railed, locomotive will to destroy the whale, that "Naught's an obstacle" to "the iron way." As with Ishmael's "Nothing exists in itself," this Shakespearean play upon nothingness has multiple meanings. On the surface, the trope states that "nothing can get in my way." But the punning reality beneath the surface is a conflicting philosophy: "the '*Idea* of Nothingness' is an obstacle." That is, Ahab's denial of nihility stands in the way of his achieving true self-awareness. Both Ishmael and Ahab pun upon Nothingness, but Ishmael is aware of his multiple meanings—indeed, his cetological chapters are a further enactment of both the promise of something beyond and the fear of "naught beyond"—whereas Ahab's double meaning seems more of a slip he does not perceive.

Here, then, are the two tales in Melville's transcendental structure: Ishmael gives us a meditation on doubt, Ahab a play about denial. But the two are not simply two sides of the same coin; rather, Ahab's play grows out of Ishmael's meditation. The drama called "Ahab" is a manifestation of Ishmael's own fear of the tragic impossibility of a transcendent reality, just as his counterpoised poeticizing of cetology, a lyrical essay we may call "Whale," conveys his comic desires of transcendence.

Evidence of Ahab's being a projection of Ishmael occurs when we find Ahab mimicking ideas and images that Ishmael has already voiced. In Chapter 42 Ishmael relentlessly, almost Ahabistically, pursues the cause behind our fear of whiteness. The analysis takes Ishmael further than he wants to go. As a symbol maker, he celebrates the "godly gamesomeness" (126) we enjoy in building symbols and playing with meaning. But in analyzing the symbol of whiteness, Ishmael destroys the very foundations of symbolism itself and undoes the only means he has (i.e., his creativity) of counteracting his fear of nothingness. For in following the symbol of whiteness to its ultimate meaning, he finds himself "stab[bed] ... from behind with the thought of annihilation" (169). Rather than making whiteness into an easy allegory of death, he discovers an "absence of color," and from that absence he leaps into the vacuum: "a colorless, all-color of atheism." As a symbol of nothingness, whiteness symbolizes paradoxically that symbols do not exist. Two chapters later, Ahab mimics this same revelation. In "The Chart" (Ch. 44) he experiences that shattering form of sleepwalking dream we now call "night terror," a separation of soul from body, and becomes, says Ishmael, "a vacated thing, a formless somnambulistic being, a ray of living light, to be sure, but without an object to color, and therefore a blankness in itself" (175).

Clearly, Ishmael in Chapter 44 uses the same vocabulary of "blankness" to talk about Ahab's psychological fear of nothingness that he uses in Chapter 42 to seek the source of his own fear of whiteness. More than just replaying his idea of nothingness, Melville is framing Ahab's psychosis within Ishmael's vision. He is having Ahab emerge as a fearful dramatic enactment of Ishmael's poetically derived fear. Thus the two tales are interwoven, with Ishmael acting as the novel's hidden stage director. In short, *Moby-Dick* not only demonstrates revolutionary states of mind, as revealed in the thoughts of Ishmael and Ahab, but its structure, with Ahab's world projecting out of Ishmael's, puts readers into a destabilized condition of transcendental doubt. Whose language do we hear more passionately? Whom do we follow: Ishmael or Ahab? And how, to raise the stakes, is this revolutionary transcendental structuring at all political? The answers lie in sexuality and dramaturgy, which if pursued will bring us back to Shakespeare.

III. Sexuality and Politics

Melville's two-part transcendental structure bids us take an ontological plunge from the risky but finally safe Socratic *questioning* of Ishmael into the disastrous *questing* of Ahab. Just as Ahab says he is "darkness leaping out of light," Melville has us leap from Ishmael's warm, meditative mode into Ahab's dramatic Shakespearizing. In this double search for the nature of being, we are asked to connect down to the determinants of our identity, and in particular our sexuality. It is problematic to say that "our sexuality" is at issue when, in this famously male-oriented text, the female gender is barely represented. But just as Melville's pursuit of identity—and how being emerges out of nothingness—invariably leads to sexuality, his representations of sexuality invariably promote a gender-crossing politics. In fact, *Moby-Dick* is not so purely male. To know what it means to Be, Ishmael must know what it means to be male; and to know the meaning of maleness requires his knowing other males. And to know others he must know the Other, and thus Queequeg becomes the perfect mate. He is quite male and quite other in that his paganism stands in contrast to Ishmael's conventional Christianity; he is self-possessed, unlike the neurotic Ishmael; he is like a husband as, astonishingly, Ishmael plays the wife. Ineluctably, Melville portrays sexuality as a gendered cosmopolitanism wherein (to borrow from the period's definition of "cosmopolite") one "is nowhere a stranger" in either sex. This "pansexuality" is the seed of a political ideology designed to call authority and capitalism into question and to bring apparent opposites—female and male, "civilized" and "savage"—together. Unlike Stubb, Starbuck, and even Ahab, who reminisce about women or wives, Ishmael creates women in meditation, as if to infer the otherness of "female" from his own male being.

From the start, Ishmael researches the feminine side of being. He is drawn to water, like so many other Manhattanites, although for him its magnetism reveals not only the warm and shapely allurements of femininity but also the threat of narcissism. What attracts this "metaphysical professor," this "artist," this "healthy boy"? It is the Phantom of Being beneath the water, and, he remarks, "meditation and water are wedded forever" (13); they are boy and wife. Soon enough Ishmael beds down with Queequeg, struggling (but not too hard) to unloose the islander's "bridegroom clasp" (33); thus, the metaphysical wedding in "Loomings" becomes the more sensual coupling in "The Counterpane," and with "A Bosom Friend," the two are "married" (53). But this matrimonial state is nothing more, Ishmael argues, than a Polynesian version of blood brothers swearing to die for one another. Even so, in Chapter 72 Ishmael returns to the wedding metaphor to describe the whaling phenomenon of the "Monkey Rope," in which Ishmael and Queequeg are tied together by a safety line designed to keep Queequeg from falling into shark-infested waters. Actually, the seamen roped together is Melville's concoction, a convenient adaptation of whaling practice that resituates the sexualized male bonding of the bedroom in the alienating world of work. Ishmael restates that he and Queequeg "were wedded, and should poor Queequeg sink to rise no more, then both usage and honor demanded that instead of cutting the cord, it should drag me down in his wake" (271). From the point of view of the whaling industry, Melville's fictional version of the monkey rope binds two workers, two commodified beings absurdly roped in to actualizing profit, and yet the human and sexual ligature transcends alienating capitalism, or at least achieves "honor" despite capital.

By transferring the previously metaphysical and sexual idea of wedding to the symbol of rope, Melville is able to expand his meditation further into politics. Earlier, in "The Line" (Ch. 60), hempen ropes surround the oarsmen of the whale boats, as if to stress the machinery of whaling as well as the moral "self-adjusting buoyancy and simultaneousness of volition and action" required by each sailor to avoid those ropes (180–1). These are the same ropes that hang Ahab. And these lines connect harpooners to live whales as well as dead whales to "waif poles" that signify ownership. Ishmael explains the latter process in "Fast-Fish and Loose-Fish" (Ch. 89) but quickly moves from whaling law to divorce law and whether a divorced husband has any claim to the assets of his remarried former wife. The facile analogizing of women to whales ironically undercuts the law's more pernicious assumption that women are property. Before the chapter ends, Ishmael has converted an offhanded meditation on possession into a more sanguine, indeed calamitous, tirade on such imperialistic thefts as Britain's rule of India and America's taking of Mexico, a tirade that ends with the question of whether the rights of man, our very words and thoughts, and indeed readers themselves are fast fish or loose (334).

The chain of images—from weddings metaphysical and homoerotic to lines that bind us one to another in cosmopolitan interdependency to lines that commodify humans in the workplace and enslave women in courts of law—allows Melville to extract politics out of sexuality just as he infers sexuality out of being. In doing so, his message of revolt is by necessity subsumed within the lyric strains of Ishmael's meditation rather than openly announced. It has been argued that Melville is practicing an art of concealment, that he hides his political agenda so as not to incur the wrath of less liberal readers and the snippings of censorious editors, both of which he had endured in previous books, most notably *Typee*. But Melville's strategy goes deeper than this, for in following the logic of Melville's symbols, readers are encouraged to tie meanings together for themselves, made to read creatively (as Emerson would have it), and drawn to the root political determinants of our lives. We hug others, we love them, we attach ourselves to them. But to hug is to grab and take and possess: we enslave. And this happens because we fear that our being is a nothing; thus, we seek either companionship or control. Rather than have his characters spout politics, Melville has us dig for their politics in the subterranean recesses of being and sexuality, all the more to show us the human necessities of certain ideologies. Thus, readers experience in their reading why Ishmael chooses freedom and love; why Ahab demands control.

Ahab's politics stems from his wounded sexuality. Ahab is democracy's worst nightmare: the charismatic, single-issue demagogue who can sway the masses away from mutual and communal contractarian democracy to self-destructive individualism or separatism. He is a John Brown or Calhoun; a McCarthy or Buchanan; or any of a number of supremicists, white or black. What makes Melville's psychological study of Ahab's monomania so politically compelling is Melville's locating the causes of his destructive charisma—his vision of disunity, social chaos, and death—in sexuality. In "Ahab's Leg" (Ch. 106), the captain suffers a painful blow to the groin when his whalebone pegleg snaps under his weight. The pain, Ishmael says, is "the direct issue of a former woe" (385). In dancing around this delicate fact; Ishmael finally intimates that more of Ahab is missing than his leg, and part of the verbal dance that he reports happening in Ahab's mind is an intricate argument concerning castration, ontology, and genealogy. It is essentially this: Ahab's "heart-woe" is connected genealogically to "the sourceless primogenitures of the gods." That is, there is a tragic, "sourceless" source that preexists even God. If this is so, then "the gods themselves are not for ever glad," and the "heart-woe" pain descends to us collaterally beside God's. We are not children of God; we are cousins related to one grandparent, Grief. What is this grief? Later, in "The Candles" (Ch. 119), Ishmael dramatizes Ahab's logic. He has Ahab modify the earlier genealogical argument as a way of claiming superiority to God. Since the gods are "unbegotten," he argues, they exist without a sense of genealogy and therefore cannot know, as Ahab does, that there is "some unsuffusing thing beyond," a source for God and man's mutually shared, collateral grief. Ahab cannot reach that "thing," but he knows it is there. But instead of working out this sense of grief the way Ishmael might work out his anxiety, he uses his awareness of a higher sense of being as a means to seize a rhetorical superiority to God. Since God's "unbegotten" status makes God unaware of the higher "thing" or grief source, Ahab's ontological self-awareness gives him ascendancy over God's nonawareness. But, again, what is this heart-woe grief source? Like Goethe's "Mother Night," it is essentially the incomprehensible idea of being or consciousness itself, which precedes all. It is not Ahab who is blind (says Ahab) but our silent, impersonal God, which cannot see that the mystery of being preexists divinity. Ahab calls this unreachable mystery "my sweet mother" and reserves for himself a motherless, orphan, foundling status.

Ahab's argumentation is compelling but tragically flawed. On the one hand, we recognize not only that Ahab's physical loss is a sexual impotency, but also that this sterility is in addition a loss of creativity, as manifested in his longing for his lost, nurturing "mother." But Ahab has compressed his sexual loss into a desperate ontological affair. He has set up God as an unknowing, father-figure version of himself, sans personality, sans self-righteous anger; and he allows his own putative superior self-awareness to stand for a fuller recognition of being, a return to Mother Night. In defying God, he manages to ignore the fact that "the unsuffusing" mother-like "thing" beyond us all—being itself—is also an impersonal symbol of our own devising, just a rhetorical trope. Ahab's defiance of the Father God is an appeal to the absent Mother Being, as though such a verbal victory would give him an edge over God in resolving the ultimate question of his identity. The futility of all this is that Ahab's genealogical metaphor gets him no closer to resolving the real dilemma of our grief: that we can never comprehend where consciousness comes from or what being is. Thus, Ahab's repressed sexual wound leads him to rig up a defiant response to the problem of being that simultaneously gives gender to being (mother) and then takes her away (nothingness). And that response strikes us as both poignant and sadly pathological, if not delusional.

Ahab is defiant and worshipful ("defyingly I worship thee!"), and this angry male's charisma is located in his search for a mother and wholeness. Ahab's callous commodification of whales and crew bespeaks his role as unregenerate demagogue, capitalist, and imperialist. But beneath this surface politics is an agenda of personal reclamation that makes his anger so dangerously alluring: "Our souls," Ahab says, "are like those orphans whose unwedded mothers die in bearing them: the secret of our paternity lies in their grave, and we must there to learn it" (491). Finally, what is political in *Moby-Dick* lies not in its allegories of freedom or slavery, but in the novel's analysis of the deep sexual necessities of our being, both integrative and nihilistic, that make us political beasts. We are Ishmaelean cosmopolites or Ahabean tyrants because our sexuality is conditioned by our need to fill a Nothing through communality or dominance.

IV. Politics, Drama, and Melville's "Shakespeherian Rag"

Rather than making *Moby-Dick* a call to arms in support of an Ishmaelean or Ahabian ideology, Melville places us in the condition of experiencing the tug of both: one multicultural and inclusive, the other separatist and divisive. Thus, readers become revolutionary to the extent that they inhabit the debate, oscillating between Ahab's righteous but pathological resolve and Ishmael's deep but finally domestic creativity. Concomitantly, by offering these variant worlds in radically different voices—Ahab's dramaturgy and Ishmael's lyricism—Melville enhances the novel's revolutionary effect, for we constantly feel the switching of rhetorical modes as we read. Even so, the shifting is not indifferent or nondirectional. Ahab may be a good hater, but it is always Ishmael who contains and controls. Moreover, Melville's rejection of Ahab's railed and railing way is manifested in Melville's ultimate rejection of Shakespeare. To be sure, Melville's Shakespearean dramatics magnify Ahab's tragic bearing, but he also uses Shakespeare to purge himself of Shakespeare, as a blow for both his own artistic freedom and America's cultural independence. Indeed, *Moby-Dick*'s revolutionary politics lies in the deconstruction rather than emulation of Shakespeare.

To clarify, we need to consider the role of theater in Melville's America, and in particular the attitude Melville and his contemporaries had toward Shakespeare. We also need to consider that drama is politics.

Drama is a ritual of political response. As with the Greeks, who pulled performance out of communal dance, America's antebellum drama was not just an evening's diversion or a slice of life but a ritualized enactment, a symbolic representation through staged event, of the culture's doubts about the democracy. To "do drama" was to "act out" race, region, and class tensions, to affirm or deny difference in the context of the nation's great Equality. This was true of formal productions such as Royall Tyler's *The Contrast* (1787), James K. Paulding's *The Lion of the West* (1830), the stage versions of *Uncle Tom's Cabin*, and even various Shakespearean plays (the most popular being *Richard III* and *Macbeth*), where manners and governance were explicit issues. But this was even truer with the more spontaneously contrived burlesques and commedia dell'arte theatricals performed by such ever-popular acrobatic mime troupes as the Ravels; in which unscripted jabs at public figures, factions, or events were the daily fare, and audiences—newsboys, workers, families, blacks, and whites (in separate sections)—hurled taunts, cheers, furniture, and overripe comestibles without restraint. Theatergoing had all the edge of a political rally; it was physically perilous and mentally destabilizing. Given this cultural context, putting Ahab on stage was not simply Melville's aspiring to Shakespearean heights; rather, his conversion of narrative into drama was in itself a political statement.

William A. Jones, an articulate spokesman for the liberal faction called "Young America" (with which Melville was aligned), saw the theater as democracy's most effective art form, for on stage the diversity of America's

factions and character types—Yankee, backwoodsman, black minstrel—
could perform and work out the nation's evolving political tensions over its
inchoate national identity.[14] It would serve as a cosmopolitan collocation
of America itself. Or that was the hope. From the audience's perspective,
the stage was not only a place to see American ideals realized, it was itself
a playing out of politics and the venting of class pressures. Thus, the
reality, despite Jones's hope, was that theater rarely achieved nationalizing
ritual but instead degenerated into mere political rally, and from rally it
even fell into riot. The most prominent case was New York City's three-
day Astor Place riot of 1849, which resulted in thirty deaths. The British
Shakespearean William Macready had, it was alleged, hissed at his American
counterpart, Edwin Forrest, and when Macready appeared at New York's
newly constructed Astor Place Opera House (a theater not for the people but
the elite) to perform *Macbeth*, audiences inside and crowds outside shouted
him down. The aristocratic Macready barely escaped with his life. Melville
joined several others in petitioning Macready to continue his tour, assuring
him of the city's return to order (*Log*, 302), but a riot ensued (ironically) on
Melville's Astor Place townhouse doorstep.

Melville knew how the phenomenon of drama could body forth an
immediate confrontation between audiences and the social forces that
impinge upon their lives and identities. And his decision to present Ahab's
tale as drama was itself a conscious political act and revolutionary both as a
public statement to his readers and as a moment of private resolve in shaping
the direction of his art. Publicly, Melville's act of dramatizing reinforces his
doubts about the direction of America's experiment in democracy. Whereas
his most optimistic political statements come to us through Ishmaelean
meditation, his concern for the nation's dangerous factionalism and racism
is delivered in the dramatist's idiom of speeches and stage direction, with
the novel's most dramatic character, Ahab, at the center. Ahab's memorable
entrance is in the play-within-a-novel section (Chs. 36–40), already
mentioned, in which Ahab makes his quarterdeck speech bidding the crew
to pursue Moby Dick. But while Ahab commands our attention in the
first half of this little "play," it is the crew that brings the performance to
its chilling climax and quick curtain. Here the whalemen give no thought
to Ahab but turn immediately to drink, dance, and sexual desire; and out
of the carousing comes a racial slur, then a fight, then a riot with the still
sane Pip making the link for us between this chaos, an impending storm,
and the foreshadowed encounter with Moby Dick. Rather than a comic
enactment of political harmony envisioned by Young America's William
Jones as the proper function of drama, Melville's play ends in the kind of
theatrical and political riot the author witnessed at home in New York City.

Melville's very use of the play genre—indeed, his jarring interruption of the controlled narrative of Ishmael with the stagy theatricals of both Ahab and the crew—enhances the political instability of Ahab's authoritarianism and the democratic crew's demolition of racially tolerant cosmopolitanism. The shifting modes also abruptly destabilize the reader, reminding us of the precarious nature of race and sexuality in America's democracy and placing us as well in a condition of doubt that sharpens our awareness of the risk in democratic revolution.

But Melville's use of drama, and Shakespeare in particular, had a private as well as a public function. In general, critics have stressed the author's emulation of Shakespeare, but the full story of Melville's "Shakespeherian Rag," to borrow Eliot's *Waste Land* phrase, reveals a crucial ambivalence: Melville lived for a while in Shakespeare's idiom, danced that dance but let it go. His relation to Shakespeare was a manifestation of the revolutionary iconoclasm he was building into *Moby-Dick*.

We marvel at Melville's uncanny replication of Shakespeare's voice. More than a source or "ordinary influence," Shakespeare had "grown into the fibre of Melville's thought" (Matthiessen, 435). Powerful confrontations such as "The Quarter-Deck" and "The Candles," or theatrical stagings such as "Midnight, Forecastle," or comic byplays such as Stubb's wide-awake sarcasms and "Leg and Arm" (when Ahab meets Boomer and Bunger)[15] do not in any real sense copy Shakespeare but rather do what Shakespeare, in the nineteenth century, might have done with America, metaphysics, and the sea. Melville's brilliant management of soliloquy and his invention of sequential soliloquies that focus on a single symbol (as in the contemplative "coin" chapters, "The Doubloon" and "The Gilder"), his adaptation of the fool (first Stubb, then Pip) to complex themes of comic regeneration, and his ingenious use of the gam to allow for scene shiftings beyond the limiting stations of the whaleship—these literary gambits extend beyond Shakespeare to an exuberant reshaping of the dramatic genre itself.

But the puzzle is that Melville's use of Shakespeare is as self-consciously bad as it is inventive and transforming. It flops as often as it soars, and rather than being dramatistic, certain moments in *Moby-Dick* are simply "dramaturgid." There are, for instance, the gratuitous Macbethean prophecies of Ahab's demise, the outrageous asides ("something shot from my nostrils"), the creaky transitions ("the envious billows sidelong swell to whelm my track; let them; but first I pass"), the overdone ellipses ("Down, dog, and kennel") designed to out-Lear Lear, the forced comic set pieces (Fleece's sermon to the sharks made all the more strained in contrast with Ishmael's far subtler meditations on sharks), and the utterly improbable staginess of Tashtego's hammering a red flag to the sinking mast-head and impaling a sky hawk in the process. Such "lumbering," "labored," and "derivative" passages (as Matthiessen put it) are precisely the kind of overwriting that drives modern minimalists to distraction."[16]

Our first inclination is to presume that these infelicities are the necessary lapses of an overreaching assimilation of Shakespeare or that Melville did not have time to make his inventions better. However, whereas Ishmael admits to the "careful disorderliness" (361) of similar infelicities in his lyric mode, he never explains away the relentless strut and fret of Ahab's Shakespeherian rag. A sedulous reviser and capable dramatizer from the time he wrote *Typee*, Melville was talented enough to diminish the "rag" if he had wanted to. Significantly, he did not.

The effect of Ahab's theatricality is twofold. On the one hand, it is symptomatic of the self-deluding con games Ahab uses to captivate crew and reader. His "sultanism" is undeniable, but the "paltry and base" methods to which he sinks—plying the crew with rum and gold (Ch. 36), playing electrical parlor games with the compass (Ch. 124) and corposants (Ch. 119)—are invariably rendered with strained theatricality to suggest the artificiality of Ahab's near-delusional egoism. Thus, Melville's parodic Shakespeareanisms undercut what Lawrence Levine identifies as an ideology of individualism invariably associated in the popular culture with Shakespearean protagonists.[17]

On the other hand, Ahab's "base" Shakespearean histrionics also suggest Melville's radical ambivalence toward his own experiments in the dramatic mode. Dramatism allowed Melville to curtail the metaphysical wanderings that he frequently permitted himself in his various first-person narrations. As if to make a point of this need, Melville underscored a passage from the Apocrypha at about the time he began *Moby-Dick*: "let thy speech be short, comprehending much in few words, be as one that knoweth and holdeth his tongue" (Sirach 32:8; *Log*, p. 370). The dramatic chapters in *Moby-Dick*—with their soliloquies, dialogue, stage directions, and histrionics—cut Ishmael short in his lyrical meditations so that he might "holdeth his tongue." But if this dramatic self-effacement allowed Melville to disperse his ideas in diverse tongues, it necessarily denied Ishmael a dramatic presence. That lyric voice which contained the novel's regenerative moral vision would remain disembodied in the face of Ahab and Shakespeare: it was undramatizable. Indeed, soon after *Moby-Dick* Melville ceased his Shakespearizing. Ultimately, Melville needed a narrative strategy that went beyond Shakespeare—one that could remove narrative voice from authorial personality and yet play a role in the narrative, despite such radical distancing—one that we find him continuing to seek in *Pierre*, "Benito Cereno," and *The Confidence-Man*.

There is no denying Melville's profound love of Shakespeare; he even compared him to Jesus (*Correspondence*, 127), and yet his "Mosses" essay reveals an ardent need for the artist to shake Shakespeare loose. The problem was both societal and private: What was the new world writer's relation to the past? How might artists invent a culture out of their own originality but maintain a regard for the received cultural standards endorsed by past readers? Shakespeare was a vital link to a past culture and a transcendent language, but as Emerson noted, "Genius is always sufficiently the enemy of genius by over-influence ... [and we] have Shakespearized now for two hundred years."[18]

Following Emerson, Melville "boldly contemn[s] all imitation" and consigns all "American Goldsmiths" and "American Miltons" to critical oblivion. But oddly enough, after having made his stand for independence, Melville virtually anoints Hawthorne as America's Shakespeare ("Mosses," 248), thus canonizing his new world friend with an old world halo. Finding himself caught between two ideologies, Melville quickly adopts something of an Emersonian approach. He is not interested in Shakespeare "so much for what he did do, but for what he did not do, or refrained from doing," both in text and with audience. He scoffs at the bardolatry of contemporary critics who call Shakespeare "unapproachable."[19] Melville's Shakespeare was a man, like himself, scarred by his culture, one who had to accommodate his original genius to Elizabethan demands. Although a model of restraint providing insight in "cunning glimpses," he was also a rank popularizer pandering to his audience's expectations of "noise and show of broad farce, and blood-besmeared tragedy." Melville's implication is that America's progressive liberalism removes the political restraints that forced Elizabethan writers to their blood, thunder, and farce. Finally, Shakespeare is as much a problematic model of the rhetorician as he is a model thinker,[20] and Hawthorne's achievement lies not in any imitation of Shakespeare's thought but in his doing what "Genius" does: he projects ideas in "the still, rich utterances of a great intellect in repose."

In short, Melville had as much to reject in Shakespeare as to admire. And he had support in this ambivalence from the populace's growing resentment of the classism inherent in Shakespeare's kings and such elitist interpretations of Shakespeare as Macready's, which could trigger a riot. The Declaration of Independence might free modern writers to tell certain metaphysical truths, but that document did not make audiences any more willing to accept them or the politics that come with them. Indeed, if Astor Place proved anything, it was that Americans were beginning to associate Shakespeare with aristocratic repression and class conflict. If, too, Shakespeare was becoming at this time, as Lawrence Levine argues, a symbol of drama's separation from the people, Melville's own ambivalent use of Shakespeare represents something more complex than an Emersonian attempt to apply the genius and insight of a Shakespeare to America. His use of "bad" Shakespeare is also a recognition that the "blood-besmeared" farce of American demagoguery and individualism he was witnessing in the streets was giving the lie to the effectiveness of drama in the culture. Ahab's theatricality, then, is the false ring of liberty's bell, signifying a society out of joint.

VI. REVOLUTION AND READER

Melville's use of Shakespeare clarifies even as it complicates the two-part transcendental structuring of *Moby-Dick*. As a dramatic projection of Ishmael's worst doubts about the sources of being and the communalizing promise of sexuality, Ahab dives deep, like Hawthorne and Shakespeare. However, Ahab's artificiality signifies his mental and political instability. And this undoing of his dramaturgy draws us back to the meditative containment of Ishmael's "intellect in repose." Thus, the journey out of Ishmael's "visible world ... formed in love" into Ahab's sphere "formed in fright" (169) necessitates a return, and in this "essaying" of Shakespeare and dramatism, Melville purges both. Moreover, the reader partakes of this revolution in form.

Caught up in the duel between Ishmael's and Ahab's conflicting worlds, and feeling the shift in narrative modes, the reader experiences Ishmaelean doubt. The real dramatization going on is not Ahab's histrionics but Melville's guerrilla theatrics of pulling us on stage and forcing us to enact Ishmael's and Ahab's conditions of love and fright.

At times this revolutionary conditioning is programmed like a tennis match, as in "The Sphynx" (Ch. 70), when Melville has Ishmael and Ahab volley their emotions in front of a beheaded whale. Ishmael focuses on "silence," another symbol of absence, that reigns over the deck: "An intense copper calm, like a universal yellow lotus, was more and more unfolding its noiseless measureless leaves upon the sea" (263). For Ishmael the sea calm is an umbrageous tree of all-knowing: serene, Tennysonian, and transcendent. But for Ahab, the stillness, an emblem of his faithlessness, is a "deadly" impediment to his quest; and silence is all he hears from the Sphynx-like head that has all the answers but will not speak: "O head! thou has seen enough to split the planets and make an infidel of Abraham, and not one syllable is thine!" (264). His angry iambics stand in stark contrast to Ishmael's free-verse poeticizing that transforms the otherwise threatening calm into something palpable, hence containable. Of course, Ahab ends with a better line: "O Nature, and O soul of man! how far beyond all utterance are your linked analogies! not the smallest atom stirs or lives in matter, but has its cunning duplicate in mind" (264). Here the Shakespearean rhythms effectively articulate Ahab's tragic inability to believe, create, and transform. He acknowledges the existence of a two-part transcendental world in which matter is an analogical version of the soul, but the analogies are unutterable and, contrary to the symbolizer Ishmael, for whom utterance comes easy, Ahab lacks the creativity to give them voice. Ishmael's "copper calm" is his "deadly calm."

But though Ahab's verbal soliloquy recalls Hamlet, the staged imagery is really all Oedipus. Stage director Ishmael has Ahab stand before the whale's head using a cutting spade for a crutch so as to enact the iconography of not only the lame, staff-wielding Oedipus addressing the Sphynx but also the allegorized "three-legged" man of old age, which is the final part of the Sphynx's famous riddle. The irony is that old-man, three-legged Ahab stands in relation to the whale's head as Oedipus to the Sphynx, and yet he cannot answer the whale's riddle of Being even though he is (three "legs" and all) enacting the final part of the answer to that riddle: "Man." Ishmael's ironic stage crafting ensures that we shall see Ahab's Shakespearized allegorical insights in relation to Ishmael's more fluid symbolizing as misdirected. Even so, Ahab's antitranscendental revelation of the unutterability of analogies leaves us with the gnawing doubt that Ishmael's copper calm effusions are just artful words designed to fill a void that is "beyond all utterance." As Ishmael puts it later on, Ahab's insights "tarnish" Ishmael's poetic transcendencies.

Ishmael's ironic stagecraft grows stronger in "The Gilder" (Ch. 114) when Ishmael's and Ahab's distinct voices begin mystically to blend. In this "coin" chapter, Melville essentially replays "The Doubloon" by having successive characters reflect upon a single object, in this case another sea calm. Ishmael achieves a zen vision of "fact and fancy, half-way meeting, [and] interpenetrat[ing to] form one seamless whole" (406). Then Ahab delivers the famous "Oh, grassy glades" speech, easily his most poetic effusion. No longer a fist shaker, he addresses not God, the sun, a Sphynx, or the crew, but his own condition. He finds himself broken on a cycle of life which takes us through sequential stages of being—infancy's unconsciousness, boyhood faith, adolescent doubt, true skepticism, then disbelief, then finally "manhood's pondering repose of If." But this cycle never turns just once; the curse is that it continually revolves, sending us back from wisdom to former unbalanced selves; there is, Ahab complains, "no steady unretracing progress" (407). Ahab's problem is not that he never achieves the repose of If but that he cannot sustain it. He oscillates between boyhood faith and adolescent doubt and is forever an "orphan" wondering "where is the foundling's father hidden" and seeking out his mother in the grave.

Unlike Ishmael, who transforms these stages of consciousness—each one a revolution—into the very stuff of his lyricism, Ahab is dramatically confounded by the shifting and takes the "few fleeting moments" of "immortality" that he sometimes captures as an insult goading him on to seize transcendental totality. His speech is the lament of the anxious rebel unable to synthesize the ideology of his material self with the ideology of transcendental unity. In it, we hear none of his pathological denials and contrived arguments. This is Ahab's sincerest self-recognition that his anger, fear, and quest are rooted in his impotent, indeed infant-like and foundling status.

But most challenging for readers is that Ahab sounds more like Ishmael than Ahab. He speaks of "ever vernal endless landscapes in the soul," of "young horses" rolling "in new morning clover," and of the "cool dew of life immortal" (407). Rarely is iron-railed Ahab allowed such fluid pastoral rhythms. Gone is his insistent blank verse, but strains of the familiar Shakespearizing Ahab persist. After. all, his cycle revises Jaques's seven-stages-of-man speech in *As You Like It*; in fact, it goes one better by making the cycle damningly repetitive and by recasting Shakespeare's finalized seventh stage (mere oblivion) as a seaman's orphanage or "final harbor, whence we unmoor no more," which tauntingly evokes *Othello*. Taken as a whole, the mixed modes of dramaturgy and lyricism adopt an Ishmaelean sensibility but in a Shakespearean idiom. Witness Ahab's transformation of Ishmael's notion of interpenetrating moods into his own blank verse: "But the mingled, mingling threads of life are woven by warp and woof." Clearly, Ishmael's and Ahab's separate voices are themselves mingling. "The Gilder" is crucial, then, not simply for what it says but for what it does. The mingled mingling of voices reminds us that stagy Ahab is the projection of stage manager Ishmael. He sounds like Ishmael because it is Ishmael speaking through him.

Curiously enough, an apparent accident in the printing of *Moby-Dick* has created a textual dilemma that problematizes the interpenetrating voices. Although Ishmael's lines preceding the "grassy glades" speech clearly set us up for a transfer to Ahab's point of view, there are no quotation marks around the speech itself to make these words undeniably his. In fact, the formal effect of the missing punctuation is that the "grassy glades" speech appears to be Ishmael's, not Ahab's. And this omission has existed in every edition of *Moby-Dick* since 1851. However, the editors of the now standard Northwestern-Newberry (NN) edition argue (on the basis of context alone rather than any textual variant) that the missing quotation marks should be supplied, and their emendation to that effect assigns the speech unequivocally to Ahab. Although the arguments for adding the punctuation are convincing, the change remains debatable because there is no physical evidence suggesting that Melville intended to supply quotation marks. The NN editors' decision is not so much a "correction" of a previously "corrupt" text as the creation of a modern variant. In effect, the "grassy glades" speech has now become a "fluid text," one that exists in significantly different physical forms for significantly different readerships. For readers of the historical editions of *Moby-Dick* (sans quotes) have and can continue to assume that the "grassy glades" speech is a continuation of Ishmael's meditation, whereas readers of the NN edition (with quotes) have no choice but to read the speech as Ahab's. In short, readers of "The Gilder" fall into Ahabian and Ishmaelite camps, depending on who they assume is speaking.

Moreover, our awareness of this editorial dilemma accentuates the destabilized revolutionary condition of the reader. For the speech itself, whether in quotes or not, sounds sufficiently Ishmaelean and Ahabian to make us consider with "equal eye" two possibilities: either Ishmael is becoming more Ahabian or Ahab, in his final dramatic moments, reveals his longing for an Ishmaelean sensibility. It is as though the editorial indeterminacy of the text signals to us the interpenetration of worlds: Ahab's anxiety and Ishmael's transcendence. Lub and dub.

Melville could not have foreseen this particular postmodern reading experience, but nevertheless it reinforces the established experience of the novel's revolutionary conditioning of the reader. Tripped up by the text itself, an errant set of quotation marks, and caught in the quandary of having to assign voices to ideas, we find ourselves revolving in and out of variant worlds—pitting Ahab's fears of nihility against Ishmael's faith, the politics of supremacy rooted in sterility against the politics of inclusion rooted in a sexualized communality, an ontology of self against other, and the rhetoric of Shakespearean theatrics against the poetics of transcendence. Surely these conflicting ideologies manifest an age of revolution in itself; but the deeper revolution is in the revolving that readers must perform in reading. That process leaves us wakeful, not confused, poised in anticipation of a synthesis we shall never fully achieve. It is the hot-cool copper calm of desire that is finally our only realizable approximation of ideality, a condition of perpetual revolving. Ahab's stage is struck. The rest is Ishmael spinning on the margin of his maelstrom. Always in revolution.

NOTES

1. *Correspondence*, ed. Lynn Horth. In The Writings of Herman Melville, Vol. 14, ed. Harrison Hayford, Hershel Parker, and G. Thomas Tanselle (Evanston and Chicago: Northwestern University Press and The Newberry Library, 1993), p. 163.

2. In addition to Scoresby, he also researched Frederick D. Bennett's *Narrative of a Whaling Voyage* (1840), J. Ross Browne's *Etchings of a Whaling Cruise* (1846), and Thomas

Beale's *Natural History of the Sperm Whale* (1839). Still the best study of Melville's borrowings in *Moby-Dick* is Howard P. Vincent, *The Trying-out of Moby-Dick* (Boston: Houghton Mifflin, 1949; rpt. Kent, OH: Kent State University Press, 1980). For a broader assessment of Melville's reading habits and a list of books he is known to have read and borrowed, see Merton M. Sealts, Jr., *Melville's Reading* (Columbia: University of South Carolina Press, 1988). For a history of source studies and a checklist of Melville's sources, see Mary K. Bercaw, *Melville's Sources* (Evanston, Ill.: Northwestern University Press, 1987).

3. Herman Melville, "Hawthorne and His Mosses," in *The Piazza Tales and Other Prose Pieces, 1839–1860* (Evanston and Chicago: Northwestern University Press and The Newberry Library, 1987), p. 144. Hereafter cited as "Mosses."

4. The fullest articulation of the theory is in Leon Howard, *Herman Melville: A Biography* (Berkeley: University of California Press, 1951), pp. 150–79. See also George R. Stewart, "The Two *Moby-Dicks*," *American Literature* 25 (January 1954): 417–48, as well as James Barbour's extension of Howard's view to three compositional phases in "The Composition of *Moby-Dick*," *American Literature* 47 (November 1975); rpt. in Louis J. Budd and Edwin Cady, eds. *On Melville: The Best from American Literature* (Durham, NC: Duke University Press, 1988), pp. 203–20. Harrison Hayford supplies a helpful overview of the development of the compositional theories (including his own multiphase "Unnecessary Duplicates" theory) in the Historical Note to *Moby-Dick*, ed. Harrison Hayford, Hershel Parker, and G. Thomas Tanselle (Evanston and Chicago: Northwestern University Press and The Newberry Library, 1988), pp. 648–59.

5. Walter E. Bezanson makes this point in his argument against the received legend of the composition of *Moby-Dick* in "*Moby-Dick*: Document, Drama, Dream," in John Bryant, ed., *A Companion to Melville Studies* (Westport, CT: Greenwood Press, 1986), pp. 176–83.

6. "Melville's *Moby-Dick*; or, *The Whale*," *Literary World* 9 (November 12, 1851), as qtd. in Barbour, "The Composition of *Moby-Dick*."

7. Herman Melville, *Collected Poems of Herman Melville*, ed. Howard P. Vincent (Chicago: Hendricks House, 1947), p. 231.

8. Charles Olson, *Call Me Ishmael* (San Francisco: City Lights Books, 1941), p. 39.

9. F. O. Matthiessen, *American Renaissance: Art and Expression in the Age of Emerson and Whitman* (New York: Oxford University Press, 1941), pp. 423, 42–4, 416.

10. Julian Markels, *Melville and the Politics of Identity* (Urbana: University of Illinois Press, 1993), in his otherwise cogent study of Melville and Lear reverts to a rhetoric of compulsion when he asserts that Shakespeare's "political vision ... compelled ... Melville to rise to its occasion" (1).

11. See Alan Heimert, "*Moby-Dick* and American Political Symbolism," *American Quarterly* 15 (Winter 1963): 495–534

12. These positions are drawn in several recent studies, including Michael Paul Rogin, *Subversive Genealogy: The Politics and Art of Herman Melville* (New York: Knopf, 1983); Wai-chee Dimock, *Empire for Liberty: Melville and the Poetics of Individualism* (Princeton: Princeton University Press, 1989); Larry Reynolds, *European Revolutions and the American Literary Renaissance* (New Haven: Yale University Press, 1988); and Toni Morrison, "Unspeakable Things Unspoken: The Afro-American Presence in American Literature," *Michigan Quarterly Review* 28:1 (Winter 1989): 1–34.

13. Ralph Waldo Emerson, "The Transcendentalist," in Stephen Whicher, ed., *Selected Writings of Emerson* (Boston: Houghton Mifflin, 1957), p. 203.

14. Largely headed by Evert Duyckinck and the loquacious Cornelius Mathews, Young America was a political and literary faction that lionized Irving and promoted the

development of an American national literature. See John Bryant, *Melville and Repose: The Rhetoric of Humor in the American Renaissance* (New York: Oxford University Press, 1993) pp. 47–48.

15. Edward H. Rosenberry, *Melville and the Comic Spirit* (Cambridge: Harvard University Press, 1955), pp. 132–3.

16. Matthiessen, *American Renaissance*, p. 435. Olson's *Call Me Ishmael* also focuses upon Melville's borrowing from Shakespeare.

17. Lawrence Levine, *Highbrow/Lowbrow: The Emergence of Cultural Hierarchy in America* (Cambridge: Harvard University Press, 1988), pp. 40–1.

18. Ralph Waldo Emerson, "The American Scholar," in *Selections*, ed. Stephen E. Whicher (Boston: Houghton Mifflin, 1957), p. 68.

19. "Mosses," p. 245. Of Chatterton's belief that "Shakespeare must ever remain unapproachable," Melville wrote, "Cant. No man 'must ever remain unapproachable'" (*Log*, 363–4).

20. Hershel Parker states the rhetorical problem confronting Melville succinctly: how can an American writer "write of real American life with a Shakespearean intensity without imitating Shakespeare—particularly Shakespearean rhetoric." See *Herman Melville: A Biography*, Volume 1, *1819–1851* (Baltimore: Johns Hopkins University Press, 1996), p. 739.

Chronology

1819	Herman Melville is born August 1 in New York City. He is the third child of Allan Melville, an importer, and Maria Gansevoort Melville.
1826	Melville attends the New York Male High School.
1830	Father's business collapses and he moves the family moves to Albany. Herman becomes a student at the Albany Academy until his father's death in 1832. He works various jobs: bank clerk, helper on his brother Gansevoort's farm, assistant in Gansevoort's fur factory and store.
1835–1838	Melville continues his education at various high schools, supplementing the family income by teaching at a district school.
1837	Brother Gansevoort goes bankrupt with family business; family moves to Lansingburgh, New York.
1839	"Fragments from a Writing Desk" is published May 4 and May 18 in the *Democratic Press* and *Lansingburgh Advertiser*. Melville then works his way to Liverpool, England and back to New York City on the *St. Lawrence*, a merchant ship.
1841–1844	Melville leaves New Bedford, Massachusetts, as a sailor on the whaler *Acushnet*, on a voyage to the South Seas. He jumps ship in the Marquesas Islands (present-day French Polynesia), where he lives among the natives for about a month. After a series of adventures, he travels home as a passenger on the frigate *United States*.

1846	Publishes *Typee*. Brother Gansevoort dies.
1847	Publishes *Omoo*. Marries Elizabeth Shaw, daughter of chief justice of Massachusetts.
1847–1850	Melville tries to earn a living as a writer, producing occasional articles and reviews. Makes the acquaintance of George and Evert Duyckinck, and other New York literary figures.
1849	Publishes *Mardi* and *Redburn*. Travels to Europe. Son Malcolm is born.
1850	Publishes *White-Jacket*. Purchases Arrowhead, a farm near Pittsfield, Massachusetts. Begins his friendship with Nathaniel Hawthorne, who lives in nearby Lenox.
1851	Publishes *Moby-Dick*. Son Stanwix is born.
1852	Publishes *Pierre*.
1853	Daughter Elizabeth is born.
1853–1856	Writes stories and sketches for *Putnam's Monthly Magazine* and *Harper's New Monthly Magazine*. Publishes "Bartleby the Scrivener."
1855	Publishes *Israel Potter* as a book, after serialization in Putnam's. Publishes *Benito Cereno*. Daughter Frances is born.
1856	Travels to Europe and the Near East for his health. *The Piazza Tales* is published.
1857	*The Confidence-Man* is published. Melville returns to the United Sates.
1857–1860	Supports family by lectures on such topics as "Statues in Rome," "The South Seas," and "Traveling."
1863	Melville sells Arrowhead and moves his family to New York City.
1866	Publishes a collection of poems, *Battle-Pieces and Aspects of the War*.
1867	Son Malcolm commits suicide by shooting himself, after which son Stanwix runs away to sea.
1876	Publishes *Clarel*.
1886	Second son, Stanwix, who went to sea in 1869, dies in a San Francisco hospital.
1888	*John Marr and Other Sailors* is privately printed.
1891	*Timoleon* is privately printed. Writes *Billy Budd, Sailor*, which is not published until 1924. Melville dies on September 28, in New York City.

Contributors

HAROLD BLOOM is Sterling Professor of the Humanities at Yale University. He is the author of 30 books, including *Shelley's Mythmaking, The Visionary Company, Blake's Apocalypse, Yeats, A Map of Misreading, Kabbalah and Criticism, Agon: Toward a Theory of Revisionism, The American Religion, The Western Canon,* and *Omens of Millennium: The Gnosis of Angels, Dreams, and Resurrection. The Anxiety of Influence* sets forth Professor Bloom's provocative theory of the literary relationships between the great writers and their predecessors. His most recent books include *Shakespeare: The Invention of the Human,* a 1998 National Book Award finalist, *How to Read and Why, Genius: A Mosaic of One Hundred Exemplary Creative Minds, Hamlet: Poem Unlimited, Where Shall Wisdom Be Found?,* and *Jesus and Yahweh: The Names Divine.* In 1999, Professor Bloom received the prestigious American Academy of Arts and Letters Gold Medal for Criticism. He has also received the International Prize of Catalonia, the Alfonso Reyes Prize of Mexico, and the Hans Christian Andersen Bicentennial Prize of Denmark.

ALFRED KAZIN was a well-known literary critic who came to be associated with the "New York intellectuals" in the 1930s. He was the author of many books of essays and criticism, including *On Native Grounds; A Walker in the City;* and *Writing Was Everything.* Kazin taught at Harvard, Smith, Amherst, Hunter College, and the Graduate Center of the City University of New York.

PATRICK MCGRATH is the author of a story collection, *Blood and Water and Other Tales*, and six novels, including *Spider*, *Asylum*, which was short-listed for the 1996 Guardian Fiction Prize, and *Port Mungo*.

HOMER B. PETTEY has published articles on Melville and Faulkner, and most recently, he edited the collection of essays on The Western for *Pardoxa: Studies in World Literary Genres*.

FRED V. BERNARD is a professor emeritus of English at Aquinas College.

CAROLYN L. KARCHER taught English at Temple University for over 20 years before she retired. She is the author of *The First Woman in the Republic: A Cultural Biography of Lydia Maria Child* and *Shadow over the Promised Land: Slavery, Race, and Violence in Melville's America*.

DAVID S. REYNOLDS is Distinguished Professor of English and American Studies at the Graduate Center and Baruch College of the City University of New York. He is the author of *Walt Whitman's America: A Cultural Biography*, winner of the Bancroft Prize and the Ambassador Book Award and finalist for the National Book Critics Circle Award. His other books include *Beneath the American Renaissance: The Subversive Imagination in the Age of Emerson and Melville*; *Whitman: A Very Short Introduction*; and *George Lippard*, and *Faith in Fiction: The Emergence of Religious Literature in America*.

HENRY NASH SMITH taught at the University of Texas, the University of Minnesota, and the University of California at Berkeley, where he taught for 20 years. The publication of *Virgin Land: The American West as Symbol and Myth*, which received the Bancroft Prize in 1950, led to Smith's national recognition as a scholar. His other books include *Mark Twain of the Enterprise*; *Mark Twain: the Development of a Writer*; *Popular Culture and Industrialism*; and *Democracy and the Novel*.

CAROLYN PORTER is a professor of English at the University of Berkeley. She is the author of many essays on Faulkner, Twain, and Melville.

CHARLES OLSON was the author of *Call Me Ishmael* and several books of poetry. He is considered by many to have been the major poet of his American generation, and is remembered most for *The Maximus Poems*.

CHRISTOPHER STEN is the author of *Sounding the Whale: Moby-Dick as Epic Novel* and *The Weaver-God, He Weaves: Melville and the Poetics of the Novel*.

JOHN BRYANT is the author of *Companion to Melville Studies* and *Melville and Repose: The Rhetoric of Humor in the American Renaissance*, and co-editor of *Melville's Evermoving Dawn: Centennial Essays*.

Bibliography

Bernard, Fred V. "The Question of Race in *Moby-Dick*." *Massachusetts Review* 43, no. 3 (Fall 2002): 383–404.

Bersani, Leo. *The Culture of Redemption.* Cambridge, Mass. and London: Harvard University Press, 1990.

Bloom, Harold, ed. *Herman Melville.* Modern Critical View. New York: Chelsea House, 1986.

———, ed. *Ahab: Major Literary Characters Series.* New York: Chelsea House, 1991.

Branch, Watson G., ed. *Melville: The Critical Heritage.* London and Boston: Routledge and Kegan Paul, 1974.

Brodhead, Richard H. *New Essays on Moby-Dick.* Cambridge and New York: Cambridge University Press, 1986.

Brodtkorb, Paul. *Ishmael's White World: A Phenomenological Reading of Moby Dick.* New Haven: Yale University Press, 1965.

Bryant, John. *A Companion to Melville Studies.* Westport, Conn.: Greenwood Press, 1986.

———. *Melville and Repose: The Rhetoric of Humor in the American Renaissance.* New York: Oxford University Press, 1993.

———, and Robert Milder. eds. *Melville's Evermoving Dawn: Centennial Essays.* Kent, OH: Kent State University Press, 1997.

Chase, Richard Volney. *Melville: A Collection Of Critical Essays.* Englewood Cliffs, NJ: Prentice-Hall, 1962.

Cowan, Bainard. *Exiled Waters: Moby-Dick and the Crisis of Allegory*. Baton Rouge: Louisiana State University Press, 1982.

Coffler, Gail. *Melville's Allusions to Religion: A Comprehensive Index and Glossary*. Westport, Conn.: Greenwood-Praeger Press, 2004.

Davis, Clark. *After the Whale: Melville in the Wake of Moby-Dick*. Tuscaloosa: University of Alabama Press, 1995.

Deblanco, Andrew. *Melville: His World and Work*. New York: Knopf, 2005

Dimock, Wai-chee. *Empire For Liberty: Melville And The Poetics Of Individualism*. Princeton, NJ: Princeton University Press, 1989.

Haberstroh, Charles. *Melville and Male Identity*. Rutherford, NJ: Fairleigh Dickinson University Press, 1980.

Hardwick, Elizabeth. *Herman Melville*. New York: Viking, 2000.

Hayes, Kevin J. *The Critical Response to Herman Melville's Moby-Dick*. Westport, Conn.: Greenwood, 1994.

Higgins, Brian and Hershel Parker, eds. *Critical Essays on Herman Melville's Moby-Dick*. New York: G. K. Hall & Co., 1992

———, eds. *Herman Melville: The Contemporary Reviews*. Cambridge.: Cambridge University Press, 1995.

Hillway, Tyrus, ed. *Moby-Dick Centennial Essays*. Dallas: Southern Methodist University Press, 1953.

Howard, Leon. *Herman Melville: A Biography*. Berkeley: University of California Press, 1951.

Jehlen, Myra. ed. *Herman Melville: A Collection of Critical Essays*. Englewood Cliffs, NJ: Prentice Hall, 1994.

Karcher, Carolyn L. *Shadow Over the Promised Land: Slavery, Race, and Violence in Melville's America*. Baton Rouge and London: Louisiana State University Press, 1980

Kelley, Wyn. *Melville's City: Literary and Urban Form in Nineteenth-Century New York*. New York: Cambridge University Press, 1996.

Levin, Harry. *The Power Of Blackness: Hawthorne, Poe, Melville*. New York: Knopf, 1970.

Levine, Robert, ed. *The Cambridge Companion to Herman Melville*. New York: Cambridge University Press, 1998.

Lewis, R. W. B. *The American Adam*. Chicago: The University of Chicago Press, 1955

Markels, Julian. *Melville And The Politics Of Identity: From King Lear To Moby-Dick*. Urbana: University of Illinois Press, 1993.

Martin, Robert K. *Hero, Captain, and Stranger: Male Friendship, Social Critique, and Literary Form in the Sea Novels of Herman Melville*. Chapel Hill: University of North Carolina Press, 1986.

Mumford, Lewis. *Herman Melville*. London: Jonathan Cape, 1929.

Olson, Charles. *Call Me Ishmael*. San Francisco: City Lights Books, 1947.

Otter, Samuel. *Melville's Anatomies*. Berkeley: University of California Press, 1999.

Pettey, Homer B. "Cannibalism, Slavery, and Self-Consumption in *Moby Dick*." *Arizona Quarterly* 59, no. 1(Spring 2003): 31–58.

Sanborn, Geoffrey. *The Sign of the Cannibal: Melville and the Making of a Postcolonial Reader*. Durham, NC: Duke University Press, 1998.

Selby, Nick, ed. *Herman Melville: Moby Dick*. New York: Columbia University Press, 1998.

Shultz, Elizabeth. "Melville's Environmental Vision in *Moby Dick*." *Interdisciplinary Studies in Literature and Environment* 7, no. 1 (Winter 2000): 97–113.

Simpson, David. *Fetishism and Imagination: Dickens, Melville, Conrad*. Baltimore and London: Johns Hopkins University Press, 1982.

Spanos, William V. *The Errant Art of Moby-Dick: The Canon, The Cold war, and the Struggle for American Studies*. Durham: Duke University Press, 1995.

Sten, Christopher. *Sounding the Whale: Moby-Dick as Epic Novel*. Kent, OH: Kent State University Press, 1991.

———. *The Weaver-God, He Weaves: Melville and the Poetics of the Novel*. Kent, OH: Kent State University Press, 1996.

Thomson, Shawn. *The Romantic Architecture of Herman Melville's Moby-Dick*. Madison, NJ: Fairleigh Dickinson University Press, 2001.

Walker, Herbert. *Moby-Dick and Calvinism: a World Dismantled*. New Brunswick: Rutgers University Press, 1977.

Wilson, Eric. "Melville, Darwin, and the Great Chain of Being." *Studies in American Fiction* 28, no. 2 (Fall 2000): 131–150.

Acknowledgments

"Introduction" from *Moby-Dick: Or, the Whale* by Herman Melville, edited by Alfred Kazin. Copyright © 1956, renewed 1984 by Alfred Kazin. Reprinted by permission of Houghton Mifflin Company. All Rights reserved.

"Introduction" by Patrick McGrath. From *Moby Dick* by Herman Melville, pp. v–xi. © 1999 by Patrick McGrath. Reprinted by permission of Oxford University Press.

"Cannibalism, Slavery, and Self-Consumption in *Moby-Dick*" by Homer B. Pettey. From *Arizona Quarterly* 59, no. 1 (Spring 2003): 31–58. © 2003 by Arizona Board of Regents. Reprinted by permission.

"The Question of Race in *Moby-Dick*" by Fred V. Bernard. From *The Massachusetts Review* 43, no. 3 (Autumn 2002): 384–404. © 2002 by *The Massachusetts Review*. Reprinted by permission from *The Massachusetts Review* Volume 43, Number 03.

"A Jonah's Warning to America in *Moby-Dick*" by Carolyn L. Karcher. From *Shadow Over the Promised Land: Slavery, Race, and Violence in Melville's America*, pp. 62–91. © 1980 Louisiana State University Press. Reprinted by permission.

"'Its wood could only be American!': *Moby-Dick* and Antebellum Popular Culture" by David S. Reynolds. From *Critical Essays on Herman Melville's*

Moby-Dick, Brian Higgins and Hershel Parker, ed., pp. 523–544. © 1992, G.K. Hall. Reprinted by permission of the Gale Group.

"The Madness of Ahab" by Henry Nash Smith. From *The Critical Response to Herman Melville's* Moby-Dick, Kevin J. Hayes, ed., pp. 183–200. Originally published in *Yale Review* 66 (1976): 14–32. © 1976 by Henry Nash Smith. Reprinted by permission.

"Call Me Ishmael, or How to Make Double-Talk Speak" by Carolyn Porter. From *New Essays on* Moby-Dick, Richard H. Brodhead, ed., pp. 73–108. © 1986 by Cambridge University Press, reproduced with permission of the author and publisher.

"A *Moby-Dick* Manuscript" by Charles Olson. From *Call Me Ishmael: A Study of Melville*, pp. 51–62. © 1947 by Charles Olson. Reprinted by permission.

"Sounding the Whale: *Moby-Dick* as Epic Novel" by Christopher Sten. From *Sounding the Whale:* Moby-Dick *as Epic Novel*, pp. 1–26. © 1996 by Kent State University Press. Reprinted by permission.

"*Moby-Dick* as Revolution" by John Bryant. From *The Cambridge Companion to Herman Melville*, Robert S. Levine, ed., pp. 65–90. ©1998 by Cambridge University Press, reproduced with permission of the author and publisher.

Index